Crypto Gold 2021

A Beginners Guide to Cryptocurrency Investing

Copyright © 2021

All rights reserved

The characters and events portrayed in this book are fictitious. Any similarity to real persons, living or dead, is coincidental and not intended by the author.

No part of this book may be reproduced, or stored in a retrieval system, or transmitted in any form or by any means, electronic, mechanical, photocopying, recording, or otherwise, without express written permission of the publisher.

Contents

Title Page
Copyright
Introduction
Blockchain technology
Setting up your Office
Cryptocurrency Exchanges
Fundamental Analysis
Technical Analysis Market Cycles
Resources and support

Introduction

"An investment in knowledge pays the best interest." - Benjamin Franklin

We are witnessing the technology of the future unfolding before our eyes at an exponential rate. The foundation for a digital global economy is being built right now, and the construction materials being used are called blockchain technology. What does this have to do with me right?

When you hear the words financial freedom, what does it mean to you? Does it make you think of a hot new sports car that just hit the market? Does it paint a picture in your mind of a big house with a white picket fence, or does it mean the freedom from being chained to a job you hate, day in an day out slaving away the one precious resource you can't make more of, time. The time to raise your children instead of being a sideline observer because you have to be at work all day. The freedom to travel on a whim. That is what this book is all about.

Have you ever dreamed of what it would be like to live a life of complete freedom? I'm talking about the freedom to be able to wake up one morning, put your finger on a globe, and travel there kind of freedom. The freedom of no longer having to work at a job you hate doing, dealing with the fake company culture, fighting through rush hour traffic, for a boss that doesn't respect you. The freedom of being able to set your own hours, and work whenever you want. The freedom to spend more of your most precious resource, your time, with your family and friends. The freedom of doing what you want when you want, and have the ability to live and work anywhere in the world.

Let me tell you something! Life is much different when you can wake up whenever you want, come and go as you please, actually change the oil in the car when it needs it, watch your kids tee ball game or dance recital, and not have to answer to anyone! That's called freedom! Most people today can't say they have it. If you had the opportunity to create a life like this for you and your family would you take it, or will it just be another opportunity that passes you by?

A blockchain technology called bitcoin crept on the scene a little over a decade ago, and has been the #1 top performing asset ever since! Bitcoin has outperformed Gold, Silver, stocks, bonds, real estate, you name it. Bitcoin has even outperformed big companies like Tesla, Google, and Amazon!

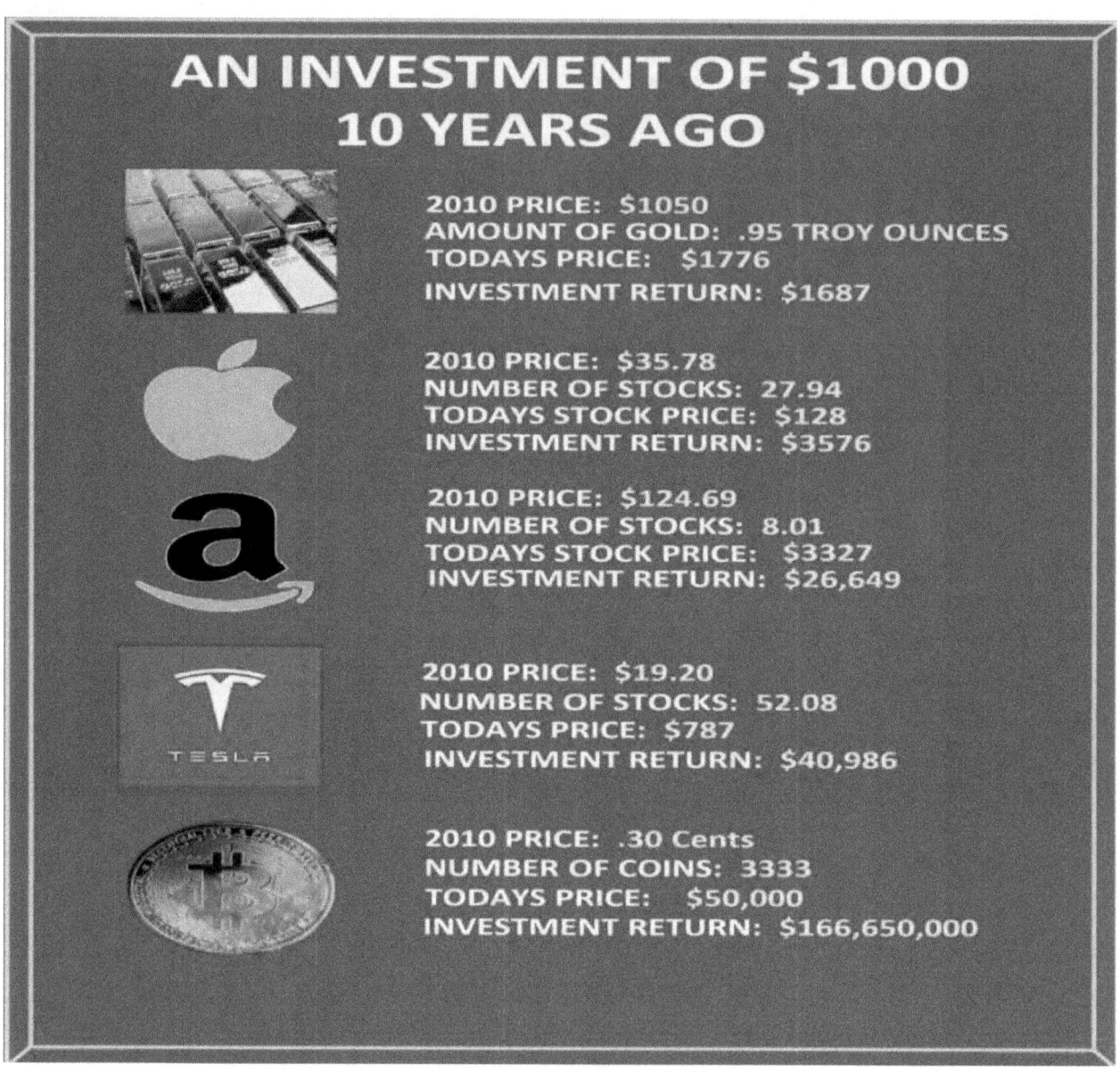

If you would have invested just $1000 into bitcoin in 2010 you would now have over $166 million dollars. Just $10 and you would have over $1 million. Now that's some life changing money! bitcoin isn't the only one. Another project called Ethereum has seen some impressive gains as well. If you had invested $1000 into Ethereum just five years ago you would have over $4 million dollars! It's had over a 60,500% price increase! You're not going to find those kind of returns anywhere. There are countless other success stories. While some people are earning a measly 2% on bank certificates of deposit it's nothing to see a cryptocurrency go up 1000% in a month! No wonder why cryptocurrencies are the highest appreciating asset class in history!

> *"How many millionaires do you know who have become wealthy by investing in savings accounts? I rest my case."* - Robert G. Allen

Teenage kids with acne, living in their parents basement, are getting rich living in penthouses and driving exotic cars while you're wasting your precious time slaving away at the 9-5 hoping things will change. It's time to make a change! As time goes on more and more people are getting interested in cryptocurrency. Get in now before this market really takes off. The earlier you start the more your gains will compound.

Don't wait any longer. This is the greatest financial opportunity of our lifetimes! Those who capitalize on this opportunity now are getting into this market so early that we could all be rich by the time cryptocurrency hits the mainstream market in full force. I'm talking about life changing money! These are exciting times we are living in! Buckle up and fasten your seat belt because this is going to be a wild ride!

Mainstream adoption is happening and big institutions are starting to buy. The following companies are currently investing into blockchain technology: Amazon, anthem, Bank of America, BMW, Bayer, Cargill, Citi Group, Credit Suisse, Daimler, De Beers, Depository Trust and Clearing Corp, DHL, Dole Foods, Facebook, GE, Google, IBM, JP Morgan, Honeywell, HSBC, ING Group, shipping giant Maersk, Mastercard, Microsoft, Nasdaq, Nestle, New Balance, NVIDIA, Overstock.com, Paypal, Royal Dutch Shell, Samsung, Santander, Skybridge, Square, TD Ameritrade, Tesla, T-Mobile, United Nations has several blockchain initiatives, Vanguard, Visa, and Walmart. I'm sure there were several I left out. Mass adoption is right around the corner!

If you've been working a job and are sick of it, if you're not able to go to work and need money, or if you just want a side hustle for some extra cash this could be the opportunity you've been looking for. Life changing money is being made in this industry. Are you going to capitalize on this opportunity or will you let it just pass you by?

I know all of this can be very overwhelming especially if you are new to investing. There's all sorts of information available on the internet, but it's scattered in pieces all over the place. There are lots of shills on YouTube, but who has the correct information? Who do you turn to in order to learn how to invest in this market? When is the best time to buy? When is the best time to sell?

In this book, you will learn everything you need to know when it comes to investing in cryptocurrency. You will learn the basics of blockchain technology, how it was created, and how it works. I'll show you everything you need to get started like setting up security so you won't get hacked, and how to navigate the cryptocurrency exchanges. I will teach you how to locate the hottest new coins, and when to place your orders. I will do my best to simplify things as much as possible and make it easy to understand, so even if you are brand new to investing you can be a successful trader.

Even if you have very little money you can start investing with as little as it would cost you to eat a fast food dinner. All you need is a smart phone and an internet connection. Not good with computers? I will walk you through how to navigate the exchanges step by step. No time? Even if you have very limited time I can teach you how to make money with the amount of time it takes you on the porcelin throne. That's all the time you need to make a trade! I can teach anyone how to do this part-time and with no previous experience.

Even if you've already started investing I can teach you how to invest in cryptocurrency the smart way, and give you winning strategies and techniques that can potentially increase your portfolio 50X or more. I'm going to show you signs to look for before you enter and exit a trade. I'm going to show you how to review a cryptocurrency project to determine if it's a good investment or not. I'll show you how to avoid the projects that scam investors out of millions. I'm going to teach you when Wall Street professionals purchase their company holdings, so that you can profit along side them. You will also learn everything you need to know to keep your portfolio from getting rekt!

There weren't any good books to read about trading cryptocurrency when I got started. I had to learn everything on my own, and I made a lot of mistakes along the way. I wrote this book so anyone that wants to invest in cryptocurrency will have a solid foundation to work with instead of having to invest their hard earned money blindly.

Take the time to learn this new skill. Get out of your comfort zone and take a chance. Create a second income stream for yourself with the goal of doing it full time. Believe in the future of this technology. Now is the time. The biggest financial opportunity you will ever have is staring you right in the face. All you have to do is take action. If you read this book and apply its principles you can have everything you've ever dreamed. Will you take the chance? Well, what are you waiting for? Mortgage the house and sell the kids! It's time to get crypto rich!

"The biggest risk of all is not taking one." - Mellody Hobson

Crypto Rich
A Beginners Guide to Cryptocurrency Investing

Financial advice disclaimer
Dedication
Introduction

Chapter 1 - What is blockchain technology
What is Cryptocurrency
How was Crypto Created
How does bitcoin Work
This is a Revolution - Take the power back
Endless Possibilities - Use cases for crypto, mainstream adoption

Chapter 2 - Setting up your office
Supplies needed
Different wallets, not your keys not your crypto
Anti-virus software
Anti-malware
VPN
Operating Rhythm

Chapter 3 - Cryptocurrency Exchanges
How to Create an Account
How to Connect your Bank Account
Trading Pairs
How to purchase- Limit Buy Orders, Market Buy Orders
How to sell - Market Orders, Limit-Stop Orders, and Stop-Limit Orders
How to do a One Order Cancels the Other (OCO) Order
How to Transfer Crypto to Another Exchange or Wallet

Chapter 4 - Fundamental Analysis
Project Information - White paper
Tokenomics
Network Metrics
Market Statistics

External Factors that Affect Value

Chapter 5 - Technical Analysis
The Basics - Price action, candles, volume, time frames and trader styles, Identifying support and resistance
Indicators - types of indicators, most common indicators, Moving averages, MACD, RSI, Bollinger Bands, Volume, VPVR, Fibonacci retracement tool, Fibonacci extension tool
Candle Trading - Who is Thomas Bulkowski, common candlestick patterns
Identifying common patterns - Common continuation and reversal patterns
Buying Breakouts - 50X your portfolio with minimal risk

Chapter 6 - Understanding Market cycles
Wyckoff Market Cycles
Elliot Wave Theory

Resources and support

Disclaimer

This book is for informational purposes only, and should in no way be construed as financial, legal, or tax advice. This book is not a recommendation to buy or sell cryptocurrency, or engage in trading activities of any kind. Trading involves significant financial risks. The author of this book is not a licensed financial advisor. Conduct own independent research and consult with your financial advisor before investing.

Blockchain technology

In order to trade cryptocurrency we must first know what we are investing in. The technology behind cryptocurrency is called blockchain. Blockchain is an innovative technology that allows people all around the world to conduct transactions in a lightning fast, safe, and trustless way. The transactions are trustless because they don't require trust in any custodians, middlemen, or even the person on the other end of the transaction. Blockchain is quickly changing the way our global economy operates.

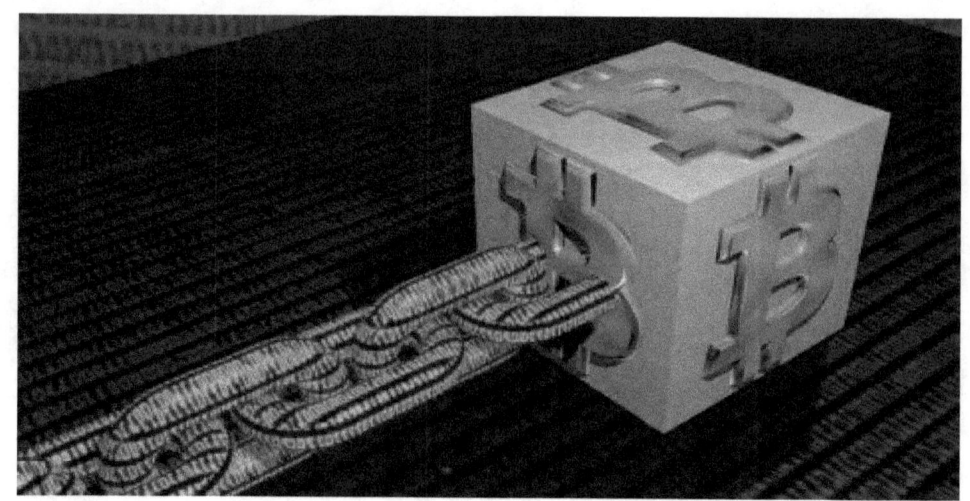

In it's most simplified form, a blockchain is just a place to store data. New data is constantly being added and stored together until it forms a block. The newly formed blocks are then attached to the blockchain forming a sequence of digital blocks that can never be changed or altered. The whole blockchain is secured using cryptography.

Cryptography takes the information and scrambles it making the information extremely difficult to interpret. This prevents those who shouldn't have access to the information from reading it. Governments around the world, militaries, and banks all use cryptography to protect and keep information encypted and secure. Each block contains a cryptographic piece of the previous block, a time stamp, and transaction data such as purchase amount and parties involved, making it resistant to modification.

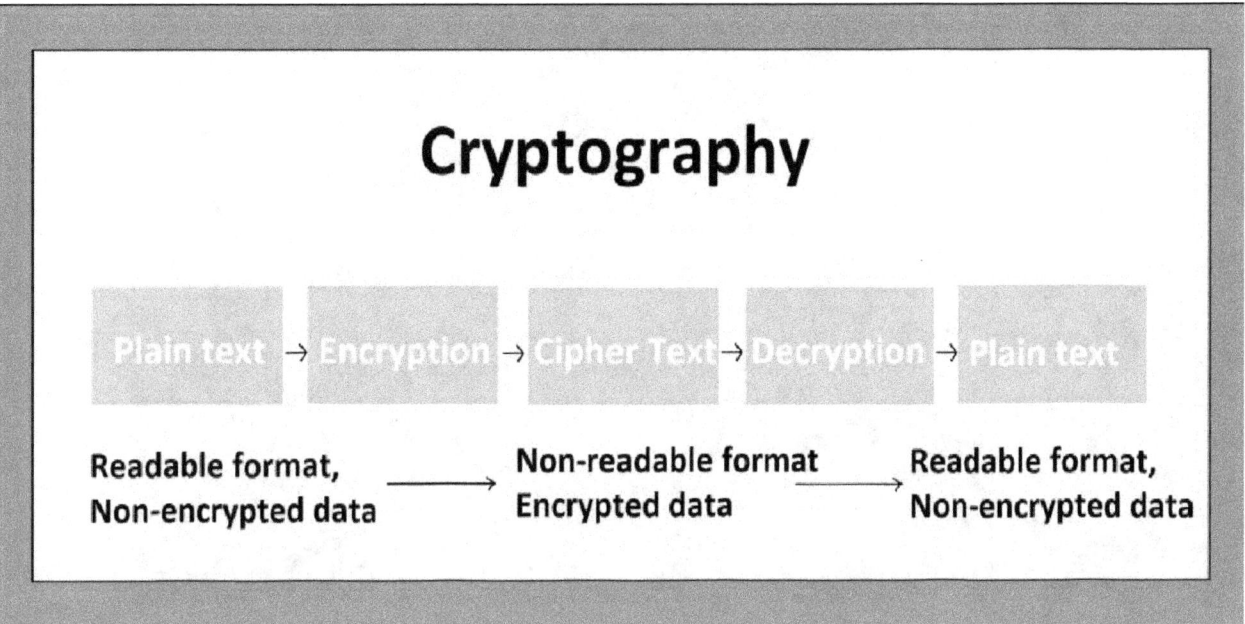

When there's enough data to form a block it's added to the chain of other blocks in the blockchain. Once a block is attached to the chain the information cannot be changed without altering all subsequent blocks, which would require agreement from the majority of the network. The network is constantly updated and maintained by a network of computers, developers, and end users. No central authority is needed for the blockchain to operate.

Blockchain technology first emerged as early as 1991, when W. Scott Stornetta and Stuart Haber decided to design a system where document time stamps couldn't be tampered with. In 1992, they teamed up with Dave Bayer and incorporated Merkle trees to the design. This addition improved the efficiency by allowing several document certificates to be collected into one block.

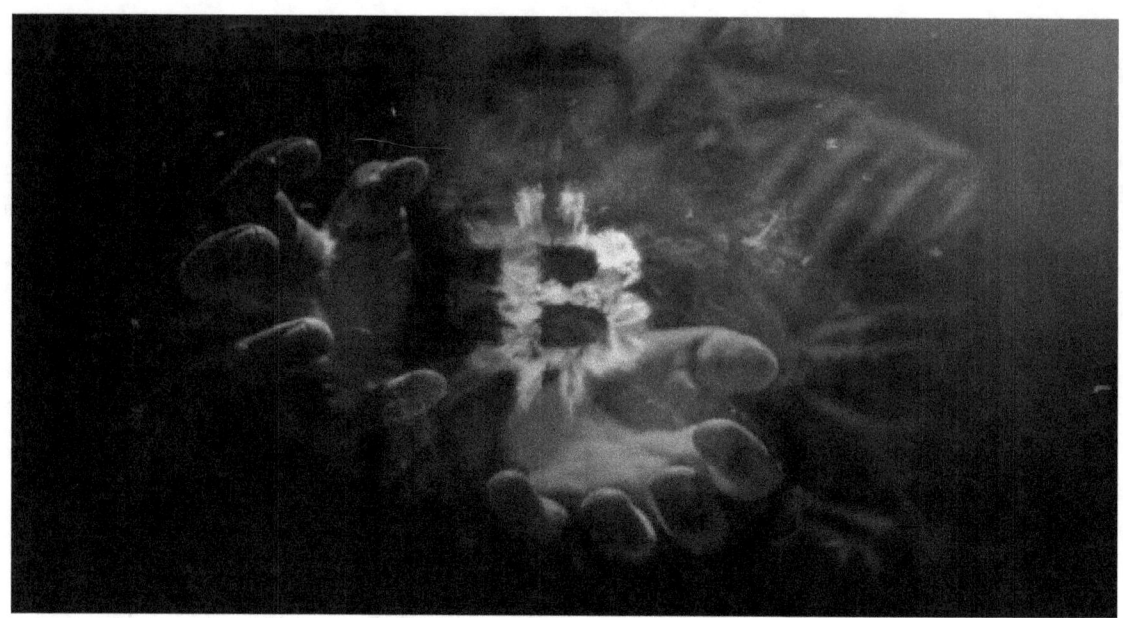

Later in 2009, a mysterious man known as Satoshi Nakamoto developed the first blockchain to serve as the public transaction ledger of the revolutionary cryptocurrency bitcoin. According to Bitcoin.org,

> *"Bitcoin is a consensus network that enables a new payment system and a completely digital money. It is the first decentralized peer-to-peer payment network that is powered by its users with no central authority or middlemen...Bitcoin uses peer-to-peer technology to operate with no central authority or banks; managing transactions and the issuing of bitcoins is carried out collectively by the network. bitcoin is open source; its design is public, nobody owns or controls bitcoin and everyone can take part."*

The invention of bitcoin's blockchain made it the first digital currency without the need of a central authority. bitcoins are created as a reward through a process called mining. Miners keep the blockchain stable, complete, and unalterable by processing transactions on the network into a block, when a block is complete it is added to the blockchain where it is verified by recipient nodes. Each block contains a cryptographic hash of the previous block linking it to the blockchain. When a miner adds a block to the blockchain they are rewarded with bitcoin.

Designed into bitcoin's code is a limitation on the supply that will be created. bitcoin is designed to where there will only ever be 21 million bitcoin mined into existence, and about twenty percent of that are believed to have been lost, making it an increasingly scarce and valuable resource.

Around every four years bitcoin has what's called a halving. This is where they decrease the reward for mining a block which means bitcoin isn't being created as quickly. This causes scarcity and increases demand. Eventually the reward will drop to zero when the 21 million limit is reached.

Miners will then be rewarded in transaction fees.

Since its inception, the bitcoin design has inspired the phenomenon of thousands of others such as Ethereum, Cardano, Litecoin, Chainlink, and many more. Each having their unique approach to blockchain. Today, there are thousands of cryptocurrencies, but be careful because there are a lot of scams out there!

Nakamoto stated that work on writing the code for bitcoin began in 2007. On August 18, 2008, either he or a colleague created bitcoin.org, and on October 31, 2008, he published a paper describing a digital cryptocurrency titled, "bitcoin: A Peer-to-Peer Electronic Cash System"

On January 9, 2009, he released version 0.1 of the bitcoin software, and launched the network by mining the genesis block of bitcoin (block number 0), which had a reward of 50 bitcoins. Embedded in the coinbase transaction of this block was the text: "The Times 03/Jan/2009 Chancellor on brink of second bailout for banks", referring to a headline in the UK newspaper The Times published on that date. This note has been seen as a timestamp of the genesis date, and a expression of his contempt of the instability caused by the central banking system.

The identity of Satoshi Nakamoto remains a mystery to this day. There is no other wallet that is watched closer than his. He mined over 1 million bitcoin before his first and only transaction on January 12, 2009 when he sent 50 bitcoin to Hal Finney. His wallet hasn't been touched since. Was Satoshi Nakamoto murdered for creating an alternative currency that challenged the global power structure, or did he simply leave his completed work behind so there would be no central person or authority as he originally planned for the decentralized cryptocurrency?

This is a Revolution!

"No force on earth can stop an idea whose time has come." - Victor Hugo

Maybe Nakamoto created bitcoin because of the financial turmoil we're in. Maybe the 2008 financial crisis was the last straw for him because during the 2008 global financial crisis, the need for a currency that wasn't centrally controlled or manipulated by a government or central bank was never more evident. The crisis resulted in the collapse of numerous large financial institutions, the bailout of banks by national governments, and downturns in stock markets all around the world. In many areas, the housing market also suffered, resulting in numerous evictions, foreclosures, and prolonged wealth estimated in trillions of U.S. dollars, and a significant decline in economic activity, leading to a severe global economic recession in 2008. Nakamoto's bitcoin was exactly what the world needed.

Currencies have been controlled and manipulated by those in power all throughout history, and today it's no different. Until recently our banking system used what's called fractional reserve banking which only allowed banks to loan out up to ten times more than they had in reserves. This kept the banks from inflating the dollar. In 1971, President Nixon took the United States off the gold standard which meant nothing was physically backing the dollar anymore. This allowed banks to create an endless amount of money without having to have anything in reserves. They were essentially given the power to create money from nothing. Giving them this power over our currency was a wonderful idea since banks have such a great history of trust worthiness.

Over time as more and more currency is issued, the less purchasing power it has. Today, the US dollar is estimated to be worth around 4 percent of what it was worth in 1913 when the federal reserve was created. Twenty percent of all currency in circulation today was created in 2020 during the Coronavirus pandemic. That is a scary statistic! The purchasing power of the dollar is fading quickly. The more money they print, the more the dollar is devalued. The more the dollar is devalued, the less you are able to purchase. People used to pay cash for just about everything. It now takes two people working in a household instead of one to survive. Now it's difficult for most people to survive without leveraging debt. How else can you survive in a debt based economy?

"If there is one common theme to the vast range of the world's financial crises, it is that excessive debt accumulation, whether by the government, banks, corporations, or consumers, often poses greater systemic risks than it seems during a boom." - Carmen Reinhart

Fiat Currency Throughout History

The dollar is eerily following the same path as other fiat currencies that have collapsed throughout history. The oldest example was ancient Rome which was the largest empire at the time. At the start of the Roman empire the currency at the time was the denarius. When minted by decree of Caesar Augustus in 15 b.c.e, the denarius was made out of nearly pure silver, but by the time of the collapse of the empire the denarius only contained around

.02% silver. The currency was inflated in part to fund high-profile imperial projects, or to fight costly wars to expand the empire just as it is today.

Banks at the time typically kept less in reserves than what customers had on deposits since they weren't required to ensure that customers' deposits would be insured in the event of a bank run. The Empire's banking system allowed for the exchange of extremely large amounts without the physical transfer of coins, which led to the denarius becoming fiat money. The value of the denarius continued to fall as the content of silver backing it decreased until the fall of the empire.

In another example, The Republic of Zimbabwe's poor monetary policy led to extreme amounts of hyperinflation beginning in the 1990s. The worst of the inflation occurred in 2008, which led to complete abandonment of the currency. The peak month of hyperinflation occurred in mid-November 2008 with a rate estimated at 79,600,000,000% per month.

The hyperinflation got so bad that it got to the point where $1 US was equivalent to over 2 billion Zimbabwean dollars! Just three eggs would cost 100 billion Zimbabwean dollars. Zimbabwe banned its financial institutions from cryptocurrency dealings in 2018 as its citizens rushed to bitcoin to escape the country's faltering monetary policies. All financial institutions were ordered to terminate servicing cryptocurrency exchanges within 60 days and to begin liquidating any accounts related to crypto. In 2020, Zimbabwe's central bank halted all mobile transactions to prevent those attempting to flee the country's hyperinflation from purchasing cryptocurrency.

In a more recent example, the British pound faced the same fate. On

September 16th, 1992 a single-day collapse in the value of the pound sterling was dubbed "Black Wednesday." The pound collapsed due to poor government monetary policy just as every other fiat currency in history.

There's no doubt about it, a new currency is needed. A currency that is decentralized and cannot be manipulated by anyone. Maybe this is why Nakamoto kept his identity a secret. To disrupt the power structure would most certainly be a death sentence. Will Nakamoto's bitcoin become the new currency of the world? Probably not, but the new world currency won't be far behind and it will be digital.

This isn't just a great new way to make money and exchange currency. This is a revolution! The so called royalty, wealthy families, bankers, and politicians have had control over the world, and specifically our currencies, for centuries and it's time for a change!

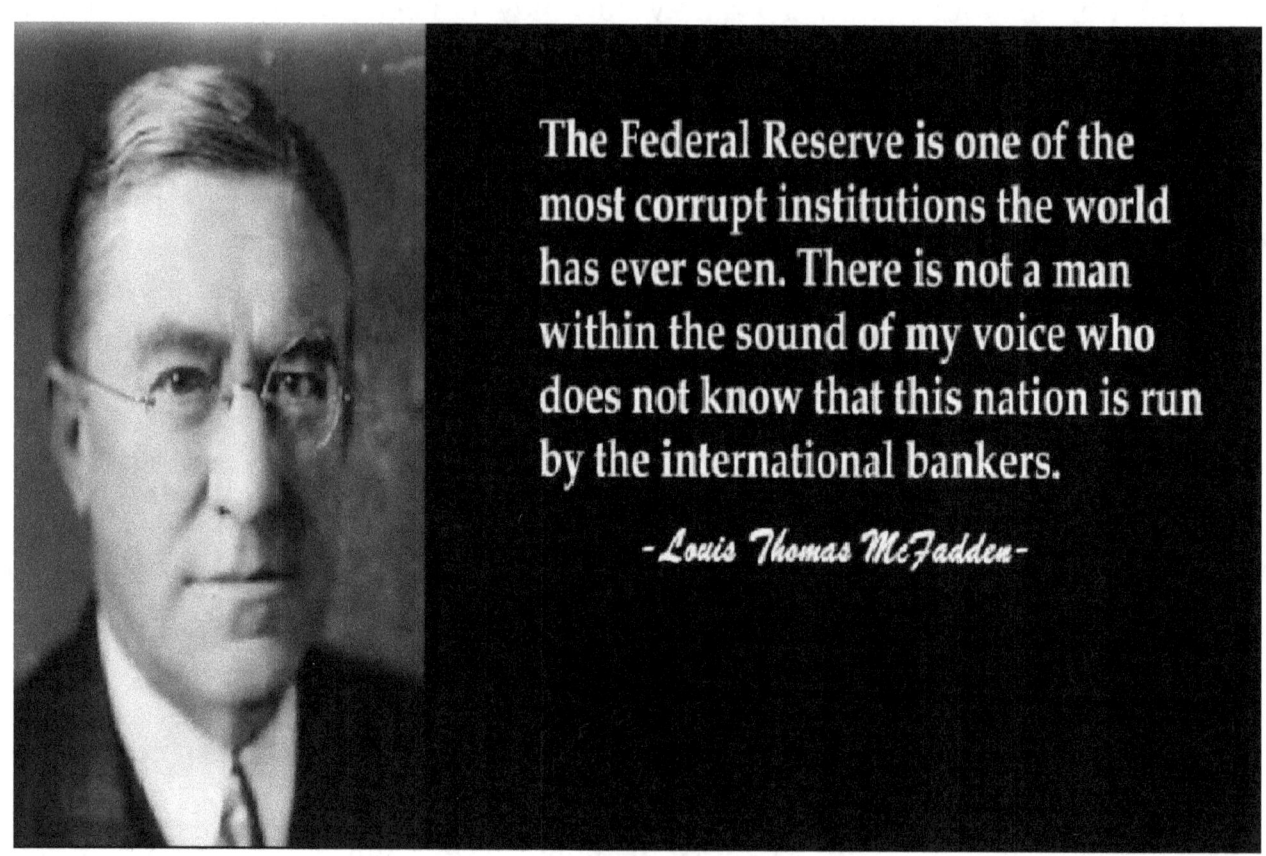

"I care not what puppet is placed upon the throne of England to rule the Empire on which the sun never sets. The man who controls the

British money supply controls the British Empire, and I control the British money supply." - Nathan Mayer Rothschild, Rothschild Family Banking Dynasty

This technology has the ability to take the power away from those in power and positions of influence so there is no central authority. Although it is still in infancy stages, in the future it will be compared to how revolutionary the internet was to our civilization. People all over the world who don't have access to the banking system at all like many in Africa, now have the ability to be their own bank. People who live in countries where their government is corrupting the currency can convert their native currency to cryptocurrency and preserve their wealth. Thousands of people now have the ability to work from home and for themselves instead of for these big corporations. Countless billionaires have been made by tech companies, and the same thing is currently happening with blockchain companies. Investors are making millions in the process too. This movement is creating all sorts of opportunity for those who decide to take advantage of it.

Endless Possibilities

All the life changing money we make in this industry will be amazing, but it's not all about money though. This technology will completely change the way the world economy operates. It will completely change the way we live our lives. Decentralized cryptocurrencies, prevent governments, or anyone else for that matter, from manipulating the currency through inflation. This is very exciting because governments have track records of printing their currencies into oblivion until eventually they become worthless leaving their citizens behind in poverty. This is giving the people the power back.

Decentralized cryptocurrencies can also prevent mega companies like Google, Facebook, and Twitter, from shaping our world as they see fit instead of the progress being agreed upon by all of humanity. These centralized companies are becoming so powerful that they heavily influence governmental policy through lobbying, and they control all of our data and information. Whistleblower, Edward Snowden, warned us about the surveillance society we are now living in. We cannot allow this to happen.

The power should always reside with the people, not with governments or corporations.

Financial institutions, governments, and businesses are already seeing the benefits of blockchain-based solutions for countless use cases. Cryptocurrency can provide numerous benefits to the global economy, and it does much more than serve as a peer to peer transaction system. Since bitcoin's inception thousands of cryptocurrencies have been created. New projects are popping up every day that are looking to provide services that will make our economy more decentralized, safer, and more efficient.

Decentralization and transparency are key for an open and free society. My hope is that through blockchain technology we can either completely eliminate the need for governments and politicians, or at the very least use it to prevent corruption by putting all expenditures and voting system on the blockchain to hold our elected officials accountable for their actions. Time will tell if that is just a Utopian dream or not. It may be just a dream, but many projects are working toward that goal. Here are just a couple projects that are working hard to fulfill the vision:

A cryptocurrency project called Brave is looking to dominate the search engine and ad revenue space. Brave believes you should control the data you give to big corporations. Based on the Chromium web browser, the Brave browser blocks ads and website trackers, and provides a way for users to earn cryptocurrency in the form of Basic Attention Tokens and have the choice to make contributions to websites and content creators. For example, if your favorite YouTube channel gives you some good advice you can send them a tip in the form of the Basic Attention Token(BAT). The Brave browser allows you to connect your cryptocurrency wallets directly to the browser, and you. I personally use the Brave browser and I think it's the best browser available at the moment. Because it blocks all the website trackers and eliminates ads except those you want to see it making the browser extremely fast. Brave already has over twenty million users! Download the Brave browser and start earning cryptocurrency today.

Concerns around internet privacy, security, and data breaches led to the creation of a cryptocurrency project called Blockstack. Everything is being decentralized in the crypto world, and Blockstack wants to decentralize the internet so the people are in control instead of mega companies. Like bitcoin, Stacks is a decentralized network. There is no company or person that controls it. People from all over the world contribute to it. There is no central authority. Stacks(STX) blockchain is built on top of bitcoin's blockchain because of it's security and it cannot be taken down.

Blockstack adopted the motto "Can't be evil" in opposition to Google's "Don't be evil" motto, and in June of 2019 Blockstack purchased a billboard across from Google headquarters to give them the message. The CEO said these companies shouldn't have the power to be evil in the first place and I couldn't agree more. Listen to what the founders of Blockstack had to say:

In an article titled, "Introducing the Blockstack Browser: A Gateway to a New, Decentralized Internet", the creators of Blockstack wrote, "Imagine a world where people don't have property rights. In this world, you cannot own a house, and all your belongings are kept in a storage facility owned by a few corporations. And in this world, walking into any store or theater implies that you disclose all your personal information, places you've been, other things you've bought to the business owners. You are tracked 24/7, your belongings are stolen from storage facilities, and you can't do anything about it.

Most of us would not stand for this in our real, everyday lives. But on the internet, we tolerate and even expect it. We become dependent on nameless, faceless, remote parties just by connecting. On the internet, we are powerless. Our existence on the internet is defined by others, whether that other be a mega-corporation or a government.

Now, we can change that.

Today we are proud to announce the Blockstack browser, which allows developers everywhere to access a whole new internet. This new internet changes the dynamic and brings the power back to the people... Blockchain technology powers this new internet. For the first time ever, you'll be able to access people, communities, apps, and services built on the blockchain from your browser. This new internet reflects how people interact with each other naturally, as they have for thousands of years. In open marketplaces and societies, people transact directly with other people to offer advice, goods, and services. Human interaction has never needed a middleman. The internet should work how real life works.

We're a group of open-source developers, and we feel the pain of app developers. The permission-based environment of the traditional internet runs directly counter to true innovation. If you are not an engineer at Google or Facebook, it's hard for you to innovate. It's not a level playing field. We simply don't have the access, and if we do, it can be revoked at any time. Innovating on the internet should not require permission from a few mega-corporations. Our developer tools for the new, decentralized internet remove the reliance on existing infrastructure or third-party servers.

What an amazing vision Blockstack has for the future of the internet.

Cryptocurrency project Vechain is doing some very exciting things. The VeChain ecosystem is currently being used to track food from farm to the grocery store using RFID technology so consumers know how it was produced and transported. Walmart in China has already implemented the technology. Contaminated food can quickly be traced back to it origin. Organic foods can be tracked and traced so consumers will know for sure if they are consuming organic or genetically modified food. Consumers can simply scan a QR code in the grocery store to learn about how the food was cultivated and transported.

Pharmaceuticals can now be tracked throughout the supply chain through Vechain's partnership with Bayer. Consumers and manufacturers can be notified if a drug is stored outside recommended temperatures which will allow for better quality control. If there is a mistake in production the drugs in question can easily be tracked and located to prevent recalls or allow consumers to be quickly notified of any potential dangers.

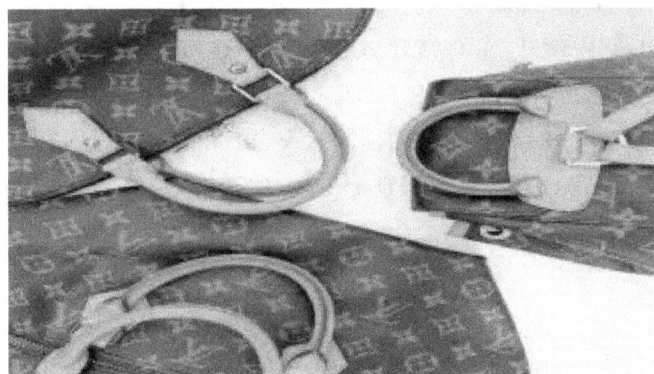

VeChain is currently being utilized to track designer merchandise and prevent counterfeits too. According to Forbes, in 2018 counterfeiting was the largest criminal enterprise in the world. Sales total more than $1.7 trillion per year! Everything from handbags, wallets, electronics, watches, to shoes are being counterfeited. Using VeChain's blockchain technology consumers can have peace of mind by verifying if they are purchasing an authentic item or not, and merchants, manufacturers, and designers won't lose near as much money to counterfeiting thieves.

Blockchain technology can also be used to prevent voter fraud and election tampering by confirming voter identity and registering votes on a tamper proof blockchain. This would eliminate the need for recounts and guarantee honest elections. How amazing would it be to have a voting system that can't be manipulated!

Located in Boston, Massachusetts, Voatz is a mobile voting platform that runs on blockchain technology. They use an encrypted biometric security system that verifies and secures your identity so you can vote on a mobile device from anywhere in the world. One of the first states to use the company's platform was West Virginia. They used the Voatz platform to collect votes from eligible service members and travelers abroad during elections.

Blockchain can also be used to verify and secure our identities on the internet instead of having to use countless user IDs and passwords, and complete an endless amount of Know-Your-Customer(KYC) verifications. Cryptocurrency project, Civic, aims to do just that. Civic has customers complete one identity verification that can then be used for any other application you want. Their current KYC checks cover over 4500 identity documents across 195 countries. Phone numbers and emails are verified by users and used to streamline account registrations. How many minutes of your life would be saved if every time you had to fill out a form online all your information would automatically populate! Artificial intelligence and biometric verification keep users identities safe and secure. This saves trees from being turned into paper and saves thousands of dollars from being spent on physical ballots.

Decentralized Finance

One of the most exciting areas in the crypto space right now is decentralized finance (DeFi). Decentralized finance eliminates the middle man (financial institutions) and enables people to lend or borrow with each other indirectly, participate in derivatives speculation, trade cryptocurrency, insure against risk, and earn interest. Decentralized finance saw a ten fold growth over the course of 2020 to over $9 billion dollars, and I expect that trend to continue.

In June 2020, cryptocurrency project Compound Finance began rewarding lenders and borrowers of cryptocurrencies on its platform with payments to lenders, units of the new cryptocurrency COMP, in addition to typical interest. Other cryptocurrency projects followed and the process became known as yield farming or liquidity mining.

Liquidity mining is a way for investors to earn passive income. The way it works is you place your cryptocurrency into a pool of funds where users can lend, borrow, or exchange tokens. Users of the platform pay fees which are then paid to those who provide liquidity by placing their crypto into the pool of funds according to the amount they contributed to the pool. The pool of funds is used to create loans for others which they have to pay back with interest. Borrowers put more cryptocurrency into the pool as collateral, so there is no risk to yield farmers if the end user doesn't pay the loan back. The only real risk is that the cryptocurrency declines in value while you're still in the farming process.

Now with defi anyone can become the bank and lend their cryptocurrency out at interest. In return, those who participate are rewarded handsomely. I've seen APR percentages over 40% in some cases!

Decentralized financed is going to completely change the financial industry. Decentralized finance empowers citizens all over the world with economic opportunity, even those who have never had access to the traditional banking system. All you need is a cell phone and an internet connection. This technology allows for a more fair, free, secure, transparent, and profitable global economy. One that benefits all instead of just 1% of the population.

The management of assets is quickly becoming more efficient and more secure with the integration of blockchain technology. Private data can be transferred without fear of compromise. Transaction history is stored on the blockchain preventing it from being changed or altered in any way. Assets can be managed and updated almost instantly allowing portfolio managers to better manage their clients' portfolios. Any type of asset such as real estate, a boat, a car, etc. can be tokenized, divided, and distributed quickly, safely, and at a minimal cost. This will help tremendously with everyday activities like the settlement of estates.

Blockchain can also help with the prevention of inconsistent data since all the information stored must be agreed upon through consensus. Every single record we have should go on the blockchain for safe keeping. Have you ever seen how sloppy our record keeping systems are? I can only imagine how many innocent people have been falsely charged or double charged by a company and there's nothing they can do about it without spending thousands on a legal team.

Blockchain technology is being used to prevent piracy, fraud, and intellectual property theft too. Artists can timestamp their work providing proof of ownership. A record would be made in the blockchain and could never be altered at that point. This can be applied to art, writings, books, music, movies, etc. This will drastically reduce piracy and allow for the distribution of authentic material.

Governments Integrating Blockchain

Many governments around the world have even started integrating blockchain technology into their economies too. Blockchain technology can be used for an endless amount of applications such as: business registrations, digital currency, health care, identity management, supply chain tracking, taxation, and voting.

- ❖ The UK government's Department of Work and Pensions is considering using blockchain technology to record and administer benefit payments.

- ❖ The South Korean government is working with Samsung to implement blockchain solutions for public safety and transport applications.

- ❖ The Estonian government has partnered with Ericsson to create a new data center to move government services like judiciary, healthcare, commercial code, and public records onto the blockchain.

- ❖ Venezuela is the first government to issue digital currency. President Nicholas Maduro said, "The have a war against our physical currency. We are moving this year to a more profound digital economy, in expansion. I've set the goal of an economy that's 100% digital." Venezuela's cryptocurrency, the Petro, is backed by reserves of oil, gas, gold, and diamonds. The Petro is operational as of 2018.

- ❖ Dubai has been researching blockchain technology opportunities across health records, shipping, business registration and for the prevention of the spread of conflict diamonds. The Dubai government has been very accepting of cryptocurrency. Cryptocurrencies are now accepted as a form of payment in Mina Rashid, Dubai where citizens can pay for trade licenses and visas with bitcoin and ethereum.

- ❖ The Government of Canada is experimenting with blockchain technology. They are using Ethereum's blockchain to publish grants and contribution data. Canada is also experimenting with its own blockchain explorer on their InterPlanetary File System.

- ❖ The Ukraine Government has chosen the cryptocurrency project Stellar Lumens blockchain network as a platform to build a central bank digital currency.

- ❖ The Ukraine Government stated its goal is to build a "virtual assets ecosystem and national digital currency of Ukraine."

These are just some of the governments around the world integrating blockchain into their economies. This is not just a pipe dream anymore. The crypto economy is forming quickly. New technology is being developed every single day. It's only a matter of time before cryptocurrency is adopted by the mainstream and becomes a part of our everyday lives. The possibilities for cryptocurrencies are endless! I can't wait to see what the future holds. Support the movement by investing in cryptocurrencies and make some crazy gains in the process.

Setting up your Office

"I will tell you how to become rich. Close the doors. Be fearful when others are greedy. Be greedy when others are fearful." - Warren Buffet

While it might be fun to just throw some money into this market like a casino.. You may even 10X your money if you time things right. However, if you really want to step up your game and do this for a living you should treat this like a business. Get yourself organized and get a plan together. Buy a whiteboard, some dry erase markers, a calendar, and a notepad so you can keep track of the current news and product releases. Write down a list of coins you would like to follow on your whiteboard. Keep track of your entry and exit points as well as your profit margin. Write them own or record them in a spreadsheet, so you can track your performance. The more organized you are, and the more you treat this like a business, the more money you will make. The success you have in this industry all boils down to how committed you are to it.

You can start trading cryptocurrency with just a cellphone and an internet connection, but I would highly recommend at least getting a laptop. It's much easier to analyze charts on a laptop than a cellphone. Set up an office area at home in a quiet place that's free from any distractions. Buy a comfortable chair because you're going to be spending a lot of time sitting in it researching and studying charts. I like using multiple monitors so I can watch several charts at one time.

The Command Center

I use a six monitor setup along with my laptop at home, and I use my cellphone, an iPad, and my laptop(insert Amazon affiliate link) for my mobile setup. I connect a USB hub to my laptop, and I use USB to VGA cords to connect the monitors to the hub. This allows me to have the bitcoin and bitcoin dominance charts up at all times on one monitor, and I can watch five other charts at once. This is overkill though. No one needs to have this many monitors to trade. It's convenient, but not necessary. One decent sized screen for looking at charts is all you really need.

I recommend that you create a separate bank account for your crypto so you can keep everything separate from your personal expenses. After making multiple deposits into your crypto wallet it's easy to lose track of what you have invested. Keeping your crypto account separate helps you keep track of everything you have invested and it also keeps you safe. If your account wasn't separate and you were to get compromised(which happens all the time), the funds you had set aside for crypto could potentially be stolen. Eventually, you'll also want to withdraw some of the profits you earn! Keeping your crypto money separate will be helpful come tax time too.

I also highly recommend setting up a business entity for tax purposes. This way you can write off any expenses you incur in your cryptocurrency business like computers, monitors, the part of your house that you use as an office, internet, cell phone, etc. If you are showing capital gains profit some places allow in the tax code where you can go buy something like a vehicle to offset your gains essentially allowing you to pay little to no tax!

Download the Brave Browser on your laptop and cellphone. Basic Attention Token(BAT) is a cryptocurrency attached to the Brave Browser. You can earn BAT for free while looking at charts, researching crypto, and watching YouTube! Not only can you earn crypto, but it blocks all ads unless you opt in to the Brave ads and third party tracking making it super fast, and it allows payments to websites and content creators. It's faster, you can earn crytpo, it keeps you safer because you're not being tracked by third parties, and there's no ads(unless you opt in to Brave ads)!

Crypto Wallets

Before you purchase your crypto you need to know where you're going to put it. A cryptocurrency wallet is similar to a bank account. It is a place where you can store your crypto just like a bank account is where you store your cash.

There are two general types of wallets. You have hot wallets, which are any wallets that connect to the internet, and cold storage wallets that don't connect to the internet. You also have custodial wallets and non-custodial wallets. Custodial wallets are where a third party controls the private key. Non-custodial wallets do not. Think of the address as a safety deposit box and a private key is what allows access to the box.

At the moment there are over 140 different wallets you can choose from to place your cryptocurrency in safe keeping. There are custodial wallets the exchanges offer, hardware wallets, desktop wallets, mobile wallets, web based wallets, and even paper wallets. Not all wallets are created the same though as you're about to find out. Just remember, if you're not given a set of keys when you create the wallet then the crypto it contains isn't actually in your possession. Not your keys, not your crypto. Make sure you write down your keys instead of storing them on a device, make a copy, and keep one copy at home in your fireproof safe and another in a safe deposit box or another safe location.

Web based wallets

Web based wallets are free and they're accessed through internet browsers like Brave, Firefox, Chrome, etc. There are two types of web based wallets: hosted and non-hosted. Some of the different exchanges like Binance offer hosted wallets, but you're not given a set of keys. Binance owns their keys so any money you have on Binance technically belongs to them until you move it off the exchange. It's just a place for you to put your crypto until you're able to send it to a wallet. Coinbase is another exchange that offers a hosted wallet, and Coinbase does give you a set of keys.

There are also non-hosted web based wallets like MetaMask and MyEtherWallet. I prefer these over the hosted wallets because exchanges like Coinbase are notorious for crashing at the worst possible times. The MetaMask and MyEtherWallets give you a set of keys, and they will never leave you in a position where you're not able to access your crypto. Make sure you have a VPN and good anti-virus and anti-malware software. Web based wallets are the least secure method to store your crypto. I wouldn't recommend keeping thousands of dollars on a web based wallet, but keeping small amounts in a web based wallet is nothing to worry about. I use my MetaMask wallet all the time.

Mobile wallets

Mobile wallets are free, convenient, and easy to use. All you have to do is install an app on your phone and sign up. It's nice having access to your wallet no matter where you're at in case of emergency. Just make sure that you use a VPN and choose a wallet that gives you private keys. Two of the most popular wallets at the moment are Crypto.com and Atomic wallet. These two wallets will provide you with keys so you control your crypto. Crypto.com has a metal debit card that allows you to convert your crypto to fiat so you can spend it anywhere debit cards are accepted. They also offer staking where you can earn interest on your crypto, but I've found better rates elsewhere. Atomic wallet has some attractive staking rates. Staking is where you basically agree to hold or lock up your tokens for a specified amount of time for a certain reward. At the moment Atomic wallet is offering 17% for BAND, 15% for ZIL, 10% for ATOM, 10% for ICON, and they allow staking for several others too.

Desktop wallets

Desktop wallets are free and downloadable software for Mac, Windows, and Linux. Like any wallet connected to an internet connection if you choose to use a desktop wallet make sure you have a VPN and good anti-virus and anti-malware software. A few good desktop wallets out there are Crypto.com, Atomic Wallet, Exodus, and Guarda.

Paper wallets

Paper wallets are extremely secure, but I would not recommend them. They are just a piece of paper with the wallet address, private and public keys, and a QR code. They aren't connected to the internet so they are safe as long as you store them in a safe place, but they can be easily destroyed. It's an archaic method that shouldn't be used.

Hardware wallets

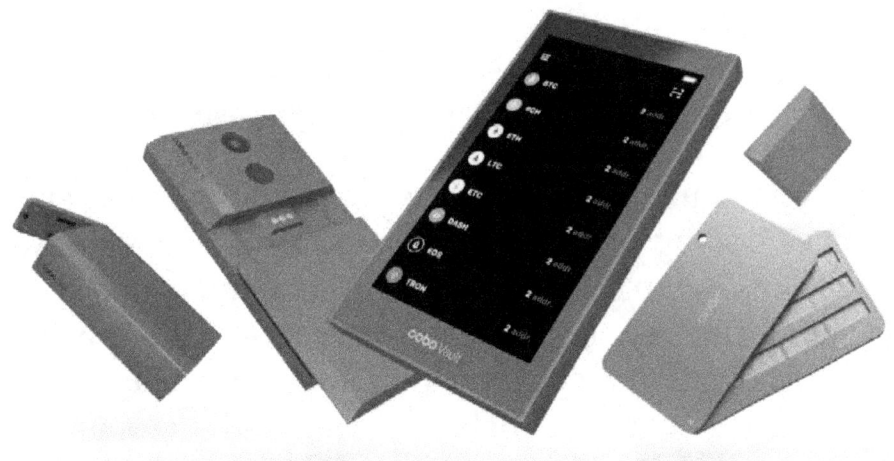

Cobo Wallet

Hardware wallets are USB like devices that are specifically designed to store cryptocurrency offline. They cost between $70-$150 and are currently the safest way to store your cryptocurrency besides paying to have it stored in a cold storage facility inside a secret bunker. Yes, this really is a thing for those of you that get bitcoin rich. Until then, the best hardware wallets available are the Trezor, Ledger nano x, Ledger nano S, Ellipal Titan, Cobo Vault, and Cobo VaultPro.

Anti-virus and Ant-malware

I think this goes without saying, but if you're trading on a computer you'll want to invest in a good quality anti-virus software and anti-malware software. I know someone that is so serious about his security he has a separate computer just for his crypto trading and he doesn't use it for anything else. If you plan on having thousands of dollars in crypto safety needs to be a priority. There are a number of good anti-virus and anti-malware software programs available such as: McAfee, Norton, Kaspersky, Malwarebytes, and Webroot. Don't rely on Windows Defender as it has been known to have flaws.

VPN

I would highly recommend that you use a virtual private network (VPN) especially if you're trading with large amounts. Your anti-virus works in the background on your computer to prevent any potential viruses, but a VPN takes things a step further to secure your identity. A VPN prevents websites and apps from tracking your online activity keeping your data secure by establishing a secure connection between you and the internet. A VPN disguises and hides your IP address so when you use the internet no one knows your true online identity. This makes it more difficult for nefarious individuals to track your online activity and steal your data.

Just like cryptocurrency, VPNs use cryptography to scramble your personal data making it unreadable to those who don't have the private encryption key that enables them to read it. Unencrypted data can be viewed by anyone with an internet connection that wants to see it. Keep yourself sasfe and secure by using a VPN.

A VPN can also prevent your service provider from slowing down your internet speeds. Sometimes providers will slow your internet speed down after you've used a certain amount of data. A VPN will prevent them from slowing you down. Some use advanced encryption standard (AES) 256-bit encryption which is a military grade security technique that is one of the most secure encryption algorithm methods available.

Get a good VPN service and you will be free to use any other exchange in the world. The exchanges are receiving a lot of pressure from the U.S. government to prevent it's citizens from using them right now. It's probably because they are worried they won't be able to track and tax the money that's ran through them. Let's face it though, the international exchanges are where the action is right now. Exchanges like the international Binance have the most volume and liquidity. Not to mention all the newest and hottest coins.

I'm not advocating this by any means, but I do know a lot of people that use a VPN to get around this restriction so they have the *freedom* to use any exchange. Non-verified U.S. customers are still able to use the international exchanges. The only difference is you just won't be able to complete the KYC(know your customer) verification process or deposit fiat US dollars. This is not a problem if you are trading with less than two bitcoin because most exchanges will allow you to withdraw up to two bitcoin per day without completing KYC verification. If you are trading with more than two bitcoin you can create an account with several exchanges and spread your money around.

If you choose to use an exchange that doesn't allow U.S. dollars you might need to turn on your VPN every time you access it, which you really want to do anyway for added security. If you forget to turn your VPN on and your account gets flagged for being in a restricted country like the U.S. don't worry, it's not the end of the world. All you need to do is send your crypto to another wallet. It can even be another wallet in the same exchange!

The exchanges want people to trust them. They aren't out to steal your money. Not in this aspect anyway. They want to profit from the fees they charge. They aren't out to steal your few thousand dollars. If people don't trust them they won't trade, and if they don't trade the exchanges don't make money.

A VPN gives you online privacy and anonymity by creating a private network from a public internet connection. Some people I know in the U.S., deposit dollars in Binance.US, or another exchange the U.S. government *allows* their citizens to use, exchange the dollars for cryptocurrency, and then transfer the crypto to other exchanges like the international Binance or KuCoin where there's a lot more variety of coins. There you can sell the crypto you transferred and buy whatever new coins you want and transact in the global economy.

My favorite exchanges at the moment are international Binance, Bitrue, and KuCoin. Binance is one of the top exchanges for a reason. It's easy to use and there are a wide variety of coins to choose from. KuCoin is very similar to Binance as far as the layout goes. I like KuCoin because they have a lot of small market cap coins that other exchanges don't have. Bitrue is my favorite exchange at the moment because they allow you to earn interest on a fairly long list of coins up to 12% at the moment. What's even better is If you don't have to lock your coin up for a long period of time like others make you do. Other exchanges want you to lock up your assets for as long as 90 days! You can unlock your coins at any time in Bitrue. If you don't want to use one of these exchanges US customers can use 3commas.com to access some of the coins they have.

2:46 ••ᵢ 5G E 🔋

🔍 **Pure vpn**   ⊗ Cancel

 **PureVPN: Best VPN for iPh...**   OPEN
Internet security & privacy
★★★★☆ 1.5K

 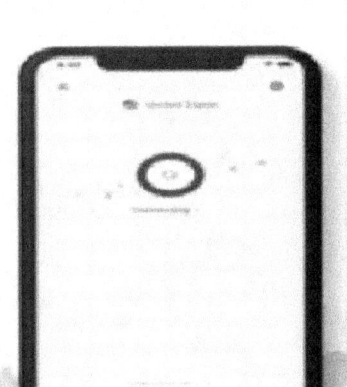

 **VPN – Super Unlimited Proxy**
WiFi Security & Privacy VPN
★★★★⯪ 974K

 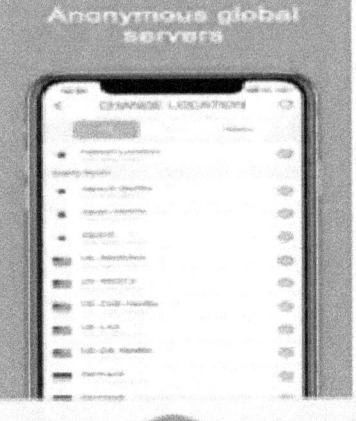 

 Today    Games   Apps    Arcade    Search

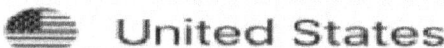
Recommended

Not Connected

Recently connected
Canada

If you decide to use PureVPN. When you download the app on your phone it will take you to this screen. Click on the 3 hash marks at the top left hand corner of the screen.

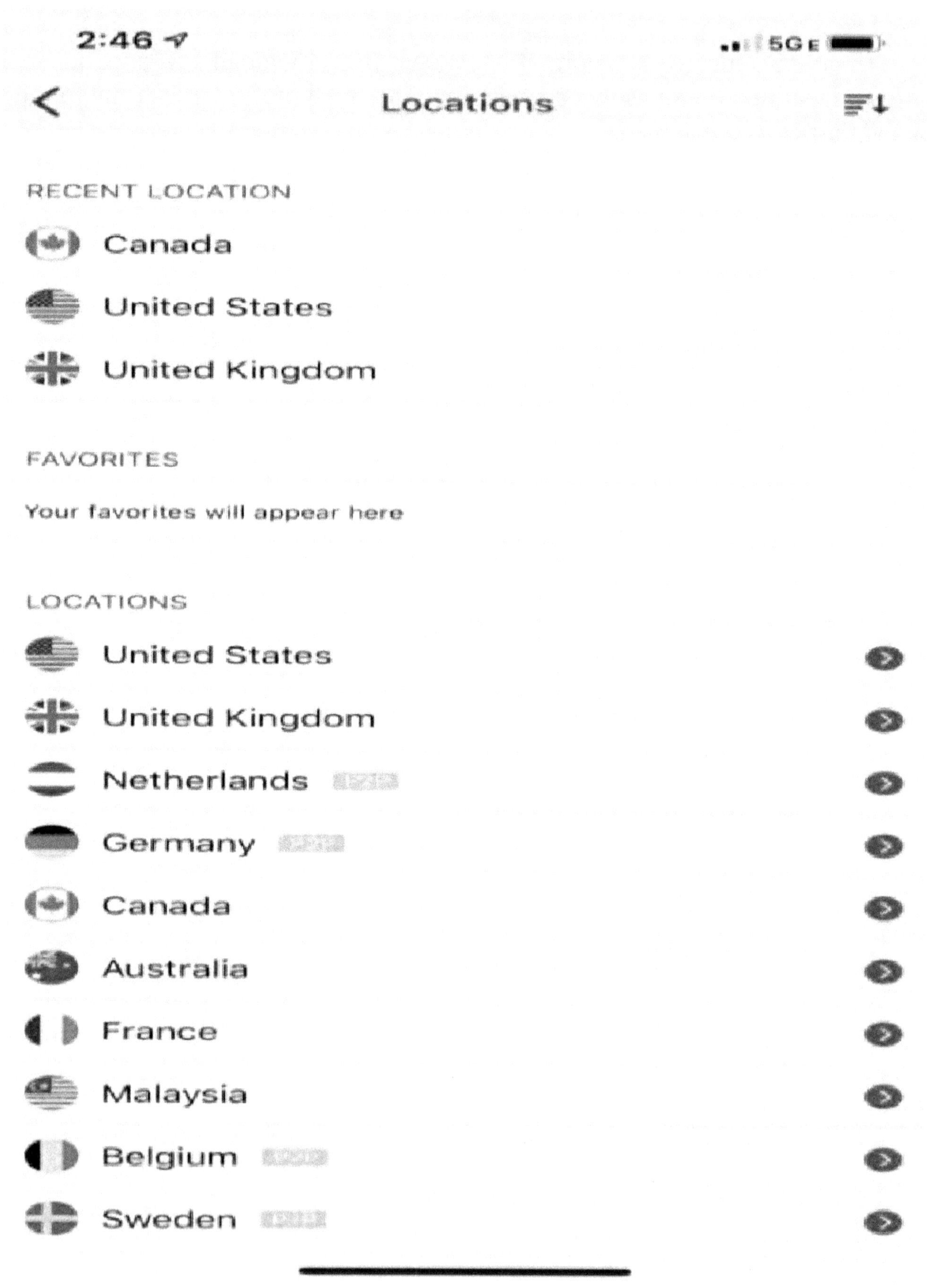

Locations

RECENT LOCATION

- 🇨🇦 Canada
- 🇺🇸 United States
- 🇬🇧 United Kingdom

FAVORITES

Your favorites will appear here

LOCATIONS

- 🇺🇸 United States ›
- 🇬🇧 United Kingdom ›
- 🇳🇱 Netherlands ›
- 🇩🇪 Germany ›
- 🇨🇦 Canada ›
- 🇦🇺 Australia ›
- 🇫🇷 France ›
- 🇲🇾 Malaysia ›
- 🇧🇪 Belgium ›
- 🇸🇪 Sweden ›

This will give you a list of countries to choose from. From there you can select a country that is crypto friendly like Canada.

Operating Rhythm

Create a daily operating rhythm and stick to it. When you wake up in the morning, as tempting as it might be, don't immediately start trading. When you wake up most of the time you're still groggy. Give yourself some time to wake up and get alert before you start trading.

Check to see what the markets did overnight. Review all the charts of the assets in your portfolio, and adjust stop losses if needed. If some of your assets went up in price you may want to move those stop losses up to the next level of support below the current price.

Now that your portfolio is safe check to see if there's any new news that hit the market through the different social media outlets the crypto projects have like YouTube channels, Facebook pages, Twitter, newsletters, and any other forms of social media you're able to follow. You want to find as many ways as possible to get news directly from the source, so you can obtain it before the mainstream does. Since this market is highly speculative right now the news is what moves the market. You need every edge you can to stay a step ahead of the competition.

Once you have the hottest news it's time to hit the charts. Set alerts where there are pattern breakouts (more on this later) and go about your day. No matter what business you have, you shouldn't allow it to run you. You run the business it's not the other way around. Don't let it consume you. Don't spend your entire day staring at the computer screen or your phone looking at charts. Set your alerts so you don't have to stay glued to the charts. When an alert goes off you can decide at that time if you want to stop what you're doing and make a trade.

Go to news outlets like the Daily Hodl, Cointelegraph, Coindesk, Cryptopanic, Lunar crush, Glassnode, Coingecko, Coinmarketcap.com, and others to read the crypto news on a daily basis so you can stay up to date with the market. As soon as everyone picks up on some hot news the price of a crypto will start pumping so be fast about it. You want to enter your position as soon as possible because the price could pump quickly. Always try to stay one step ahead of everyone else.

You don't need anything fancy to get started trading cryptocurrency. You don't need a financial degree, and you don't have to work on Wall Street to trade. Cryptocurrency allows anyone with a cell phone and internet connection to take control of their financial freedom. Start with what you have and work your way up to a laptop setup with a couple extra monitors. All it takes is one successful trade to get you there. Treat this like a business and you'll be on your way to six figures in no time.

Cryptocurrency Exchanges

"In investing, what is comfortable is rarely profitable." - Robert Arnott

A cryptocurrency exchange is a place where traders can buy and sell cryptocurrencies. Think of it as being similar to the New York Stock Exchange with stocks. In this chapter, I will show you how to create an account on the exchange, buy cryptocurrency, sell cryptocurrency, set stop losses, and how to send your crypto to another exchange or wallet.

For example purposes I will use the exchange Binance.US. You may choose to use a different exchange, but these instructions will help you no matter which exchange you decide to use. Many exchanges use a similar format so once you learn Binance.US you can operate just about any of them.

*Please note Binance.US is different than Binance international. Binance.US was designed specifically for US citizens due to regulations the

United States has placed on cryptocurrency exchanges. Please also note Binance may have changed the layout of their platform since the time of writing, but this will give you a basic understand of how to navigate an exchange.

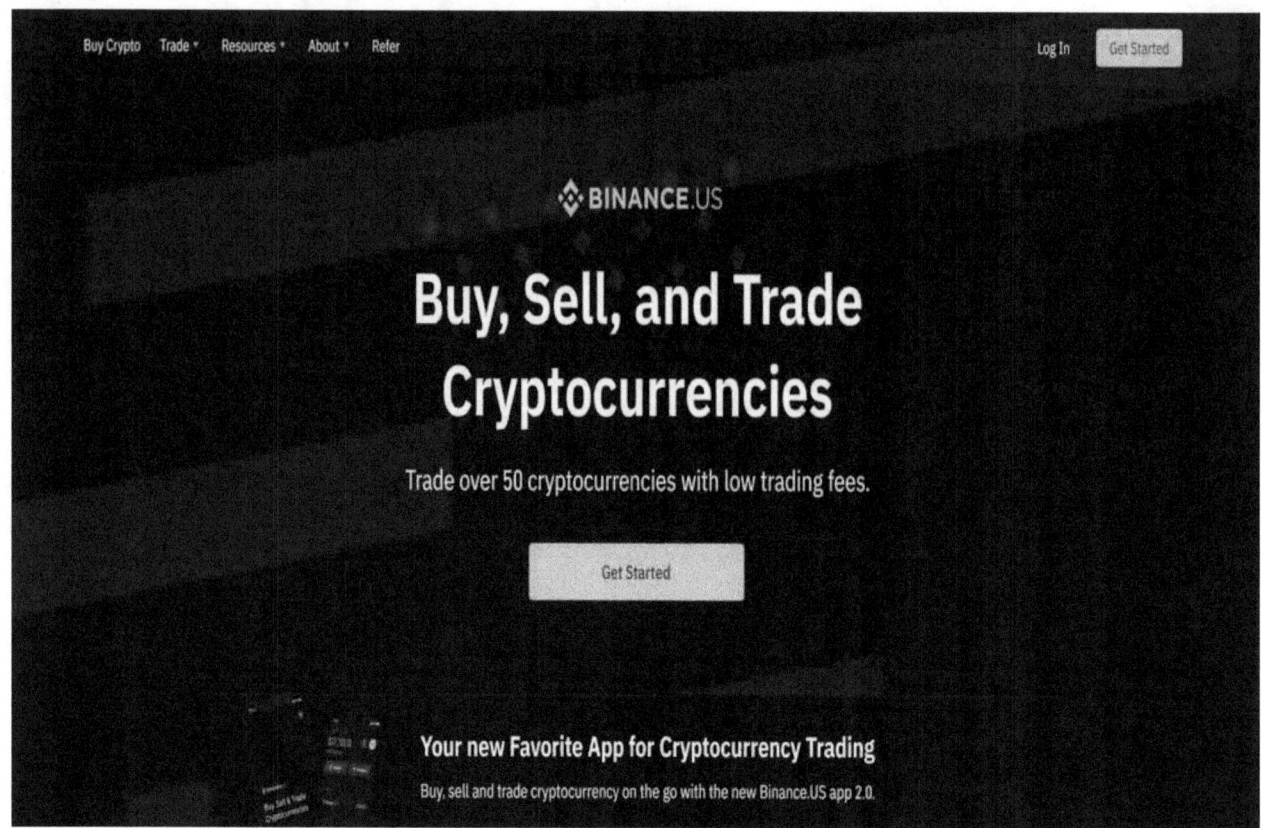

Okay let's get started! Go to Binance.US/en and follow along. Once you are on the Binance.us/en website click on register to create a free account.

Enter your email and create a secure password. Make sure you write down your password on a piece of paper or notebook and keep it in a safe place. Enter my referral ID# 35081808 for a welcome bonus. Keep two copies of your login credentials, one to keep in a fireproof safe or safety deposit box, and another copy that is easily accessible.

Binance.US will send a verification code to your email. Enter the six digit code Binance.US emails you into this section.

It will then ask you to enable 2FA or two factor authentication. You will want to enable 2 factor authentication on your account using the Google authenticator app or SMS text message authentication. Choose SMS authentication.

Enter your phone number at the top and click send SMS. Once you receive the text message enter the code in the field provided.

Towards the top of the screen next to "increase your account security", you will see that you have completed step one of four in your account security and is indicated by the green checkmark. You will need to complete all four steps of the KYC(know your customer) verification in order to purchase crypto using US dollars.

Click on verify to the right of Enable 2FA at the top left hand corner and you will arrive at this screen.

After you have completed all the verification steps scroll down to payment management at the bottom of the screen.

Click add new account.

For payment methods, I recommend using the ACH payment method, so you don't incur any fees for depositing and withdrawing cash.

Click continue to connect to your bank account. If you don't see your bank in the list that populates just type it in the search box. When you click on the link to your bank it will prompt you to login using your bank login credentials. Login to your bank account.

The program will send a security code to your phone or email, and you will have to type it in to verify it's you. Once you have your accounts pulled up choose the account you want to use. I recommend setting up a separate bank account for your crypto to keep everything separate. Now you're ready to deposit some cash! Click on the wallet tab at the top of the screen.

Click on deposit next to USD. Choose the "Deposit From:" drop down and select the account you linked to Binance.US. In the box above choose the amount you would like to deposit.

Keep in mind you won't be able to withdraw the funds for 10 days. Also, you need to make sure you have 110% of what you want to deposit in Binance in your bank account. In other words, if you want to deposit $100 into your account, you have to have $110 in your bank account.

Now we have successfully deposited U.S. dollars onto the exchange and we are ready to buy some crypto!

Trading Pairs

Trading Pairs

BTC/USD PAIR	You can buy bitcoin using U.S. dollars, or if you sell the bitcoin you've purchased you will receive U.S. dollars in return
BTC/USDT PAIR	You can buy bitcoin using U.S. dollar tether, or if you sell the bitcoin you've purchased you will receive U.S. dollar tether in return
ALT/BTC PAIR	You can buy an altcoin with the bitcoin you've purchased, or if you sell the altcoin you've purchased you will receive bitcoin in return
ALT/USD PAIR	You can buy an altcoin with your U.S. dollars, or if you sell the altcoin you've purchased you will receive U.S. dollars in return
ALT/USDT PAIR	You can buy an altcoin with you U.S. dollar tether, or if you sell the altcoin you've purchased you will receive U.S. dollar tether in return

International exchanges don't use a central bank currency like U.S. dollars, so when you trade cryptocurrency on an exchange you have to use something called trading pairs. Trading pairs allow you to trade between one type of cryptocurrency to another. There are many different trading pairs, but for this explanation we're going to use the difference between Altcoin(ALT)/bitcoin(BTC) trading pairs and ALT/USDT(United States Dollar Tether) trading pairs.

Since many trading pairs consist of stablecoins I'll need to explain what stablecoins are first. Stablecoins don't fluctuate like normal cryptocurrencies do, so they're used as safe havens to escape the market when you don't want to risk being in a trade. United States Dollar Tether (USDT) is one example of a stablecoin cryptocurrency that stays within a fraction of a percent of the U.S. dollar. Most international exchanges don't trade in U.S. dollars so

USDT was created as another option. There is also a EuroTether for Euros and YenTether for Japanese Yen, and many others.

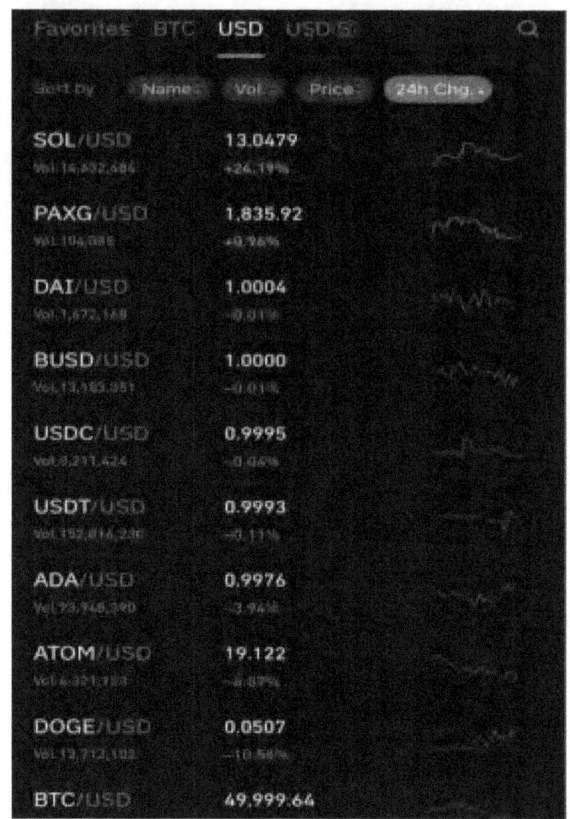

Binance.US App

At the top of the screen on Binance.US you will see a list of trading pairs. You have BTC for bitcoin pairs, USD for US dollar pairs, and USD$ which is USDT pairs. Click on the USD pairs tab. Here you will find a list of all the cryptocurrency you can purchase using US dollars. When you sell using a US dollar pair your cryptocurrency is automatically converted back to US dollars.

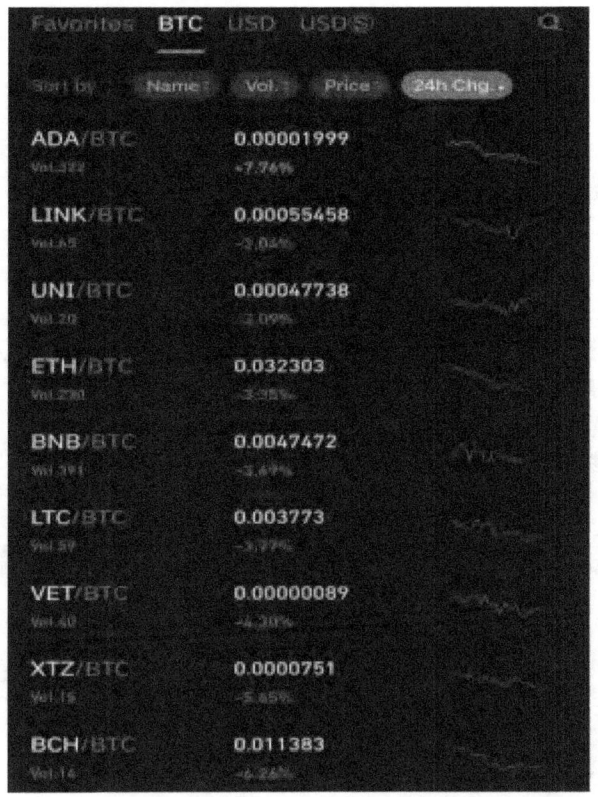

Click on the BTC tab for bitcoin pairs. Here is a list of all the cryptocurrency you can purchase using bitcoin. If you don't have any bitcoin you will need to purchase some before you can purchase a bitcoin trading pair. Since we have US dollars and no bitcoin we first have to go to the US dollar trading pair tab, go to the BTC/USD trading pair, and buy some bitcoin. Once you have bitcoin you can purchase any cryptocurrency you want in the BTC pairs tab. If you sell using a BTC pair your cryptocurrency will automatically be converted to bitcoin when you sell.

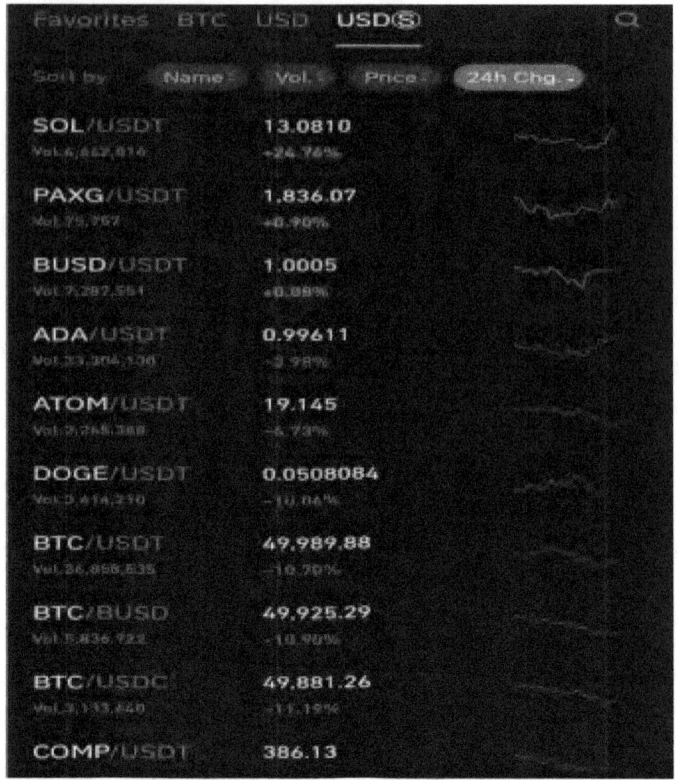

Lastly, to purchase a cryptocurrency in the USDT tab you will first need to purchase USDT. Click on the USD tab, select USDT/USD, and purchase some USDT. Once you have some USDT you can purchase any cryptocurrency you want in the USDT trading pair tab. If you sell using a USDT trading pair your cryptocurrency will automatically be converted to USDT when you sell. There are hundreds of trading pairs, and this process repeats itself for any of them.

Trading pairs are also a comparison of the performance of one coin versus another. In other words, ALT/BTC pairs are a comparison of the performance of an altcoin to the performance of bitcoin and vice versa. The goal is to be in the coin that is outperforming the other.

If you're trading using technical analysis, keep in mind that you can't convert a BTC trading pair chart to a USDT chart or any other trading pair. If you're watching an ALT/BTC chart you don't want to purchase another type of pair. The support, resistance, and break out levels won't be the same, so you have to use one or the other. Make sure the chart you're watching matches the pair you are purchasing or selling.

If bitcoin is in a fast downtrend holding altcoins is not a good idea. If you are in an altcoin that is up 5% ALT/BTC and bitcoin is down 20% BTC/USDT you've gained 5% more bitcoin, but you've lost a lot vs USDT. If an altcoin moves up 5% and BTC also moves up 5% the ALT will move sideways because there is no change in relation to bitcoin. If bitcoin moves up 5% and the ALT coin doesn't move, the altcoin will be down 5% because the value of bitcoin went up by 5%. It's all about the performance of one versus the other.

Altcoins don't do well when bitcoin is volatile. I remember one time bitcoin was hovering around $9,000 for a while, and bitcoin dominance was tanking. All the altcoins were doing fantastic. When bitcoin slowly consolidates the altcoins usually perform very well. Then, bitcoin shot up to over $11,000, bitcoin dominance increased, and the altcoins took a big hit. Some lost as much as 30%! I had stop losses set on all my positions so thankfully I didn't take much of a loss. Make sure you always have a stop loss set on every trade. I capitalized on the situation and was able to buy a couple positions back at a much lower price than before. Always keep at least 20% cash on the side so when this happens you can increase your position.

After you've purchased your coins you now have the choice to set a stop loss or place a sell order using a trading pair. When you sell, do you want your coins to convert to BTC or USDT? If you want your coins to convert to BTC, you will choose the ALT/BTC trading pair when selling or setting a stop loss. If you want your coins to convert to USDT when you sell you will need to choose the ALT/USDT trading pair.

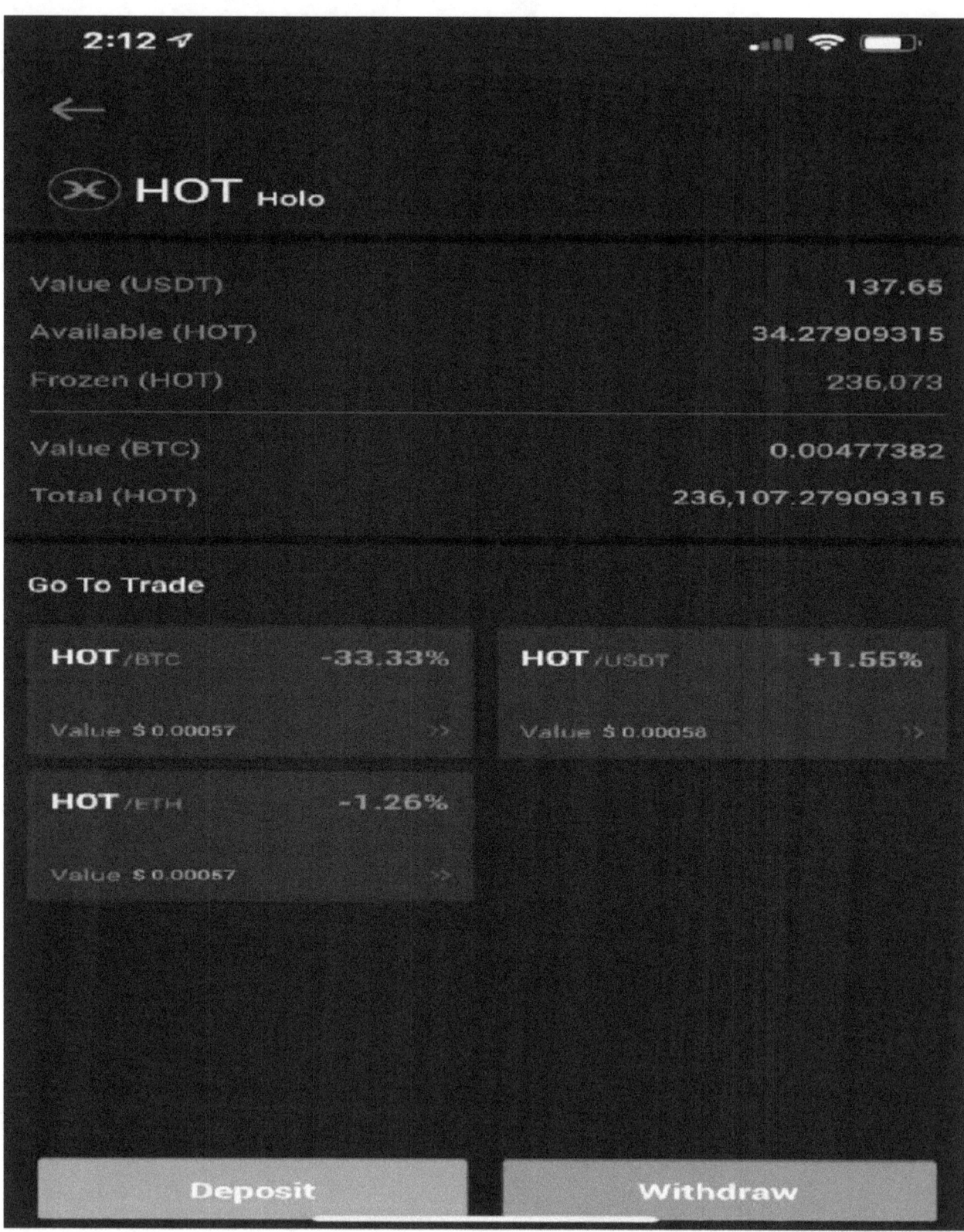

As you can see in the example above, the HOT/BTC pair was -33.33%, the HOT/USDT pair was +1.55%, and the HOT/ETH pair was -1.26%.

However, the value remained the same at $0.00057-$0.00058. The value is what's important. Bitcoin just happened to be performing very well at the time. That's why the bitcoin pair is showing such a low percentage. Bitcoin was performing 33.33% better than HOT at the time.

You can use trading pairs to anticipate the market too. If all the ALT/BTC pairs have been beaten down by bitcoin running there will be a reversal coming at some point. You will start to see a bunch of reversal patterns on the bitcoin pair charts, and when bitcoin consolidates the altcoins will take off if bitcoin doesn't drop too fast.

Don't over-complicate trading pairs. Once you've purchased the coins they're yours. You have the same amount of coins no matter which trading pair you used to purchase them.

How to Purchase

Now that you have deposited your cash it's time to buy some crypto. Click on buy crypto at the top left hand of the screen.

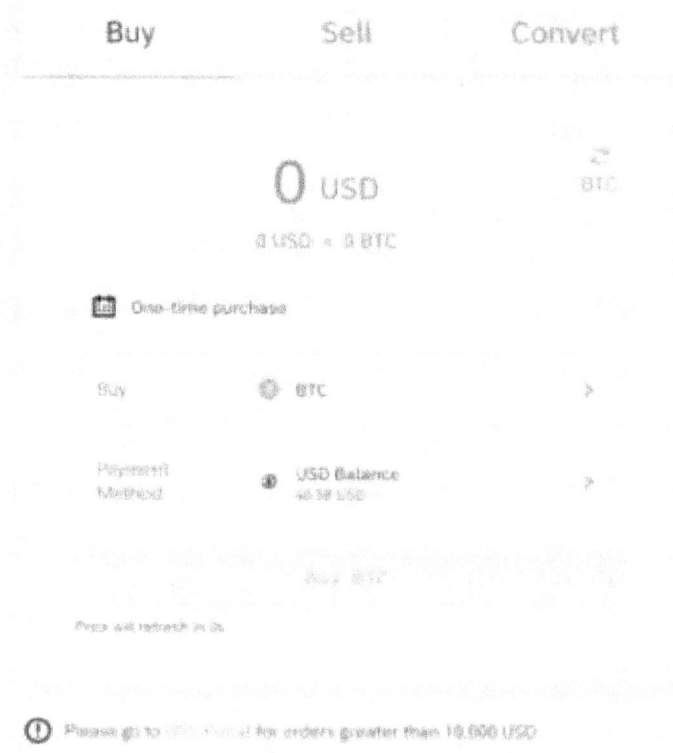

You will definitely want to purchase a little BNB (Binance token) because you can get a discount on trading fees by using the exchange's native token.

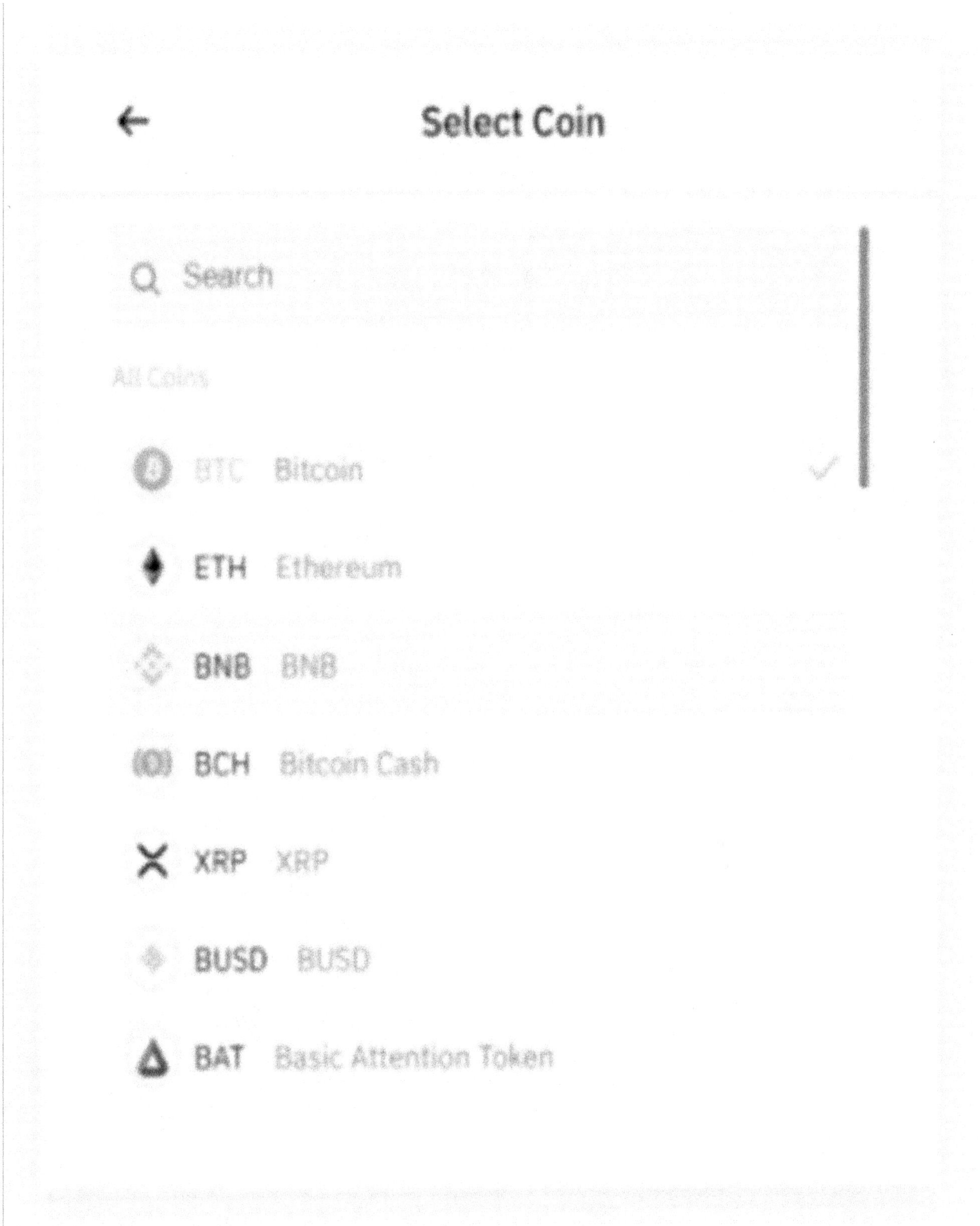

← **Select Coin**

🔍 Search

All Coins

| | BTC | Bitcoin | ✓ |

◆ ETH Ethereum

◈ BNB BNB

◉ BCH Bitcoin Cash

✕ XRP XRP

◈ BUSD BUSD

△ BAT Basic Attention Token

Select BNB from the list, choose the amount you want to purchase, and click buy BNB. Confirm your purchase.

Purchase in progress

We're currently processing your purchase! Once the purchase complete successfully, a confirmation mail would be sent with order details.

[Back to Wallet]

After you click on back to wallet you will see your purchase has been completed in the transaction history.

Now you can click on the balance tab and you will see that you now own BNB. Congratulations you've just made your first cryptocurrency purchase!

Now that you have $40 of BNB let's look for another coin to purchase. Click on trade and choose one of the four trading pairs. Remember, whatever trading pair you choose is what you will receive if you sell the coin. The BNB/BTC trading pair will give you bitcoin (BTC) when you sell.

Click on the BNB/BTC trading pair and it will take you to the main trading screen.

In the top left hand corner you will see the trading graph. In the trading graph, the price action is in the middle of the screen, and is shown in the form of red and green candles. Each candle represents the open and close prices of the coin. The lines moving with the price action are the moving averages. The volume of each candle is shown at the bottom right below the price action. The tabs at the top left are for the time frame you want to see and technical indicators you can add to the chart. In the middle of the screen at the top you will see original view, trading view, depth, and the option to go full screen.

I really like the charts on Binance because they use the tradingview website which is what a lot of professional traders use for trading stocks and cryptocurrency. In this view you have all your drawing tools available on the left hand side. In the bottom left hand corner is the order form section where you can place your buy and sell orders, view your open orders, view order history, view trade history, and funds.

Price (BTC)	Amount (BNB)	Total
	0.0000001	
0.0055677	4.60	0.0256114
0.0055625	0.01	0.0000556
0.0055582	0.06	0.0003335
0.0055578	1.57	0.0087257
0.0055513 ↓ $320.17		
0.0055430	0.11	0.0006097
0.0055428	0.03	0.0001663
0.0055425	0.12	0.0006651
0.0055421	0.29	0.0016072

Price (BTC)	Amount (BNB)	Time
0.0055513	17.62	18:01:39
0.0055519	17.62	18:01:39
0.0055494	4.91	18:01:38
0.0055499	4.91	18:01:38
0.0055431	0.40	18:01:38
0.0055432	0.16	18:01:38
0.0055458	0.03	18:01:37
0.0055476	0.07	18:01:36
0.0055482	0.03	18:01:36
0.0055484	0.03	18:01:36
0.0055485	0.15	18:01:36
0.0055485	0.03	18:01:36
0.0055496	0.44	18:01:36

Place Order VIP 0

BUY   SELL

Limit   Market   Stop-limit

0.00000000 BTC

Price   0.0056129 BTC

Amount   BNB

Total   BTC

Buy BNB

Assets

Deposit   Withdraw

BNB Available: 0.00000000
BTC Available: 0.00000000

Next to the order form section where you place your buy and sell orders you will see the live order book data. The order book data shows all the buy and sell orders in real time. The numbers in red are all the sell orders and the numbers in green are all the buy orders. The number circled in the middle of them indicates the last price a purchase was made. It is what the current price of BNB is compared to BTC. The amount column next to the prices are all quantities of coins being purchased and the column to the right of that is the equivalent amount in BTC. The section to the right is where we can place buy and sell orders.

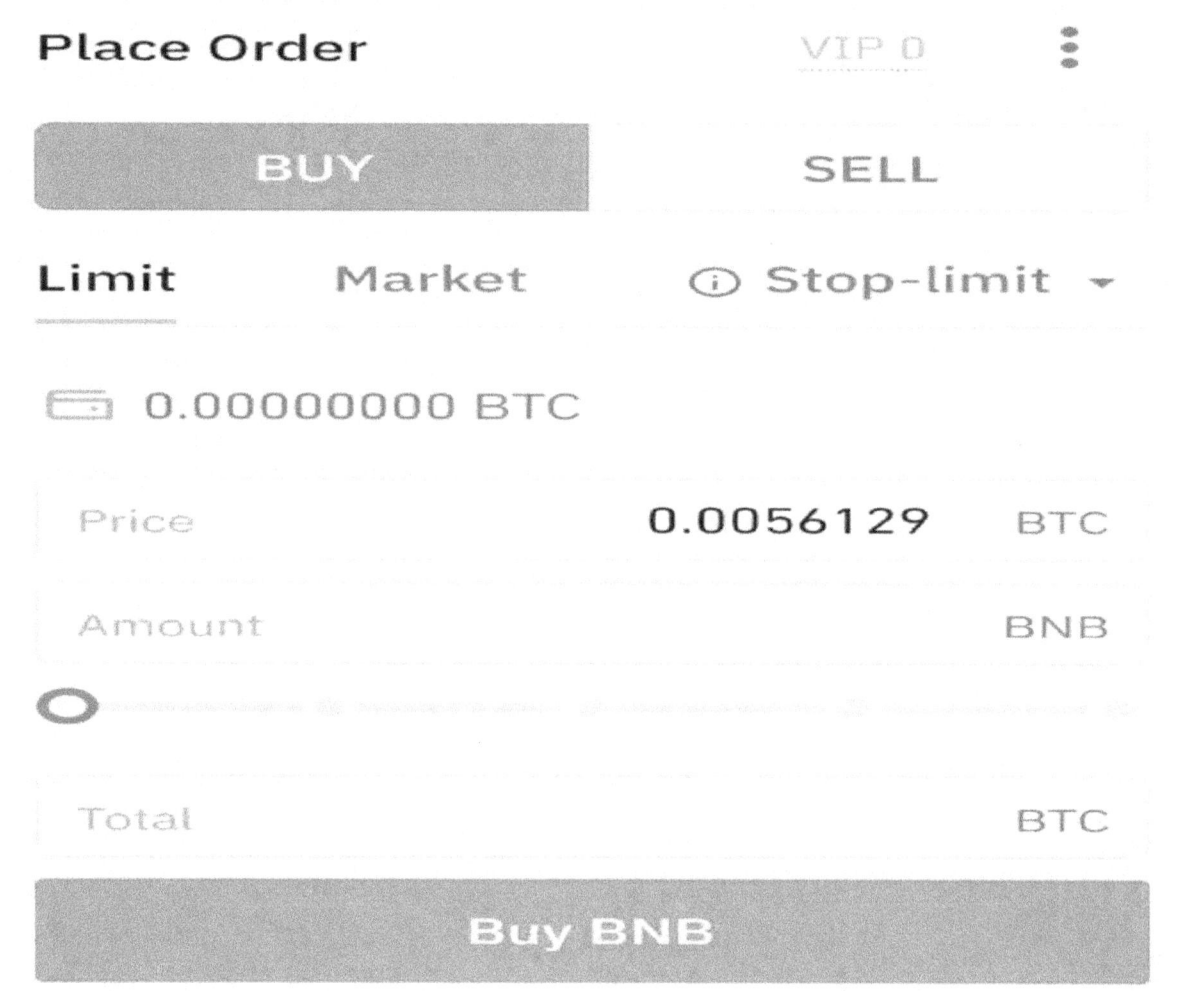

A limit order is an order to buy or sell at the price you specify. You can click on different orders that have already been placed if you want to copy the current order. Choose the amount you want to buy using a specific amount or by using the percentages below.

A market order is a purchase order or sell order for whatever the market price is currently. This can change quickly so I never use market orders. Let the market come to you.

A stop limit order is an order to buy or sell a coin once the price reaches a specified price. If your stop price is hit in the price action it will place an order to buy at the limit price you specify. If the stop price hits X amount it will place a limit order to buy at X amount. Now that we have a good understanding of the basics let's take a look at the trading pairs. Click on the drop down at the top left hand corner of the screen.

BNB/BTC ▾	0.0056201	24h Change	24h High	24h Low	24h Volume
					71.67 BTC

★	USD	BTC	FIAT ▾

Search   ● Change ○ Volume

CHANGE: 0.11%

Pair	Last Price	Change
★ ADA/BTC	0.00002037 / $1.17	+0.54%
★ BCH/BTC	0.009296 / $536.15	-6.58%
★ BNB/BTC	0.0056262 / $324.49	-1.33%
★ ETH/BTC	0.035299 / $2,035.88	-0.89%
★ LINK/BTC	0.00051641 / $29.78	-3.88%
★ LTC/BTC	0.003448 / $198.86	-2.79%
★ UNI/BTC	0.00051870 / $29.92	+3.16%
★ VET/BTC	0.00000155 / $0.089397	-3.73%

The tabs at the top are for Favorites(the star), USD, BTC, and another drop down that allows you to choose to view all FIAT trading pairs, all USDT (US dollar tether) trading pairs, BUSD (Binance's stable coin), and USDC (United States Dollar Coin) pairs. A stablecoin is one that doesn't fluctuate wildly like other cryptocurrencies. BUSD is pegged to the US dollar so it remains about the same price as a dollar. It's the same situation with USDT. USDT is a coin that is designed to follow the price of the US dollar. It's a digital dollar essentially. With a BTC/USDT trading pair you can buy bitcoin with tether or sell bitcoin for tether and vice versa. It also takes into consideration the value of one crypto compared to another. Below are all the trading pairs, the last price they were bought or sold, the 24 hour change in price, and there's a place to switch to view the 24 hr volume for each pair.

Now let's choose the USD tab. Here you will see a list of all the coins on Binance.US that are able to be exchanged with the US dollar. As soon as you deposit your cash you can go to this tab and immediately start placing buy orders. If there is a coin you want in another trading pair you will have to buy into that pair. If you want a coin in the BTC trading pair, for example, you will have to first purchase BTC, and then purchase the coin you want. When you sell the coin you will receive it's value in BTC. Go to the USD tab and choose the BNB/USD trading pair or you can type BNB in the search.

How to sell and set stop-losses

Now that you know how to buy cryptocurrency, you should probably learn how to sell it. We're going to sell some of the BNB we purchased earlier. Let's choose the highest buy order so that our order gets filled immediately. Click on the highest buy order located just below the market price. The amount we will sell is going to be 50%. After you click sell BNB the order will be filled and you will have sold half of your BNB for USD.

In the bottom left hand corner of the screen you can click order history to view your orders. Here you can see that you've successfully sold half of your BNB for USD. You could've set your limit order to sell at a much lower price if you wanted to try to get a better price, but we didn't want to wait for the order to be filled.

Now you can go to any USD trading pair and purchase another cryptocurrency using USD. We're going to purchase ADA next.

Price (USD)	Amount (ADA)	Total
1.1692	624.7	730.3992
1.1691	2,554.1	2,985.9983
1.1689	2,554.0	2,985.3706
(1.1688) ←	4,368.5	5,105.9028

1.1689 ↓ $1.17

1.1677	2,568.1	2,998.7704
1.1675	2,567.9	2,998.0233
1.1662	4,369.9	5,096.1774
1.1661	8,250.1	9,620.4416

    You're already on the limit order tab, so next you want to choose the lowest red sell order because you want the order to get filled immediately. Select 100% because you want to use all the USD available to purchase ADA.

    Now that you have purchased ADA, you'll want to put a stop loss on it in case the price drops. First, click sell, then you'll want to select the Stop-Limit tab to the right of market. A stop-limit order is an order that says if the price action reaches X amount it will sell for Y amount. In this example we're going to put our stop at 0.1408 and the limit as 0.1401 and choose to sell 100% of the ADA we purchased.

Now if the price drops to or below 0.1408 USD, an order to sell our ADA at a price of 0.1401 USD will be placed. Don't rely on the stop-losses too much though. Sometimes the price can drop so fast your order can be skipped! Make sure you set alerts so you're notified when your stop price is triggered. If you download the app on your phone you can set alerts so you will receive a message when the price reaches one of your targets. Market makers on the exchanges hunt for stop-losses sometimes to bring liquidity back into the market so keep that in mind too.

How to Use OCO (One-Cancels-the-Other) Order Type

A one cancels the other order (OCO) is where you can place two orders at the same time, a limit order and stop-limit order, under the condition that when one order is filled the other is automatically canceled. With an OCO you set a limit order and a stop-limit order in the same amount an quantity at the same time. Whichever order the price action reaches first will get filled and then the other one will be canceled. If you decide to cancel the OCO, both orders will be automatically canceled.

For buy orders, the limit price must be less than the market price and the stop price less than the market price.

For sell orders the limit price of the limit order must be greater than the market price and the stop price of the stop-limit order must be greater than the market price.

Traders that use OCO orders usually use them to trade breakout patterns.

This Aave set up is the perfect example of when you can use an OCO order. In this set up the price action is close to breaking out of this triangle pattern. You would always like to buy lower than the current price, but if the price takes off you don't necessarily want to miss out on the price increase either. That's where the OCO orders comes into play.

In this situation, your OCO limit price is placed lower than the current market price because if the price drops you want your order to get filled before the price takes off again. You want your OCO stop price set to trigger at just above where the current price is because if the price takes off after the breakout you want to jump in on the action. The other number is the range you want your order to attempt to be filled.

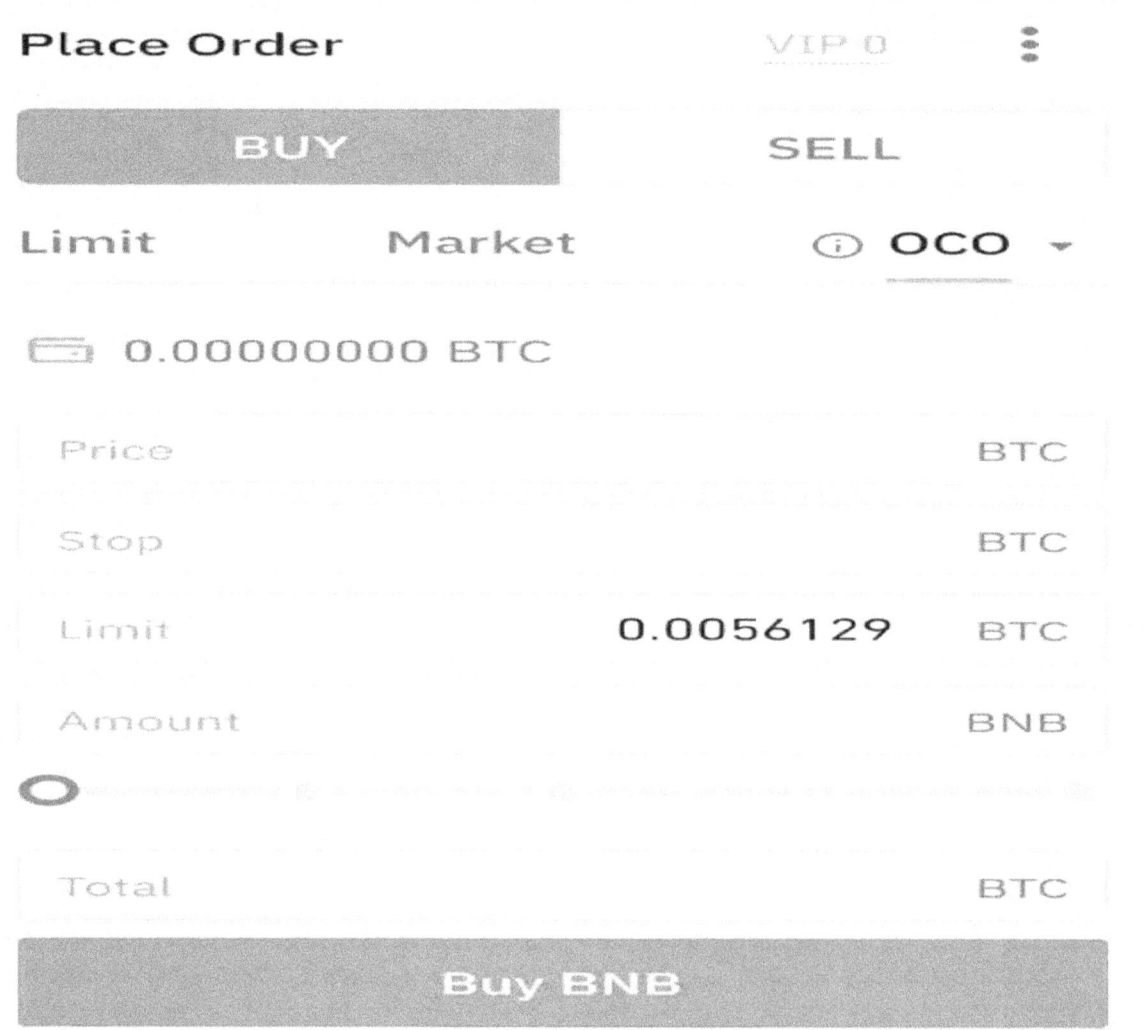

Go to the order page and select "OCO" in the drop down box when you click on stop-limit. The price you would like to pay will go in the box labeled price. Again, since this is a buy OCO, the limit price will be lower than the current market price. It's the price you would like to pay, not the current price. Your stop price is the price where you want your stop-limit buy order to trigger, and fill your buy order if the price goes above the current market price. In other words, if "Price" hits X amount you agree to purchase the asset, OR if the price hits between "stop" and "limit" you agree to purchase the asset. Whichever comes first.

The sell OCO works in a similar fashion. If "Price" hits X amount you agree to sell the asset, OR if the price hits between "stop" and "limit" you agree to sell the asset. Whichever comes first. You would want to use a sell OCO in a situation where you're in a position and you don't want to sell because you think the price will go up, but at the same time the market is volatile and you don't want to risk losing more than a predetermined amount before the price goes up as you plan. When your OCO order is placed you will see two separate order in the Orders can be canceled at anytime. Whenever one of the orders is filled the other will be automatically cancelled. Use OCO orders to obtain and sell at the best price possible.

Transferring Crypto to a Different Exchange or Wallet

Now that you know how to buy and sell cryptocurrency let's learn how to send your crypto to a different exchange, or get your crypto off of the exchanges altogether by transferring to an external wallet. Transferring cryptocurrency is easy. Crypto can be transferred with just a couple mouse clicks. From this screen, you can click on the little person at the top right hand corner to go back to the main screen.

In the dashboard section you can see a breakdown of all your holdings. If you want to send your crypto to a wallet or another exchange. Click on wallet and then withdraw.

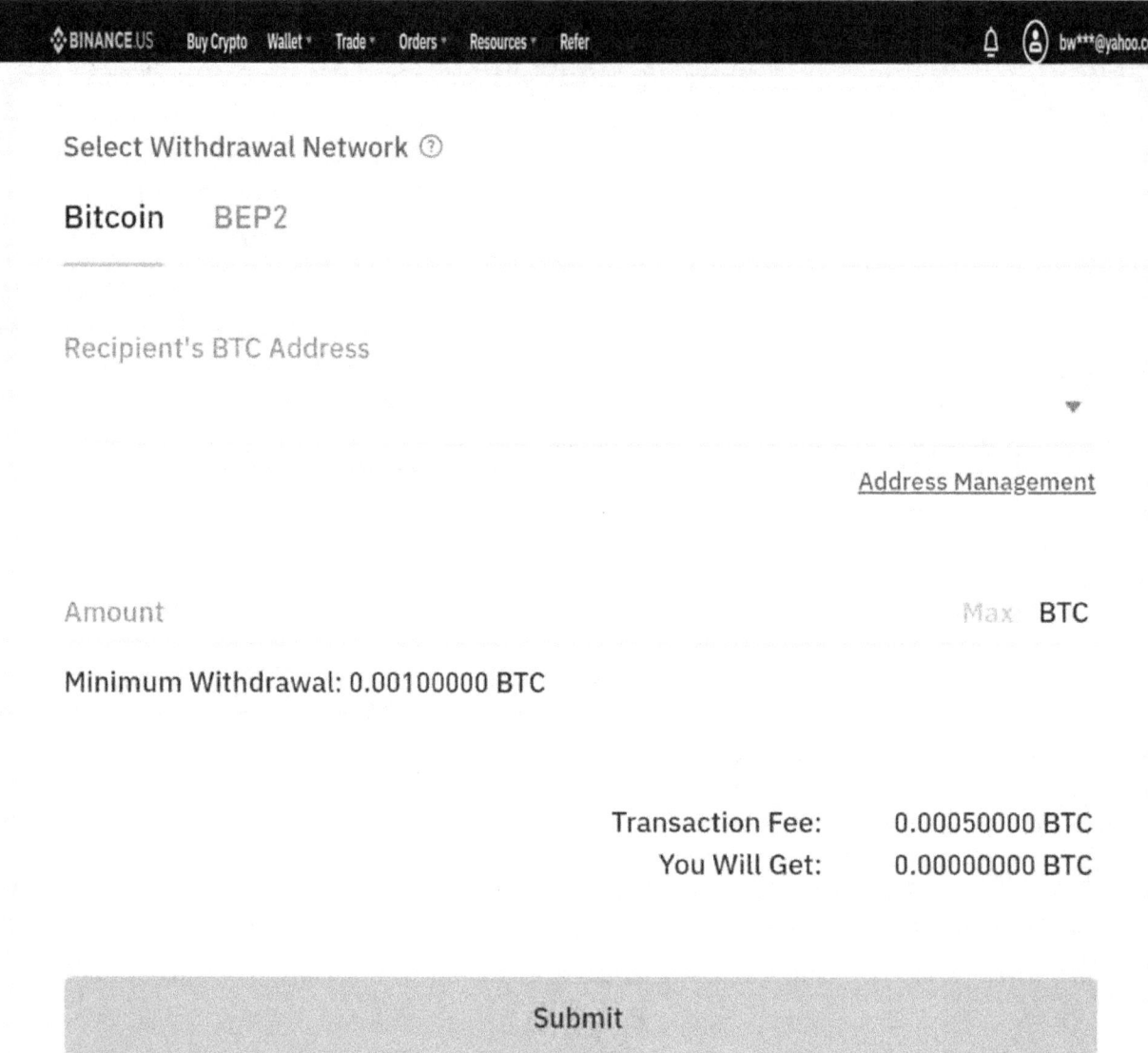

This is where you're going to type the deposit address you are going to obtain from your wallet or other exchange. Go to your wallet or other exchange you want to transfer to, and find "deposit." Select the coin you want to deposit and copy your deposit address. Now that you have your deposit address go back to Binance.US and paste it in the address section there. After you type or cut/paste the address you will have the option to type a memo if you want. If not, check the no memo box. Some cryptos like XRP will have an additional "tag", so make sure to check under the address of the account it's going in. In the amount section type the amount you want to withdraw or you can type on your available balance if you want to withdraw the full amount. At the bottom it will show the transaction fee and what you will receive when the funds are deposited into your new account. Click submit.

Just remember to copy/paste the addresses or be extremely careful when you're typing them because once you hit submit. You don't want to send your crypto to the wrong wallet! Most exchanges and wallets have fail safe measures put into place now that will tell you if the address is incorrect, but just pay attention and make sure it's correct before you hit the send button to make sure you don't have any issues.

Binance.US also has an app you can download on your phone so you can trade anywhere anytime with an internet connection! Most exchanges have apps you can use. When I first got started I actually did most of my trading on my phone. Nothing beats the size of the charts on a larger screen though. I would pick my laptop over my cell phone to trade on any day. I love being able to have multiple windows open for several different coin charts so I can flip back and forth between them. You just can't watch the market on a cell phone like you can on a laptop.

Once you think you have mastered Binance.US feel free to try other exchanges like Bitrue, Coinbase, Coinbase Pro, Kraken or even some of the international exchanges like the international Binance exchange. Now that we know where to purchase cryptocurrency and how to navigate the exchanges let's learn how we can pick projects to invest in that will increase in value.

Fundamental Analysis

"Behind every stock is a company. Find out what it's doing." – Peter Lynch

Fundamental analysis involves the research of a business in order to find the underlying value of an asset. The information obtained as a result of the research is used to determine if an asset is overvalued or undervalued which can then be used to enter and exit positions. If the sale price is less than the intrinsic value, a project is undervalued and there is profit to be made. Fundamental analysts dive deep into the business metrics and look at all aspects of a business that contribute to its value.

Just because an asset is undervalued doesn't mean the price will go up. This just gives you a foundation from which to build. It will help you determine which cryptos to focus on that have the most potential. From that point you can review other factors such as market cycle and technical analysis to see if and when you want to enter a trade.

Crypto fundamentals are a little different than the fundamentals of the stock market. Since cryptocurrency is so new most projects don't have any financial information for you to review so let's take a look at the areas we can review for crypto. Cryptocurrency fundamental analysis can be broken down into three key sections: project information, network metrics, and financial statistics.

Project Information

Instead of digging through a company's financial information crypto fundamental analysts mostly focus on whats called the white paper. A white paper outlines everything you need to know about a project. It will tell you how the project works from the market it looks to enter, problem it looks to solve, the technology used, developers involved, to the token supply. It tells you everything you need to know about the project. Think of it like a business plan.

When reviewing a white paper the main area of importance is to find out the vision of the project and all it plans to accomplish. What problem does the project solve and how can it bring value to others? What use cases does it have? Some projects promise everything under the sun, but are they really capable of fulfilling what they set out to do? Is the plan realistic?

Find out what niche of the market the project plans to target. How saturated is this sector of the market? How well has this sector done compared to others? Compare the project to all the other competitors. Has the competition had sustained growth over a period of time? Find out what makes the project different from the competition.

Investors notice when one particular niche is doing better than others. If one project is dominating a niche and another new project comes along promising bigger and better things it can cause a lot of hype. Comparing a project to the competition is a good way to find out if a project is undervalued or not.

Find out what makes a project unique. When you're reading the white paper does this sound like a project that interests you or gets you excited? If not, there's no need to waste anymore time. Move on to the next one!

One thing that isn't necessarily a make or break is if the project is creating a whole new blockchain or if it's built on another blockchain. Most of the top cryptocurrencies have their own blockchains, so take that for what it's worth. You will hear the terms coins and tokens thrown around a lot so let me clarify. A coin exists on its own blockchain and they're mostly used as currency. They're used as a store of value or a medium of exchange, where as tokens can be used for multiple different things. Tokens can be created to represent almost anything. Right now they are mostly used for decentralized applications or dApps.

There are multiple different kinds of tokens including utility tokens, payment tokens, security tokens, and equity tokens. Utility tokens provide access to a service or a product. Payment tokens are used to pay for goods and services. Security tokens are issued when an investor invests in a company before the project has been released. Equity tokens represent equity in the company that issues it.

Tokenomics

Another area of importance in the white paper is the economics involved. In a regular economy you have the issuance of currency. In a crypto economy you have the issuance of coins or tokens. You need to know how much of a digital asset will be created, how it's distributed, and how much of it will be placed into circulation.

Some have proposed the "tokenization of everything." Interestingly enough, the concept of the social token economy was first proposed by a Harvard psychologist named B.F. Skinner in 1972. Skinner believed a token economic model that focused on positive reinforcement could control behavior. Could crypto be used for sinister reasons? Absolutely, that's why it's important that we support projects that are decentralized.

1INCH token distribution

- security of the network and maintenance of its functionality (4 year vesting)
- 1inch core team and future employees (4 year vesting)
- ecosystem development (4 year vesting)
- investors and shareholders (2,5 year vesting)
- advisors (4 year vesting)
- early Mooniswap liquidity providers (1 year vesting)

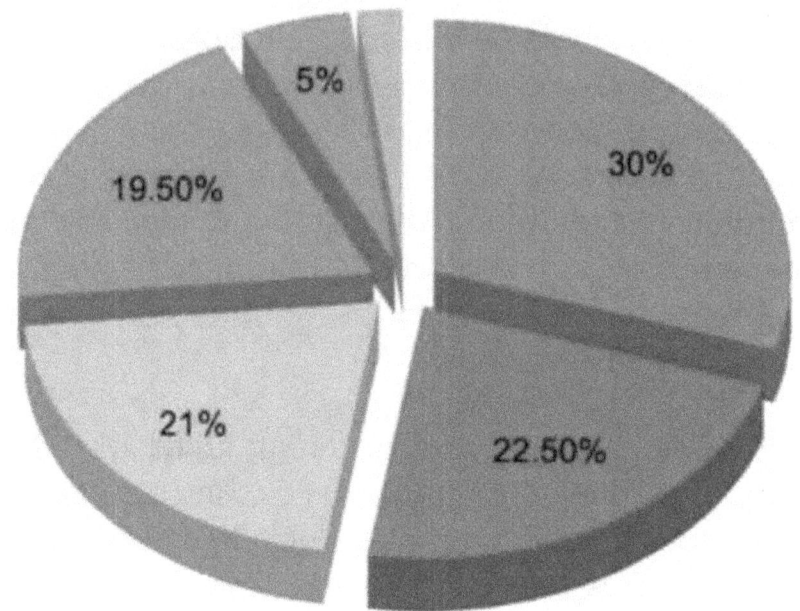

The supply and demand of a coin or token determines it's value and sustainability. All of the individual crypto projects basically create their own self-sustaining miniature economies, determine how they will be governed, and who they are going
to be governed by. In most cases that answer is no one. No single person or entity.

The creation of coins or tokens in the crypto economy is very important. Supply and demand determines market price in the crypto world just like it does the real world. If you have a low supply available along with increasing demand it should cause price to increase. A fixed supply and increasing demand causes price to rise.

Take bitcoin for example. Only twenty one million bitcoin that will ever be mined between now and the year 2140, so this creates scarcity of the supply. Scarcity combined with demand equals higher price. On the other hand, if you have a certain amount in circulation and trillions more are created as is the case with the US dollar, you end up with a devalued currency. The purchasing power is diminished through the increase in supply.The allocation of the newly created tokens is equally as important. There needs to be a fair distribution of the supply instead of the supply being in the hands of a few team members. Search the white paper to find out how many coins or tokens the team is keeping for themselves. If the team keeps the majority of the supply it's not decentralized! This is a big red flag for pump and dump schemes. There should be a balanced ratio between the team, developers, product launch and marketing, operating costs, end users, and network incentives. The supply needs to be widely distributed to ensure the project is truly decentralized.

In the white paper, sometimes a project will have an allocate some of the supply to go to early investors through what's called an initial coin offering (ICO). Unlike an initial public offering (IPO) with an ICO there is a sort of crowdfunding undertaking to raise capital for development and marketing. This is where early investors have the opportunity to buy in before the main release to the public.

With an ICO you are investing in the potential value of a company while it's still in the early stages of development. The idea of ICO's are excellent because they connect mom and pop investors to these projects and these projects can raise capital without having to go the venture capital route. Make sure the white paper provides a clear explanation as to how they will use the funds after they receive them if you decide to invest in an ICO. ICO's can be extremely risky, but they can also be massively rewarding if you invest in the right ones. Millionaires can be made quickly, but with great risk!

The white paper will also reveal how the supply will be distributed throughout its existence. This will play a big part in how the project will grow as time goes on. The inflation must be kept under control! Sometimes there are agreements between team members to lock or freeze a certain amount of tokens that are allocated to each member of a team to prevent them from selling all at once. Some contracts ensure that each member can only sell a certain amount at predetermined times. A large selloff could be detrimental to the price and cause it to plummet, so these safetly measures must be put into place.

Some projects incentivize people to hold their coins or tokens for long periods of time which discourages selling. Unlike the proof of work system that bitcoin uses where miners are rewarded for validating blocks on the blockchain, the proof of stake process secures the network and gradually produces new coins over time without consuming significant computational power. As a reward for helping secure the network holders are given a percentage of the total amount they hold back to them. This works similar to a certificate of deposit at a bank, but with cryptocurrency! Some require the assets to be tied up or frozen for a certain period of time just like a CD. Others don't require assets to be frozen at all. With proof of stake the fee is paid to the nodes that confirm each block instead of paying the fees to the miners. Proof of stake helps create value by getting people to hold their coins for extended periods of time.

How coins and tokens are created are very important too. Written into it's code, bitcoin has what's called a halving roughly every four years. This is where the reward for the miners to process transactions is cut in half. The last halving occurred on May 11, 2020. This process decreases the rate of bitcoin's that enter circulation and in turn lower the available supply. When supply is lowered combined with increasing demand it can have a drastic affect on price. Historically, bitcoin halvings have been followed by price explosions due to increased demand. Keep these on your radar! These are very significant events. They are so significant in fact that they have been the single cause that has started the cryptocurrency bull runs in the past. Cryptocurrencies other than bitcoin have halvings too. Be sure to mark them on your calendar too because they have the same effect.

While reviewing the white paper make sure you find out how much of the coin or token will remain in circulation. Will supply ever be added in the future? If supply is added it could lower the price. How much will remain in circulation is equally if not more important.

Sometimes the economics in the white paper call for coins or tokens to be taken out of circulation to manage inflation. A burn is where projects send a certain amount of an asset to a wallet address where they can never be recovered again. This too increases the price just like halvings. Buy backs have the same effect. Sometimes projects will buy back a certain amount of their own assets therefore reducing the overall supply on the market. This too will increase the value.

Another very important aspect of the token economy you can find in the white paper is the consensus mechanism. The way the blockchain arrives at consensus determines the security and stability of the blockchain. You want to see the governance framework is implemented so projects can become and remain decentralized. Governance tokens are sometimes issued for decentralization and self-governance.

Governance tokens are sometimes issued when you stake a coin. For instance, if you stake Zilliqa you receive Zilliqa in return as well as gZil their governance token. This is a very valuable token that can enable holders to become decision makers in the Zilliqa project. Another cryptocurrency project called Tezos has an on-chain voting system to solve governance issues.

Decentralized autonomous organizations (DAOs) are a form of governance that are not tied to any specific geographical area or company. This governance model allows for a token to be created to be used and another token to influence the way a project operates. They are open source so they are collectively produced for the great good as opposed to centrally created as with a company for profit. Once they are operational they work independently and decisions are reached through a voting consensus. The framework for the global economy is being built!

You'll also want to read the white paper to find a list of the team and it's advisors. After you have the list Google them to find out who they are and what kind of background they have. Have they worked for any other big name companies? Have they worked on any other projects that were successful? If there isn't much information about the team this is a big red flag. Google all the team members and learn about them to see if they are competent to perform the work.

If the project is open source there is no team. With an open source project you have a community of developers from all around the world that contribute whenever they want. Open protocol has made it to where anyone can participate in the development of a project. With open protocol you're working for yourself, but at the same time you're working for the company or crypto project. There's no longer a divide between owners and workers. Those who contribute more get paid more. The more they promote the project the currency they're paid increases. It's a wonderful model.

If the project is open source find out what the developer community looks like. Go to GitHub.com and see how many people are contributing to a project and how the development has been progressing.

The road map in a white paper is a timeline that details the goals and developmental milestones a project intends on accomplishing and how they aim to bring it to fruition. It provides direction and pace for the project. Successful projects fulfill their commitments as they originally planned and in a timely manner. When they fail to not fulfill their promises it raises a big red flag. It's important to follow the road map closely if you're holding long term. If the project doesn't fulfill it's commitments the price is likely to suffer.

Once you're finished reviewing the white paper there are some numbers we can review that can help us find the underlying value as well. We can't track profit and loss but we can track other metrics that help us determine how well a project is doing and if we are making a good investment or not.

Network metrics

The activity on the network can give us some insight as to how well a particular project is doing. By looking at data like number of active addresses, number of transactions, fees, hash rate and amount staked, we can get a better idea of how much the blockchain is being used. A high demand to use the network can translate to higher prices. There are several websites that take care of the heavy lifting by tracking this information and plotting it on graphs for you to research. Having some background knowledge of why the different aspects are important will help you become a better investor.

The number of active addresses on the blockchain is a good indication as to how well a project is doing. Blockchain addresses are used to send and receive tokens on the blockchain network. The more active unique addresses used, the more people who are using the network theoretically. I say theoretically because I'm sure some people have multiple addresses. An increase in active addresses over time shows the network is growing.

The number of transactions a network has is a good indication of how much activity is taking place on the network. A large number of transactions means there is a healthy amount of activity taking place. You can track the transaction rate to see how they stack up to the competition.

You can also track the transaction value. The transaction value tells us how much value has been transferred within a certain timeframe. If you add the dollar amount that was transacted in a day you arrive at the total volume. This is a very important because increasing volume means increasing price.

The fees that are paid to the network can also give us an idea of the demand. Some cryptocurrencies have fees called gas which are required to keep the network operational. Think of it like gasoline in a vehicle. Gas must be purchased to keep moving forward. Gas is paid by users of the network for using the service. An increase in gas fees usually means prices are increasing due to demand. During the previous bull market in 2017, bitcoin hit all time highs and transaction fees went sky high to almost $60 on average.

Hash rate is used to measure the health of a network in proof of work currencies like bitcoin. Higher the hash rate the more secure a network. Increase in hash rate can mean there is a growing interest in mining. A decrease can means miners are capitulating because it's no longer profitable for them. The fees being paid, costs of mining equipment, cost of electricity, price of an asset all affect the profit of a miner. Miner capitulation can cause fluctuation in prices.

Market statistics

Market statistics like market capitalization can give an investor an idea as to how popular a cryptocurrency is because it's how much people have invested a project. The more popular a cryptocurrency is the more money will be invested in it. People generally invest their money where they see the most potential value.

Large market cap assets, those that are in the top ten for market capitalization, are usually considered to be safer investments because they are more well-known and established in the market. Middle cap assets are those with a market cap between $1 and $10 billion. They are a little less risky than the large caps. Small market cap assets are the most risky because unfortunately there have been a lot of scams. Because they are the most risky investors usually pull their money out of the low caps before everything else. Usually top 100 assets on Coinmarketcap are safe though. I've purchased many ranked lower in market cap. Just make sure you do your research on the project before you invest money in them.

Big coins like the top twenty are hard to move in the market. A lot of money has already been invested in them, so it's not easy for the price to increase. If a crypto already has a billion invested in them, another billion has to be invested for you to double your money. Where as if a newer asset that only has 10 million invested in it gets another 90 million invested you have 10x your money.

The market capitalization is calculated using this formula:

Circulating Supply X Price = Market cap

The circulating supply is the amount of a cryptocurrency presently circulating in the market. The total supply is the total amount presently in existence. The maximum supply is the amount of a cryptocurrency that will ever exist. The circulating supply is used to calculate the market cap because any amount that is frozen or locked away isn't in the market supply and therefore should not be taken into consideration.

Let's say you have a coin in the top twenty with a market cap of $5 billion. The current price is 50 cents. In order for the price to double an additional $5 billion would have to be invested. With a small market cap the price is much easier to move. If the market cap is only $10 million all it would take for you to 10x your money is for $90 million to be invested. That's big difference.

Coinmarketcap.com is an excellent resource to use to quickly find the total market cap along with a wealth of other information. You can visit Coinmarketcap.com to see which exchanges a cryptocurrency is located on, price history, the circulating supply, total supply, maximum supply, 24 hour volume, and a brief description of the cryptocurrency. It also contains links to news based on your portfolio, project websites, project social media, and other useful information. You can even keep track of your cryptocurrency portfolio on Coinmarketcap.com. I have crypto spread out among several different wallets and exchanges so it's nice to be able to click on an app on my phone and keep track of it all in one place so I know where my portfolio stands at all times.

VET $0.02878				UNFI $12.37			
Price (all)				**Price (all)**			
Open	$0.01522	Close	$0.02919	Open	$3.920	Close	$12.232
High	$0.03505	Low	$0.00168	High	$15.25	Low	$2.72
Average	$0.00891	Change	▲ $0.01397	Average	$7.354	Change	▲ $8.312
Market Stats				**Market Stats**			
Market Cap	$1.851 Bn	24h Volume	$345.601 M	Market Cap	$35.35 M	24h Volume	$14.792 M
Circulating	64.316 Bn VET	Max Supply	86.713 Bn VET	Circulating	2.857 M UNFI	Max Supply	10 M UNFI
Tot Supply	86.713 Bn VET	ROI	▲ 91.26%	Tot Supply	10 M UNFI	ROI	▲ 241.93%
Rank	29	Holdings	110,659 VET	Rank	387	Holdings	1,430 UNFI

Here's a Coinmarketcap.com comparison of UNFI and VET. As you can see the $1.851 billion market cap for VET is much higher than UNFI's at just $35 million, yet the price is much higher. Why is that you ask? It goes back to the supply and demand principle. Let's dig a little further. VeChain's total supply is 86.713 billion, its total circulating supply is 64.316, and its total 24 hour volume is $344.767 million. UNFI on the other hand, has only $14.757 million volume, a 10 million supply and even less is in circulation at 2.857 million.

UNFI has a lower amount in circulation therefore making it more rare. The more of a cryptocurrency that's in circulation the less it is worth. This is why the price of UNFI is $12.37 and the price of VET is less than 3 cents.

The formula for price is: market cap / total circulating supply = price

The growth potential is also a lot greater for our small cap example. There is only $35 million invested in the project in this example. If the market cap were to grow to the same as VET at $1.851 billion the price of UNFI would be $647! In order for the price of VET to double another $1.851 billion would have to be invested. Most beginner investors don't take this into account. Think about this the next time someone says Dogecoin is going to $1.

You also want to take historical prices into consideration. Find out what the all time high, all time low, and average price is on Coinmarketcap.com. If you're in the beginning of a bull run and you're buying at prices much below the average price chances are you're making a good investment. If you're buying at all time highs it may be more risky. This can give you an idea of how much growth potential there is by giving you an idea if the cryptocurrency is overvalued or undervalued.

You should also check the age of the cryptocurrency you're reviewing. Ninety nine percent of all crypto projects will fail in the long run. Has the crypto maintained it's value over time?

Volume is the amount a cryptocurrency was exchanged over a certain amount of time. Newer assets may have a ton of potential, but if there is no liquidity you might be stuck holding a large bag or selling at a steep discount if you need to sell since there aren't many buyers available. You need to be able to sell at a fair price. You will need to wait for liquidity to increase or take the risk of not being able to sell if the price falls. These can be the best times to get into a coin though because you're in before everyone else. Watch for periods where there are huge fluctuations in volume in these scenarios. Smart money likes to buy when prices are just about to bottom. They could be accumulating a large amount in anticipation of a price increase.

How many exchanges is the asset on? When a cryptocurrency is listed on a top exchange it means it has been through the vetting process of that exchange. This usually means it is a strong project, and it also increases liquidity. Liquidity is essential because without it the markets are volatile.

When projects are added to Coinbase, a major exchange, they usually see a pump in price. This is not only because of the vetting process, but because it has now been made available to a lot more people. If a cryptocurrency is only on a few small exchanges it might not be a good choice. See what the volume is across all exchanges especially the one you will be trading on.

External factors that influence the market

"The secret to investing is to figure out the value of something– and then pay a lot less." Joel Greenblatt

The Economy

The manner in which U.S. citizen, businesses and the government produce and consume goods make up the economy. There are various economic factors that can have a positive or negative impact on the markets such as: gross domestic product(GDP), interest rates, inflation rate, unemployment rate, war, trade wars, among others. When the economy is doing well, businesses are doing well. When the economy is growing more people purchase goods and services, and are more likely to invest any extra money they have. When the economy is doing poorly people stop spending and investing so the markets see a decline.

GDP

The gross domestic product measures the value of the final goods and services that a country produces. Although it doesn't take into consideration the cost of living and inflation, it is still a great indicator as to how well the economy is doing as a whole. When the GDP is growing people are optimistic because it means the economy is growing and expanding. When people are optimistic they spend which stimulates the economy.

Interest rates

Interest rates play a big factor in how well the economy is doing. When interest rates are low it makes money easier to borrow. Higher rates mean people and businesses can't borrow as much. The more people are able to borrow the more they will spend. The more businesses can borrow, the more they can expand and flourish.

In general, when interest rates are low, the economy grows and inflation increases. When interest rates are high, the economy slows and inflation decreases. When the economy is struggling an interest rate cut can provide some stimulation.

Inflation & Deflation

Inflation is a general increase in prices and fall in the purchasing power of money. An increase in the cost of manufacturing, transporting, and selling goods can cause inflation to rise. A little inflation is desirable, but high levels of inflation cause buying power to decline and the costs of goods and services increase. Deflation gives the perception of a weak economy. Deflation is when the cost of goods and services drop.

The accelerating inflation of the dollar causes a lot of people to flock to bitcoin as a safe haven. It is inevitable the dollar will be replaced at some point. Every fiat currency in history has falied and there will be no exception for the dollar. Savy traders follow the DXY chart closely to track the performance of the dollar and compare it to the performance of bitcoin.

When the U.S. government is printing trillions of dollars into circulation it helps bitcoin because people see the dollar is being devalued so they run to a safe haven like bitcoin. Stimulus money helps too as people take the devaluing dollars and invest them in the cryptocurrency market. As time goes on the U.S. government has to do more and more to keep the economy afloat. Billions no longer stimulate the economy because the dollar has been devalued so much. Now it takes trillions for the economy to respond. The dollar will continue to decline in value until it is replaced.

Other aspects like unemployment levels, trade wars, war, etc. can influence the markets. If unemployment levels are high it will negatively affect the economy. Anything that disrupts the flow of materials needed for manufacturing like oil will have an impact on the economy. War can actually stimulate the economy through the massive influx of manufacturing needed to produce military equipment.

Politics and Regulation

As cryptocurrency grows and becomes more successful it draws more attention from law makers. There has been increasing discussion surrounding the regulation of cryptocurrency, and whether some are considered unregistered securities or not. Things like this can cause fear and uncertainty in the market.

It is inevitable that we'll see more and more regulation as time passes. That doesn't necessarily mean it's a bad thing. It would be nice to have some sort of framework to weed out all the scam projects. What can't happen is the overbearing oversight and red tape we currently have in the system that hinders growth and creativity. The crypto market needs to be able to operate freely without government interference of any kind.

Foreign markets

Since cryptocurrency is a global market, what happens in foreign markets can affect prices too. Russia lawmakers approved the legal status of cryptocurrencies, but banned their use as payment in July 2020 due to the fact that cryptocurrencies can be used for illegal activity. I sure am glad no Russian Rubles or U.S. Dollars have been used for illegal activity. Algeria, Bolivia, Morocco, Nepal, Pakistan, and Vietnam have banned all cryptocurrencies. They can't allow a fully transparent, trustless, secure, ultra-fast medium of exchange to replace their heavily manipulated fiat currencies can they?

Stock market

The stock market is a good general indicator of how the economy is doing. The stock market tracks all publicly traded businesses so it can be used to measure economic growth. It represents how profitable the businesses are that make up the GDP. If the stock market is going up chances are businesses are doing well.

If the market is rising, it's a good indication that businesses are doing well and GDP is growing. If the market is falling it can mean businesses are losing money, becoming less profitable, and maybe laying off employees which can lead to a shrinking GDP.

The economy is based on data like the GDP, employment rate, and consumer spending. The stock market is based on the sentiment of individual investors. Investor sentiment can rise based on investor optimism or fall based on fear.

Stock prices are based on supply and demand so if the demand for a company's stock is high, the price will be high and the company valuable. Publicly traded businesses are greatly affected by the price of their stock. The more people that invest in a stock the more the price will increase. The higher the stock price the more valuable the business. The business can then sell the stock if it needs capital. Valuable stock=valuable company. Businesses with valuable stock can offer their stock to their employees as an incentive, and give the business an advantage over the competition. The value of the stock of a business can help it retain funding from financial institutions and investors.

The stock market stimulates the economy because the more people make the more they spend. If the business a person is working for is growing, and the paycheck of the employee is growing, they are more likely to spend their money. The opposite happens if they are laid off. Most of the money in the stock market comes from people like you and me. When an investor invests money in the stock of a company they are voting with their money and helping the company grow.

Catastrophes

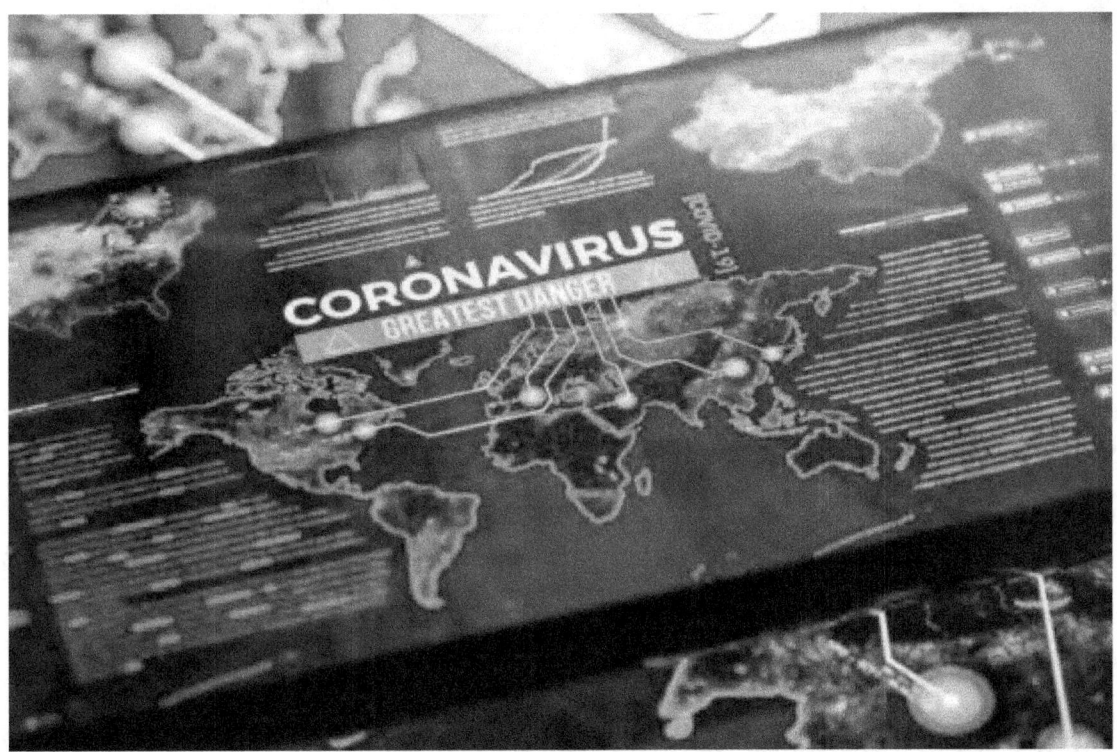

It's impossible to predict when a major economic event happens. At anytime any number of catastrophes could strike and cause the markets to crumble. It could be a hurricane, tsunami, famine, pandemic, you name it. The economy can have a big impact on the financial markets because when people panick they pull their money out.

In March 2020, COVID-19 struck and all the markets crashed. Greed brings people in the market and fear sends them out. When emotions are high people act irrational and it can cause a big sell off driving prices down. The price of bitcoin plummeted over the course of a couple days from over

$10,000 to under $4000.

Stock market crashes preceded both the Great Depression in the 1930's, and the Great Recession in 2008. If and when another stock market crash happens it will most likely affect the cryptocurrency market too. When the stock market is falling usually cryptocurrency prices are too. bitcoin has been correlated with the S&P index and has at times followed it closely.

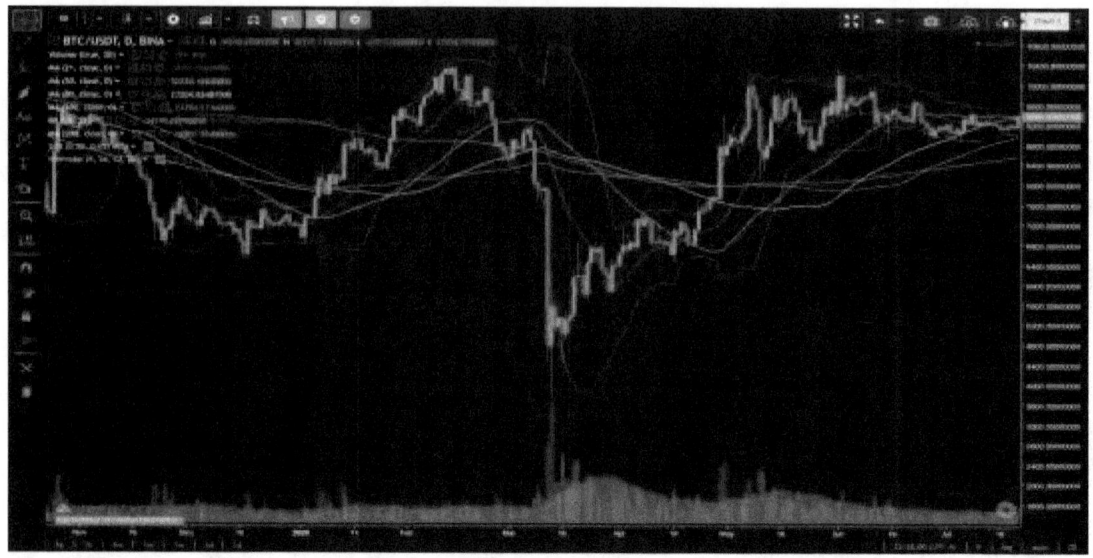

Catastrophes like this can happen at anytime causing people to want to pull their money out of more risky investments and put it into safer investments like gold and silver and tangible items like food, water, and supplies.

Meanwhile, optimistic events such as the development COVID-19 vaccine can have the opposite affect. When it was announced that a vaccine had been developed the markets rebounded back above their previous highs. The confidence had been restored in the market now that a cure had arrived.

Mass Adoption

Mass adoption is what every cryptocurrency hodler is waiting for. Large institutions buying, large institutions creating trusts. Greyscale Investments is the largest owner of cryptocurrency. They currently hold around 449,596 bitcoin worth around $5.1 billion. They've also opened multple trusts for altcoins(alternative coins to bitcoin) such as: AAVE, ADA, ATOM, DOT,

ETH, LINK, and more. Tech company Microstrategy bought 38,250 bitcoin totaling around $433 million. Square Inc. Purchased 4,709 bitcoin moving 1% of total company assets. We are already beginning to see the beginning stages of mass adoption, but we are still in the early phase.

On Jan 6, 2020, the total market cap of cryptocurrency exceeded 1 trillion dollars. The crazy part about that is if you ask ten random people on the street if they know what cryptocurrency is most of them will know very little or have no clue at all! Mainstream adoption will take cryptocurrency to the next level. The total market cap of the New York Stock Exchange is around 26 trillion, and the NASDAQ is around 12 trillion. Just imagine how much of that market cap cryptocurrency is going to take! You better take advantage of this opportunity while it's too late! Get in the market before all these big companies and the mainstream and it could make you rich.

News

News is what moves the markets. It's all about the hype with crypto right now. If a project is constantly pumping out news on social media of upgrades and product releases chances are the price will reflect the attention. Keep in mind all the news is stacked at the end of each quarter. This is when you can sometimes see large price spikes.

If you see news that a token is going to be listed on an exchange with high volume it may be a good idea to stock up because the added exposure can affect the price drastically. Main nets, test nets, hard forks, upgrades, just about any kind of update to a project will cause people to buy. It's always good to buy into a promising project early during the test net stage. Then you can sell just before or after the main net release after it gets a little more popular.

Partnerships

Partnerships can be very important in crypto. The more partnerships the better. A very popular cryptocurrency called Chainlink is the most widely used oracle service in the space. At the time of writing they have over four hundred partnerships and collaborations. Almost any time a project announces a partnership with Chainlink the price pumps.

The community following behind a project can create value. If a large number of investors believe in a particular cryptocurrency it can affect the value. The amount of a crypto locked up in staking on the network is something else to consider. If a large number are staking a project it holds value. It tells people that they believe in their investment in the project so much so they are willing to allow the funds to be tied up and earn rewards in the process. Users stake their holding to participate in block validation and in return they receive a percentage of their stake as a reward. If the project has a strong community following they can rally behind a project a drive the price up. Look at what has happened with Dogecoin!

There are many factors to consider when performing fundamental analysis in cryptocurrency. You could pick a project with the best case in the world, but if masses don't buy in the price won't be affected much. It's not about what you think, it's about what everyone else thinks because it's volume that drives the price. What do the masses think will happen in the future? What is the overall outlook of the market? Is it bullish or bearish? You have to do your best to anticipate what the masses want before they want it or jump on the bandwagon as soon as a trend starts forming.

The crypto market is highly speculative right now. The market is driven by fear and greed, news and hype. Use case matters to some extent, but emotions are what moves the market right now. You want to go where the masses are going, but you want to go before they get there.

Investor sentiment is the most important factor right now. Some cryptos have high transaction counts and lots of addresses, but the price isn't very high. Some cryptos have a large community following, but the price doesn't reflect. At the end of the day the crypto market is still highly speculative.

Invest your money in projects you believe in and projects that can benefit the world as a whole. Don't just invest to get money that's greed. Don't take part in the pump and dump schemes. Someone is always left holding the bags in the end.

Fundamental analysis focuses on measuring the intrinsic value of an asset. Technical analysis focuses on the trading and price history. By combining fundamental analysis and technical analysis you can become a more well-rounded trader and stay one step ahead of the competition.

"Price is what you pay, and value is what you get." - Warren Buffett

Technical Analysis

"The stock market is filled with individuals who know the price of everything, but the value of nothing." - Phillip Fisher

Technical analysis allows you to forecast the probability of future price behaviour based on price history. It's not a crystal ball, but it does give you certain clues to let you know if an asset is heading up or down. If you plan on investing large amounts into crypto learning technical analysis is absolutely essential. There are patterns and trends in trading that repeat themselves over and over again. If you're not aware of these patterns and trends your portfolio could get wiped out quickly.

Reading a chart is like reading a book. Once you know how to read then you will understand the story the chart is telling you. It's also like driving across the country. Imagine driving across the country with no map. Do you know anyone that would attempt to drive across the country with no map?

Without one you'll be all over the place and may never even reach your final destination. That's what trading cryptocurrency without knowing anything about technical analysis is like. Without technical analysis you're blind. All you have to guide you are the voices of your favorite YouTube shills. This is not the position you want to be in. When you learn technical analysis, not only will you be able to see where you're going, but you can take control and become the driver of your own destiny. You no longer have to rely on the opinions of others to guide you and your portfolio.

When you're trading crypto you always want to see which way bitcoin is trending first. bitcoin is the mother ship. Whatever bitcoin does influences the way altcoins perform. Usually if bitcoin goes up the altcoins follow and vice versa. One of these days altcoins may decouple from bitcoin, but until then we have to watch bitcoin and the altcoins you are trading.

One of the ways traders track the performance of bitcoin is with the bitcoin dominance chart. bitcoin dominance is a measure of how much of the total market capitalization of cryptocurrency is in bitcoin compared to the rest of the altcoins. To give you an example, if bitcoin dominance is at 58% that means 58% of the entire cryptocurrency market is in bitcoin. It's like an on/off switch for the altcoins. I cannot stress this enough. When bitcoin dominance is going up that means more money is flowing into bitcoin than the altcoins. When bitcoin dominance is going down that means more money is flowing into the altcoins.

Before you enter a position into any altcoin it is essential pull up the bitcoin dominance chart and determine if it's heading up or down. You don't have to sell your current positions, but if bitcoin dominance is heading up I would advise against opening any new altcoin positions. To view the bitcoin dominance chart you can go to tradingview.com and type in BTC.D in the search bar.

I highly recommend that you sign up for a subscription to TradingView or Coinigy. Make sure to take the tutorial before you do anything to get familiar with the layout. In Coinigy, click the help tab and click tour this page. TradingView has an app you can use on your phone. This is excellent for when you're on the go and need to tend to a trade. TradingView also has a bitcoin dominance chart and as of right now, Coinigy doesn't.

The Basics

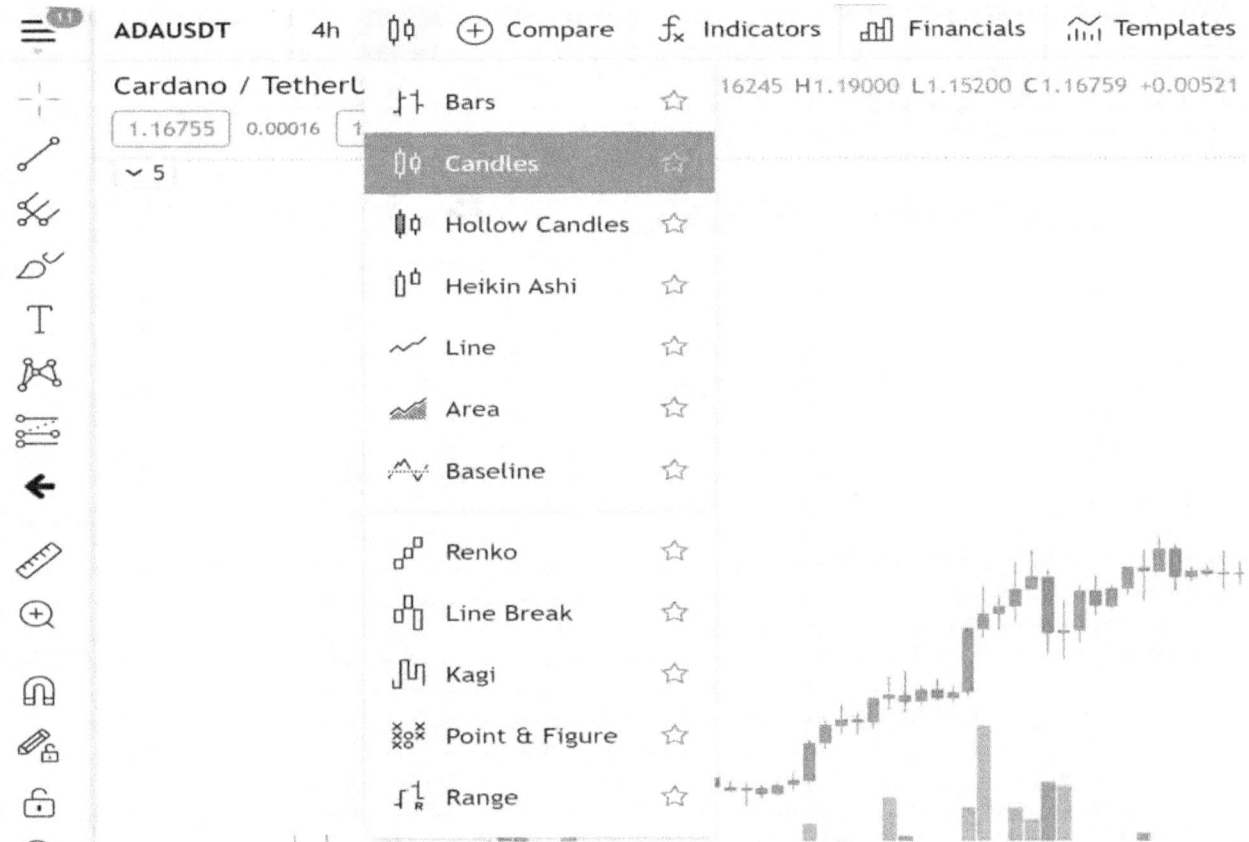

Okay, let's start with the basics. Pull up your trading platform. I prefer Tradingview. If you don't want to pay for the platform just keep doing 30 day trials. I will say it is worth paying for a membership to have access to the extra features. When you first look at a chart you will notice the red and green bars in the center of the screen called candlesticks. (In Tradingview you will need to change it to candlesticks in settings next to the time frame). Candlesticks represent what the price action did during the particular time frame you're viewing.

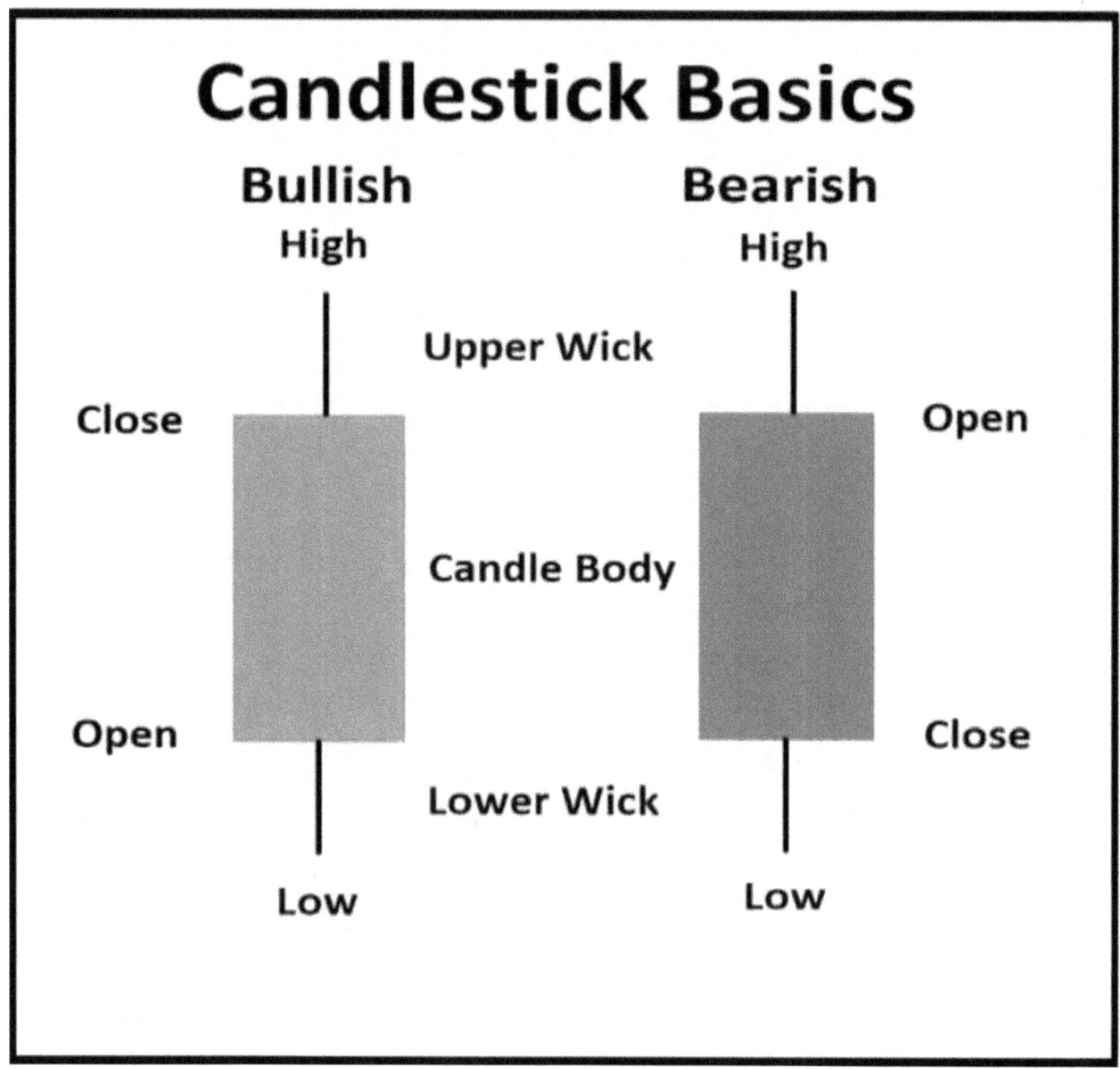

The bottom of the candle is where the price action opened and the top is where the price action closed. A bearish candle is red because the closing price was lower than the opening price and a bullish candle is green because the closing price was higher than the opening price within a given time frame. I'm in the 4 hour time frame here so each candle represents what the price action did every 4 hours. If you're on the daily chart each candle will represent a day, and the same goes for the other time frames. The gray lines at the top and bottom of the candles are called shadows also known as wicks. An upper wick shows the highest price point and a lower wick shows the lowest price point within a given time frame. The wicks indicate where the price action has fluctuated relative to the opening and closing prices. The red line going across the screen is where the price action is currently. If the price is going up the price action line is green if it's going down it will be red. The numbers going down the right side of the screen is the price action. The red and green bars at the bottom of the screen represent the buying and selling volume and the blue section is the average.

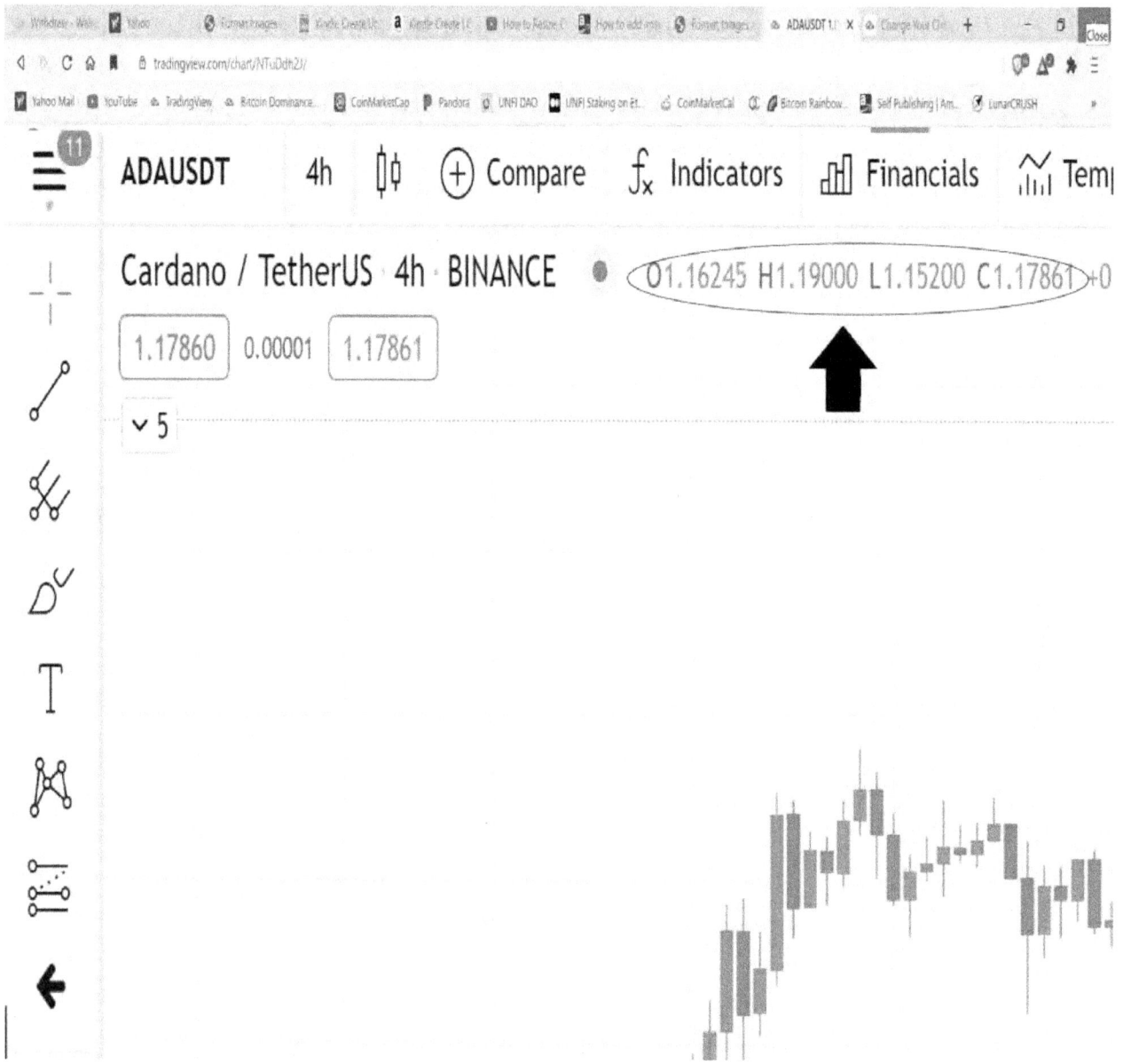

The numbers at the top of the screen O.H.L.C. stand for Open, High, Low, and Close. As you hover over each individual candle it will tell you the open, high, low, and close for that particular candle.

At the top left of the screen is the trading pair you're currently viewing. To the right are the time frames. Long-term and mid-term traders should focus on higher time frames like the hourly, 4 hour, or daily charts. You don't want to get caught up in the day trading charts like the 1 minute, 5 minute, 15 minute, and 30 minute charts. There's too much going on. Stick to the higher time frames.

Next to time frames you have the option to change how your candles are displayed. You can choose between bars, candles, hollow candles, heikin ashi, line, and area. Moving to the right you have a tab that says compare. You will choose compare if you want to compare different charts side by side. Next to compare is your indicators tab.

The tab next to settings that looks like a chart is for indicators. Indicators help you determine if the price action will go up or down in the future. The next tab you want to be familiar with is the alerts tab. Once you start trading you will want to set alerts constantly. Open trading view in multiple tabs so you can view several coins at a time.

Time Frames

Time Frames

The time frames you decide to use will largely depend on your trading style. There are four different types of traders: position traders, swing traders, day traders, and scalpers. While it would be a wild ride to just recklessly pour all of your money into the market it probably wouldn't be the smartest thing to do. You need to have a plan in place. We're treating this like a business so think of this like it's your business plan. When are you going to buy? How long are you going to hold? When are you going to take profits?

Time Frames Guide

Trader Style	Trade Length	Holding Period	Time Frames
Scalper	Very short	From less than a minute, to a couple hours	Less than one minute to 15 minutes
Day Trader	Short	From less than one hour, to one day	5 minutes to 4 hours
Swing Trader	Mid-term	From less than a day, to a few weeks	1 hour to 1 day
Position Trader	Long-term	From a few weeks, to several months	1 day, 1 week, 1 month

Position traders prefer to research all the different projects, study the white papers, as well as, all the other analytics, and purchase a couple cryptos to long term hodl(crypto lingo for hold). Position traders will hodl anywhere from a couple weeks to many months, even years. This strategy can be very effective as long as you are aware of where you are in the market cycle. If you purchase in the accumulation phase and sell near the top it would be a great strategy. If you aren't aware of what cycle the market is in and you purchase at the top of the market, this could be a terrible strategy. The crypto market is highly volatile. It's nothing to see 30% price swings in a day. Are you prepared to take losses like that? Position traders don't concern themselves with the day to day swings in the market. They are confident their holds will go up in the long term. The good thing about this strategy is you set it and forget it for a while. It doesn't require extensive amounts of your time. These traders use the daily, weekly, and even monthly charts.

Most swing traders prefer to trade based on technical analysis and news. Some of them are professional traders that trade for a living. These traders usually hodl anywhere from less than a day to a few weeks. Most of the time these types of traders could care less about the company background, white papers, etc. All they care about is the chart looking good and what the news is saying. The perception of a coin by the majority is much more important than the background and team working on the project to these traders. It doesn't matter to them if a project has the best developers and code in the world. If the majority of investors aren't aware of it or it's just not popular the price will not go up. These traders are usually mid-term hodlers. They buy the breakouts of patterns, ride them until they peak, take profit, and move on to the next one. Rinse and repeat. They don't hodl through large market dips. This strategy requires a lot more time and effort, but you can reap amazing returns. Swing traders usually use the daily time frame down to the hourly. This is the trading style I like to use the most.

Day traders in the stock market place trades during the day and sell before the day is over. In the crypto world the markets never close like the stock market does. Day traders in the crypto world sell before the go to sleep. They usually rely strictly on technical analysis. Because of the volatility day traders can thrive in the crypto market. Day traders use the four hour time frame down to the five minute chart since they're only concerned with what happens now, today.

Scalpers are in and out of trades quickly. They attempt to take as many small profits as they can, and commonly make multiple trades in a day. Scalpers can hold anywhere from a few hours to less than a minute. They typically use the fifteen minute chart down to the one minute.

Whichever strategy you choose never invest more than you're able to lose, and always use stop losses on your trades. I prefer to hodl a handful of long term holds that I buy in the accumulation phase, and no more than a couple short term trades at any given time. I would recommend buying at least some bitcoin since there is a limited supply. If you can't afford to buy a whole bitcoin, don't worry, you can buy smaller increments of one called Satoshi's. A Satoshi is one hundred millionth of a bitcoin. Whatever strategy you choose make sure it works for you and your lifestyle.

The larger time frames give you the big picture of the trend, and lower time frames give you greater detail as to what's happening. The five minute time frame, for example, is just a small part of the daily chart in more detail. Lower time frames are useful because due to the extra detail you're able to get more precise entry and exit points.

Unless you're looking for entry and exit points, day trading, or scalping, time frames like the five minute and fifteen minute charts give way too much information for beginners. Many beginners get too caught up in the lower time frames and they end up over trading. The lower time frames just have too much noise going on.

I like to expand to the daily, three day, and weekly charts to get a bigger picture of the current trend. Then I zoom out, set all my support and resistance levels, and then zoom into lower time frames for entry. I wait until I think we've hit a bottom on the lower time frame like the fifteen minute, before placing my order. Once my order is placed I zoom back out to a higher time frame like the four hour or one hour to set my stop loss.

Always remember up trends consist of higher highs and higher lows. As soon as you start seeing lower lows that particular trend is broken. The larger the time frame, the more valid the pattern, trend, and signals. Lower time frames give more false signals, but bigger moves start on the lower time frames and carry over to the larger ones.

By taking multiple time frames into account you can greatly increase your odds of a successful trade. Using multiple time frames can help you not only get a better idea of the long term, but the short term trend as well. Volume spikes will be more pronounced in the lower time frames, and can give you an indication if the price is going up or down. Higher time frames give more valid signals and can give you the bigger picture of the overall trend. Practice watching how the price reacts in different time frames and with time you will see how the smaller moves evolve into larger ones.

Identifying support and resistance levels

> *"Technical analysts use support and resistance levels to identify price points on a chart where the probabilities favor a pause or reversal of a prevailing trend."* - Investopedia.com

Support and resistance levels are cetain predetermined ranges of the price of a cryptocurrency at which it's thought the price will stop and reverse. Support is the point at which down trending price action is expected to stop falling and reverse. As the price drops, demand increases as investors take advantage of the cheaper prices forming support which prevents the price from falling any further. Resistance is the point where up trending price action is expected to reverse. As the price increases some investors decide to take profits forming resistance levels.

The price action respects these levels based on the previous price history. If the price action is repeatedly rejected by a certain price level, that range then serves as resistance and the opposite for support. The more touches you have as you go further back in the price history, the more valid the levels.

Here you can see we have multiple points where the price action came down in this yellow range and then reversed on the four hour time frame. Since we have at least three valid reversal points we can say this range serves as support. It's important to note that these levels are ranges even though most traders use lines to identify their support and resistance levels.

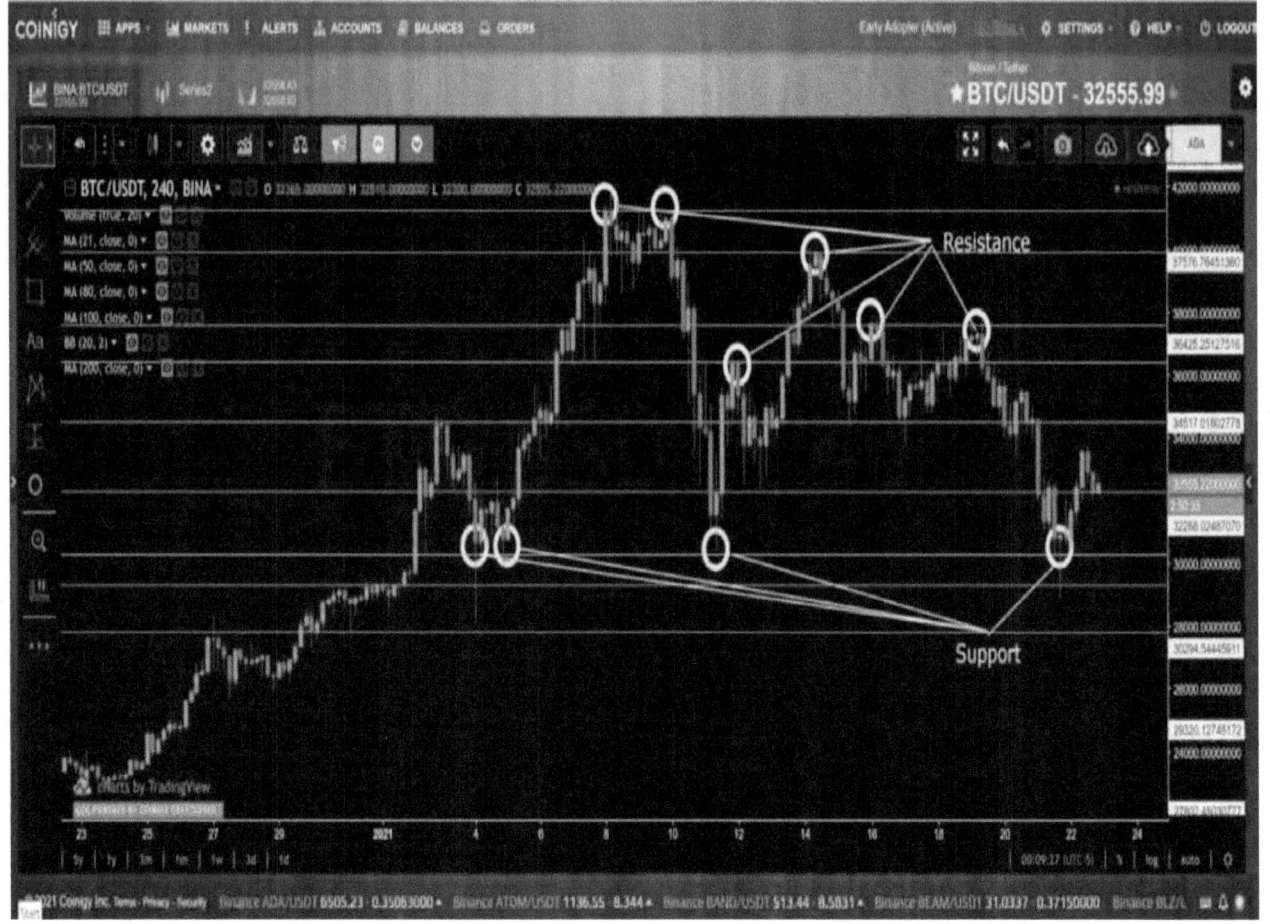

In this example I've drawn lines where I've identified points of support and resistance. It's very easy to identify where the price action has respected these levels. You'll want to look for all the points where the price action was rejected for your resistance levels and connect as many of them as possible by drawing lines at points where the price has bounced for your support levels. The more points you're able to connect the stronger the support or resistance. The line can be flat or diagonal. Support and resistance areas can be identified by drawing trend lines and by using chart indicators like moving averages, Fibonacci retracement tool and the VPVR.

Knowledge about support and resistance levels can help you determine where to enter or exit a trade. A good time to enter a trade is when the price breaks through areas where it was once rejected and holds above the previous resistance level in an uptrend. Most of the time the price action will come back down to retest the break out of previous resistance before continuing higher. You can see in the example above where the price action just broke through a resistance level. Remember, past resistance becomes future support and vice versa. If the new support is broken the trade is negated and the position should be closed. Set your stop losses just below support.

When you want to place a support or resistance line move your pointer to where you want it to go, and ALT+H. You can also move your support/resistance lines once you place them by hovering over the line you want to move, find the small white circle that appears, hold your left mouse button down, and move it to the location you prefer.

Indicators

Technical indicators are mathematical calculations based on an asset's past and current price, or volume activity. They are tools that help investors determine the trend and momentum of a particular asset. Traders use this information to evaluate historical performance and attempt to predict future prices.

Indicators are like the gauges in your car. Each gauge tells you about the condition of part of your vehicles operating system. All gauges together provide a report of the overall condition of the vehicle. Just like your vehicle's gauges, technical indicators provide a report on the overall condition of your trading position.

There are two main types of indicators: overlay indicators and oscillators. Overlay indicators share the same space or pane as the price movement on a chart. Oscillating indicators move in between a minimum and maximum range and they are plotted on their own pane usually under the price action pane on a chart. These overlay and oscillating indicator can be either leading indicators or lagging indicators. Leading indicators attempt to predict where the price is headed while lagging indicators offer a historical report of background conditions that resulted in the current price being where it is.

Indicators can be further subdivided into four categories: trend, momentum, volatility/mean reversion, and volume.

Trend indicators

Trend indicators tell you the strength and direction the price is currently moving in using price averages to form a baseline. It is thought to be a bullish trend when the price action moves above the average. These indicators can also be used to set support and resistance levels.

Momentum indicators

Momentum indicators measure the speed and strength of a trend over a period of time regardless of price action. The rate at which the strength of the price action rises or falls is the momentum. These indicators signal whether the price is trending upward or downward and can also tell if it's overbought or oversold based on previous price history.

Momentum indicators are best used in combination with trend indicators because together they show not only the direction of the price action, but the force behind the movement too. If there is little momentum behind a trend, that trend is sure to reverse soon. The ability of momentum indicators to spot possible trend reversals make them very useful to traders.

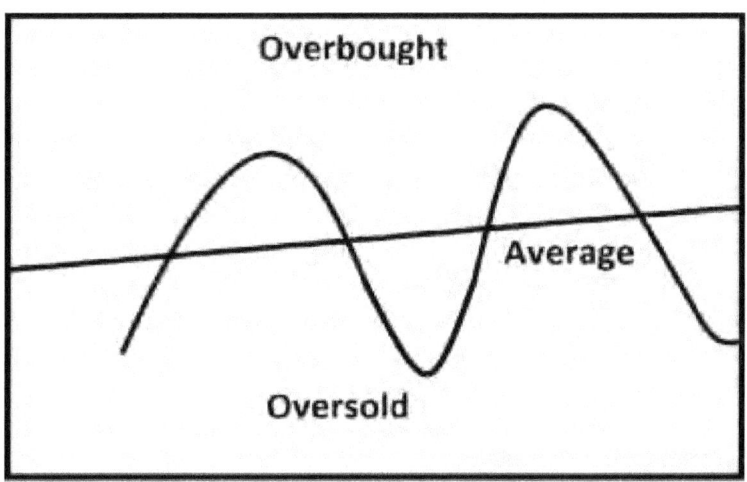

Volatility/ Mean reversion indicators

Mean reversion is the idea that the price of an asset and it's volatility fluctuate around some long-term average, and any deviation from that average eventually will revert back to the long-term average levels. Mean reversion indicators allow a trader to profit on the unexpected upswings and save on unusual downturns.

Volatility is measured and calculated using the historical data of an asset. The quicker the price fluctuates, the higher the volatility. The slower the price fluctuates, the lower the volatility.

When there is an extended price move to the upside an asset is considered to be overbought and when there's an extended move to the downside it's considered to be oversold. Since volatility indicators show when assets are oversold and overbought, they are good to use especially after a big pullback because the price movement is believed to return back to the primary trend.

Volume indicators

Volume indicators are used to confirm the strength and direction of a particular trend. Volume is the amount of buy and sell orders that have taken place in a particular time frame. The amount of trades that are taking place gives you an idea as to how healthy the trend is and if it is going to continue or reverse. Increasing volume usually signals the trend is going to continue and decreasing volume signals the trend is going to reverse.

Divergence

Whenever the price movement and an indicator move in opposite directions from one another it's called divergence because they diverge, or move away, from one another. Pay attention when this happens because divergence can tell you when a trend is weakening and provide you with an early warning signal that a trend reversal is coming soon, or it can signal that the trend is going to continue.

Divergence can be a confusing concept, but it can also be extremely rewarding so take your time to study this one. Study it until you have it memorized. Make yourself a cheat sheet and draw the different types of divergences on your whiteboard or print them out and post them on the wall of your office so you always have it right in front of you.

There are three types of divergences: regular, hidden, and exaggerated. Regular divergence signals a possible trend reversal, hidden divergence signals a trend continuation.

Divergences

Bullish	Bearish
REGULAR — Price: Lower Low; Indicator: Higher Low (Buy)	**REGULAR** — Price: Higher High; Indicator: Lower High (Sell)
HIDDEN — Price: Higher Low; Indicator: Lower Low (Buy)	**HIDDEN** — Price: Lower High; Indicator: Higher High (Sell)

Regular bullish divergence happens when the price action makes a lower low, but the indicator doesn't reach a new low. It shows the bears are getting exhausted and the trend could possibly change from bearish to bullish. Make sure you line up the the bottoms when trying to identify bullish divergence. You are concerned with the "lows".

Regular bearish divergence occurs when the price action makes a higher high, but the indicator doesn't reach a new high. It shows the bulls are getting exhausted and the trend could possibly change from bullish to bearish. Make sure you line up the the tops when trying to identify bearish divergence. You are concerned with the "highs".

Hidden bullish divergence occurs when the price movement makes higher lows while the indicator makes lower lows. Hidden bullish divergence signals a possible uptrend continuation.

Hidden bearish divergence occurs when the price action makes lower highs while the indicator makes higher highs. Hidden bullish divergence signals a possible uptrend continuation.

Exaggerated Divergences	
Bullish	**Bearish**
REGULAR: Price — Equal Low; Indicator — Higher Low (Buy)	REGULAR: Price — Equal High (Sell); Indicator — Lower High
HIDDEN: Price — Lower Low (Buy); Indicator — Equal Low	HIDDEN: Price — Higher High (Sell); Indicator — Equal High

Exaggerated divergence is basically the same as regular divergence. The only difference is the price action and indicator behave slightly different. The move is thought to be weaker than regular divergence.

As I explained earlier, with bullish divergence the price action forms a lower low, but with exaggerated bullish divergence the price action and indicator behave slightly different. With exaggerated bullish divergence the price action forms a double bottom instead of a lower low. The indicator will show a higher high. If there's hidden exaggerated bullish divergence the indicator will form a double bottom and the price will plot a lower low.

Exaggerated bearish divergence is where the price action forms a double top while the indicator shows a lower high. With hidden exaggerated bearish divergence the indicator will form a double top and the price shows a higher high.

Focus on the major highs and the major lows when connecting your divergence points. If the price is making higher highs the indicator should too. If the price is making lower lows the indicator should too. If not, they are diverging from one another. Divergences on higher time frames are more valid than lower ones.

Yes, I know this is a lot to take in. Don't worry, you'll always have your cheat sheet in front of you to help you identify the different types of divergences. After a while you won't even need to look at your cheat sheet anymore.

In conclusion, there are hundreds of indicators available, and sometimes beginners tend use too many. Avoid using too many indicators especially if they indicate the same thing. Beginners should learn one indicator before moving on to the next one. Never use more than a few indicators at once, and never choose indicators that give the same signals. You want to choose indicators that compliment each other, and you can confirm the signal of one indicator using the others. Now that we have an idea of what indicators are and how they're used let's take a look at some of the most popular indicators traders use.

Moving Averages

Moving averages are lagging indicators that smooth out the price data making it easier for traders to evaluate. This trend indicator helps filter out the noise in volatile markets by creating an average price over a period of time. This allows traders to easily know what the price action has done in recent history.

The two types of moving averages are:
Simple moving average (SMA)
A SMA is created by calculating the average price over a certain amount of time periods. A 21 SMA on a 5 min time frame shows the average price for the last 21 5 min bars. A 50 SMA on a 5 min time frame shows the average price for the last 50 5 min bars and so on.

Exponential moving average (EMA)
EMAs challenge the lagging problem of SMAs by putting more weight on the recent candle close prices. Because of this the EMA adapts faster to

reveal the current trend giving the trader a heads up. The only problem with EMAs is they can be too fast and provide traders with false signals during periods of consolidation.

Which one is better? It depends on your trading style. If you're trading lower time frames the EMA is the best way to go in my opinion because it reacts quicker to the price action. I prefer SMAs for longer time frames like the daily, but it's up to you! You can use both if you want and take a hybrid approach. You could use an EMA for your shorter moving average so that it reacts quickly to the price movement and SMAs for your longer moving averages. Try them both out for a while and go with whichever one you think suits your trading style the best.

Moving averages are like a multi-tool in a traders tool belt. They can help in several ways.

1. The side of the moving average the price is on can signal direction for trades.
2. They signal trend direction or range conditions
3. The slope of the moving average shows the strength of the trend.
4. Moving averages can also function as excellent support and resistance levels.

When the price action is above the moving averages it's generally bullish. When it drops below it's bearish. Also, whenever the price is close to the moving average it will have a more fair value and could be a better place to enter a trade as opposed to when there is a gap between the price action and the moving average.

The direction of the moving averages signal trend direction or range conditions. If the moving averages are pointing up then the price action is in an uptrend. The longer the time period (ex. 21 days, 50 days, 100 days, etc.) the more valid the trend. Sometimes the price will bounce back and forth between two moving averages ranging between them before moving up or down.

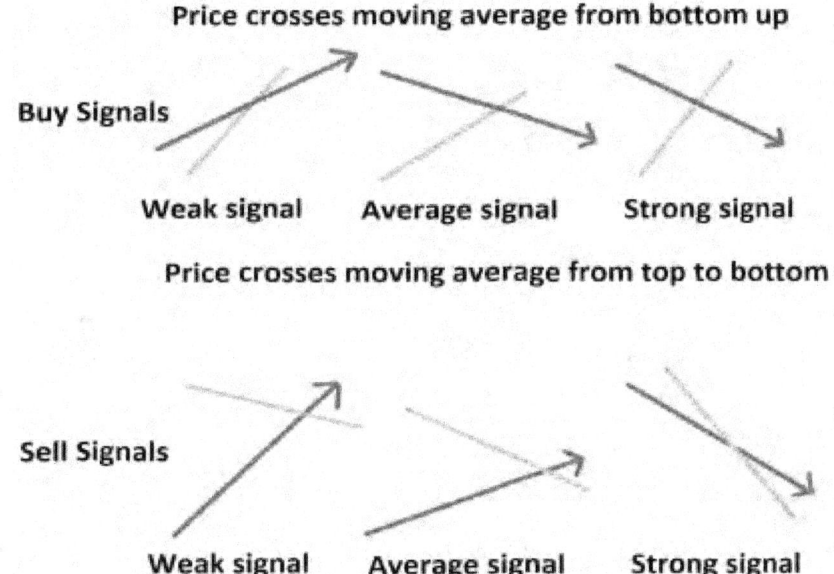

The slope of the moving average will tell you if things are trending up or down and the strength of the trend. The more slanted upward the slope is, the stronger the trend. The slope of the price movement as it crosses a moving average will also tell you a lot about the trend too. The more vertical the price action is the stronger the trend.

Moving averages can also work as support and dynamic resistance levels. They are dynamic because the levels aren't usually horizontal like regular support and resistance levels. These are usually diagonal.

Most traders that use moving averages will use several of them at once. This is called a moving average ribbon. Personally, I like to use 5 SMAs. Using multiple moving averages at once allows you to see how they move in relation to one another, and can reveal more signals to a trader like price reversals.

Whenever a short moving average like the 21 day has crossed under a longer moving average like the 200 day then the trend is down. Whenever a short moving average has crossed above a longer one the trend is up.

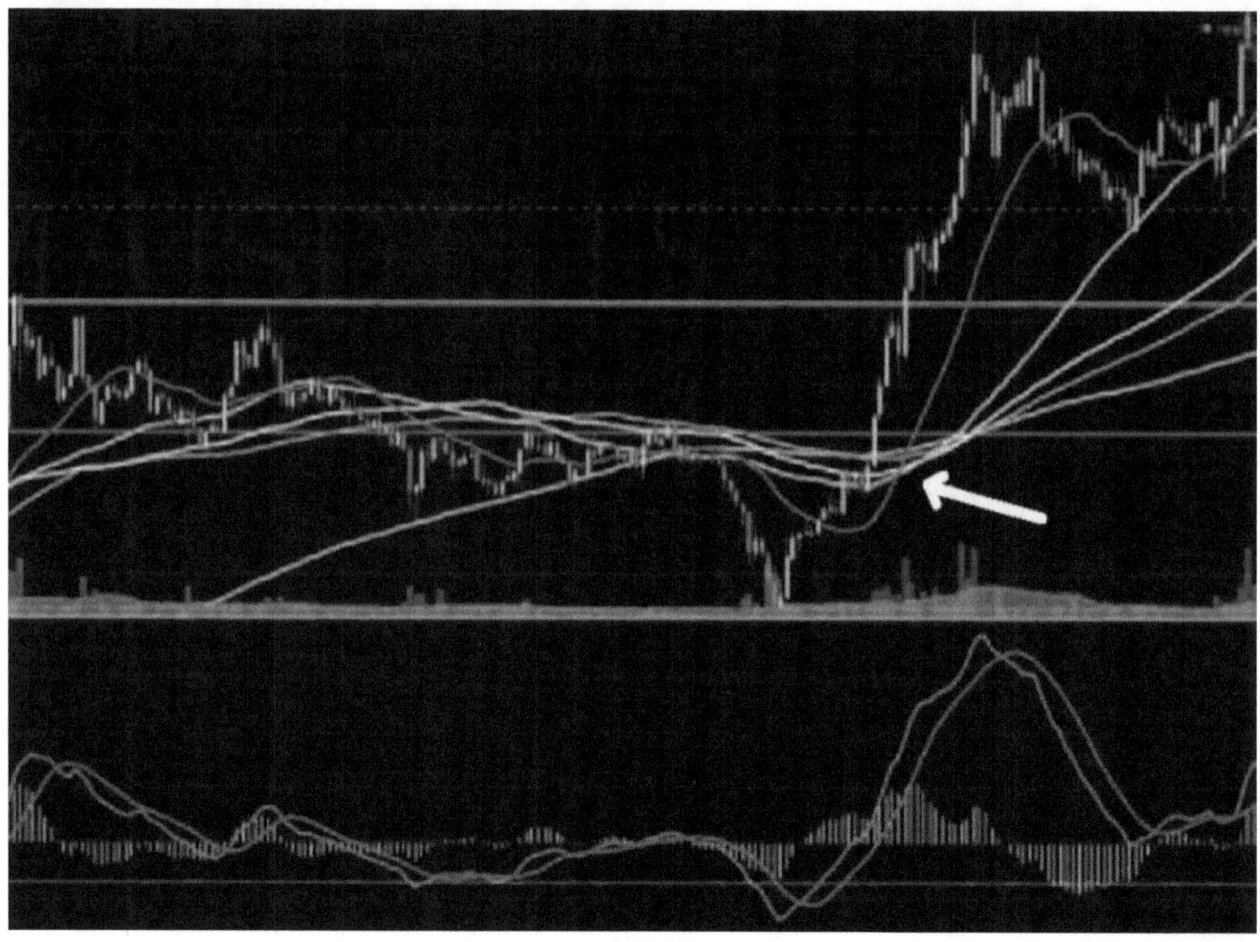

A golden cross is a bullish pattern when a short term moving average like the 50 SMA crosses over a long term moving average like the 200 SMA to the upside. It shows a temporary uptrend.

Look for the price action to cross the 21 day moving average. This is your first bullish clue that the trend has changed. Then, watch for the 21 day moving average to cross all the other moving averages. The price will retest all the moving averages before shooting up to the 200 day moving average. This is usually where the explosive movement starts. It will back test the 200 day moving average and if the price is able to break the 200 day you will see a large spike in price. Shortly after the price crosses the 200 day moving average the 21 day will follow. This is called a golden cross. In this example the red line is the 21 day moving average and the green line is the 200 day moving average.

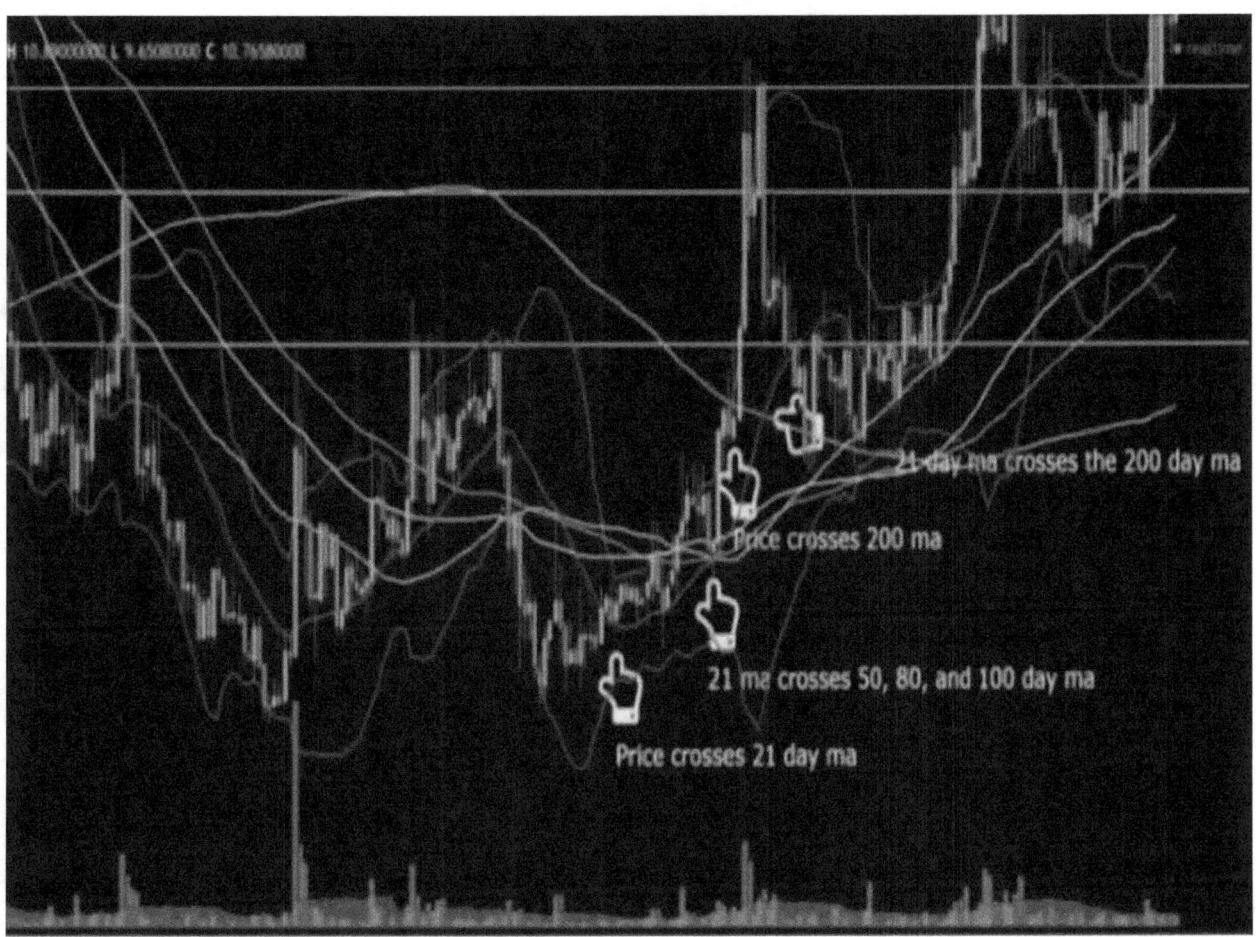

A death cross is when a short term moving average crosses over a long term moving average to the downside. It signals a temporary downtrend. Notice how the price movement fell below the red twenty one day moving average to start the downtrend. The price continued further through the moving average ribbon it met a little resistance at the two hundred day moving average. From there the price wasn't able to hold and fell even further. Notice how the moving average ribbon has now reversed and the twenty one day is on the bottom.

The price action will sometimes bounce off of the two hundred day moving average to the upside when in an uptrend and fall beneath when in a downtrend. Watch for the price action to touch the two hundred day moving average, and then nail your entry if all other indicators show positive signs as well. The price action will reward you with a nice rainbow of colors that begin to spread out signaling a strong trend, as well as, a decent gain. Larger time frames that have moving average crosses will have greater price increases.

The spacing of the moving averages tell you the strength of the trend. Wide spacing shows a strong trend and the closer the moving averages move together the weaker the trend. Be careful when you see the moving averages spread out as can be an early warning signal for a trend reversal. What goes up must come down.

Eventually when momentum slows the moving averages will begin to move closer together. The shorter moving average will either bounce off the next moving average in a bullish scenario or it will cross to the downside in a bearish scenario.

To find moving averages click on the tab for indicators at the top left hand corner of the trading graph, and type moving average in the search bar. Click moving average 5 times if you want the same moving average ribbon I use.

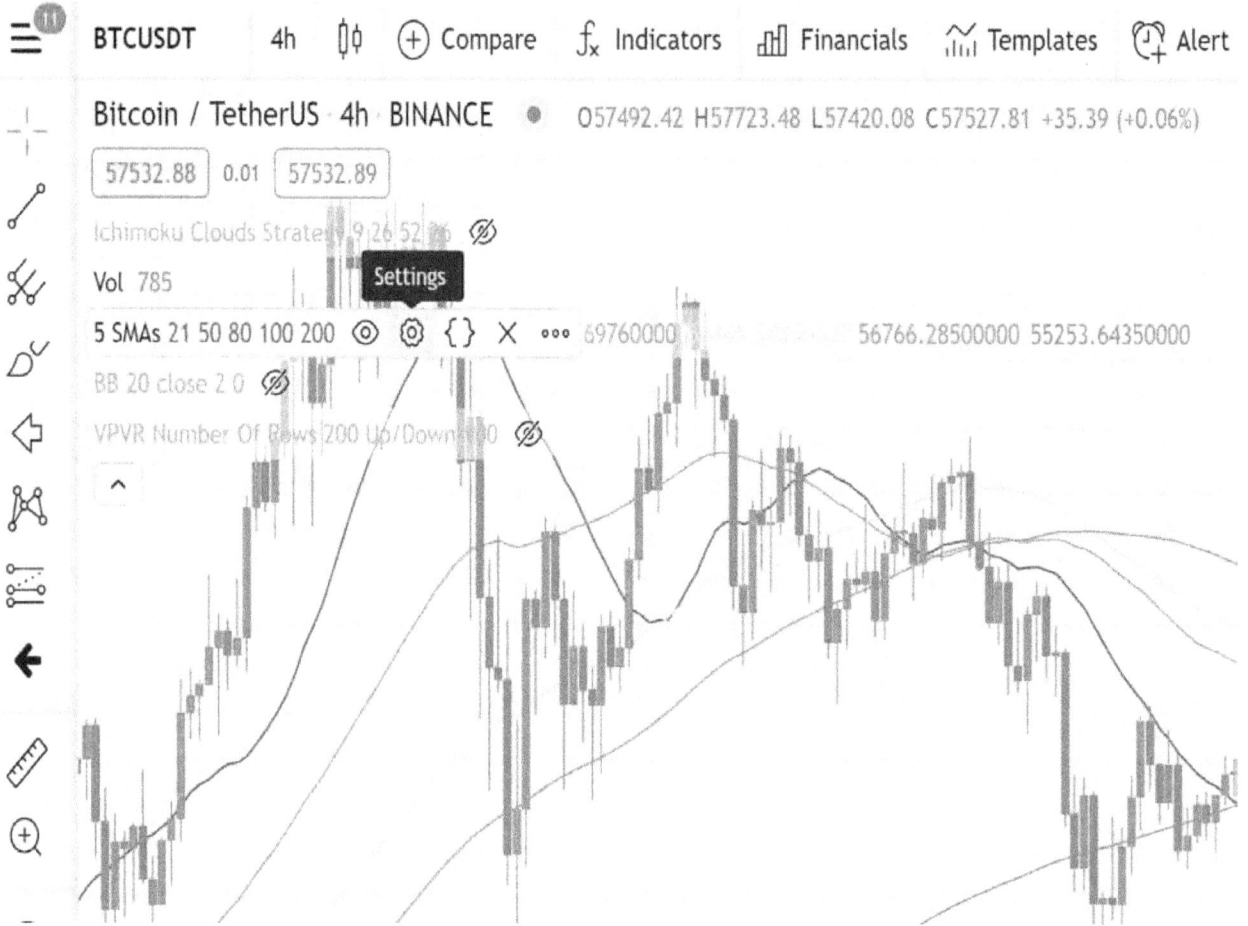

In the top left hand corner if you hover next to where it says 5 SMAs you will see an eye symbol. This is where you can hide the moving averages if you want. Next to that is what look like a gear for the settings. Change the length to 21. This is going to be our 21 moving average. We are going to do the same for our 50, 80, 100, and 200 moving averages. I like to use red for the 21(because it's dangerous when the price crosses below it), light blue for the 50, yellow for the 80, orange for the 100, and money green for the 200 (because it's bullish when price passes above it).

Here bitcoin had a nice run and you can see how all the moving averages are all spread out nicely while the price action was moving up. Once the price started to slow down you can see where the 21 moving average (red line) started crossing over the other moving averages and then the others followed. Also note that the price action fell below the 21 moving average too which was one of the first a bearish signs. The 21 ma didn't make it to the 200 moving average, but sometimes it will cross over the 200 moving average, and even go well below it. The best entries are when the price action is well below the 200 moving average. You can also see that as the price action started to slow down we also had a MACD cross and our RSI was in oversold territory.

Moving averages are essential indicators in my opinion. I never trade without them. Use moving averages in combination with other indicators for added confirmation. Keep an eye out for those golden crosses!

MACD Indicator

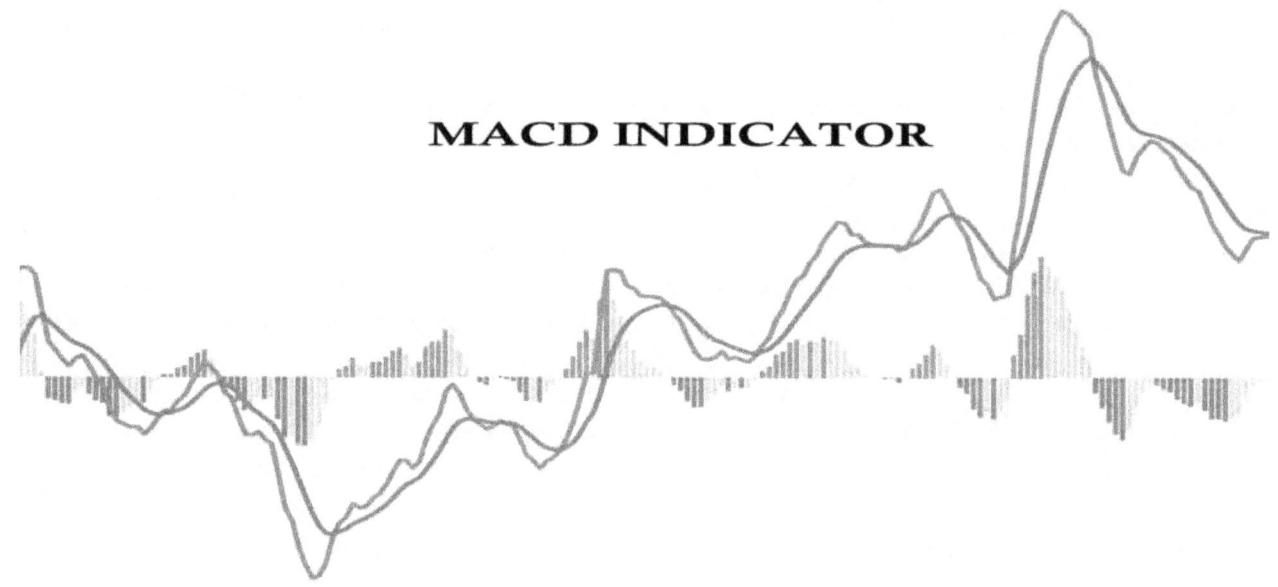

MACD INDICATOR

Another indicator I like to use is called the MACD. The MACD was created by Gerald Appel in the late 1970s. It is designed to reveal changes in the strength, direction, momentum, and duration of a trend in a stock's price. The acronym MACD stands for short for moving average convergence/divergence. It's designed to measure the relationship between two moving averages to reveal changes in the strength, direction, momentum, and duration of a trend in the price of a cryptocurrency.

Since the MACD uses moving averages, which are an average of historical prices, it is a lagging indicator. Nevertheless, it is a very popular indicator, and one that I use on a regular basis. The way the MACD works is a bit complicated, but it's simple to use. First, I will describe how it works.

The 12 represents the previous 12 bars of the fast moving average (blue line).
The 26 represents the previous 26 bars of the slow moving average (red line).
The 9 represents the previous 9 bars of the difference between the two moving averages. This is plotted using vertical lines and is called the histogram (the vertical green and red lines). The periods adjust for the period being shown on the chart: days, weeks, months, etc.

The two lines are the moving averages of the difference between two moving averages. The faster moving average(blue line) is the moving average of the difference between the 12 and 26-period moving averages. The slower moving average(red line) plots the average of the previous MACD line. This means that we are taking the average of the last 9 periods of the faster MACD line and plotting it as the slower moving average. This smooths out the original line even more, which gives us a more accurate line. The histogram plots the difference between the fast and slow moving average. It may sometimes give you an early sign that a crossover is about to happen. As the two moving averages separate, the histogram gets bigger. This is called a MACD divergence because the faster moving average is "diverging" or moving away from the slower moving average. As the moving averages get closer to each other, the histogram gets smaller. This is called convergence because the faster moving average is "converging" or getting closer to the slower moving average.

When a new trend occurs, the fast line will react first and eventually crosses the slower line. When the crossover happens, and the fast line starts to "diverge" or move away from the slower line, it often indicates that a new trend has formed.

The usual settings for the MACD indicator are:
Signal Line: 9 period Exponential Moving Average
Short-term Exponential Moving Average: 12 period
Long-term Exponential Moving Average: 26 period

Signals

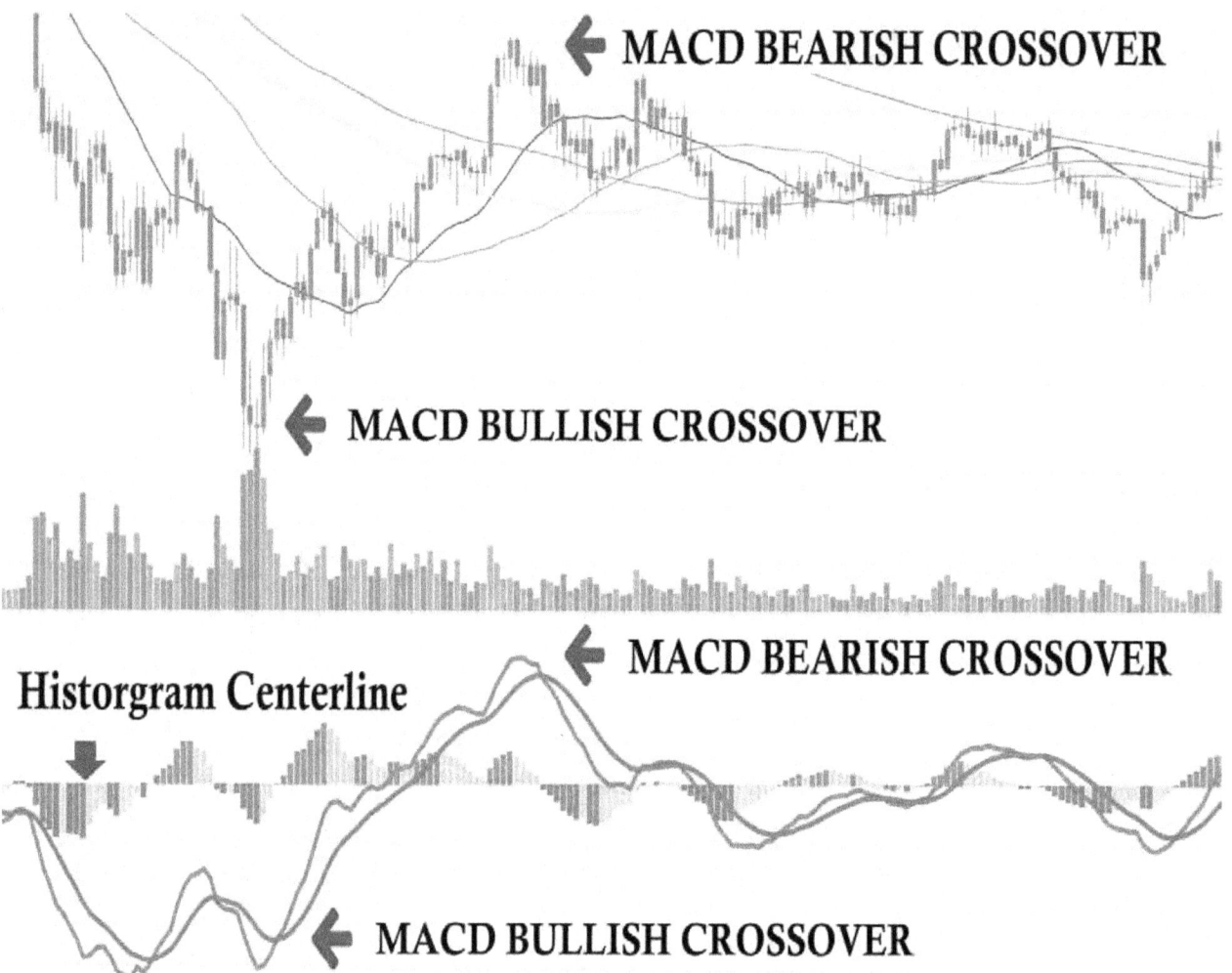

Look for signal line crossovers, center line crossovers, and divergences to find buy and sell signals using the MACD. Signal line crossovers are the most common MACD signals. A bullish crossover occurs when the blue MACD line turns up and crosses above the red signal line. A bearish crossover occurs when the blue MACD turns down and crosses below the red signal line.

Another common MACD signal are center line crossovers. A bullish center line crossover occurs when the MACD line moves above the zero line on the histogram, shown by the white line I drew, to the positive side. This happens when the shorter EMA of the asset moves above the longer EMA. A bearish center line crossover occurs when the MACD moves below the zero line to the negative side. This happens when the shorter EMA moves below the longer EMA.

When the price is moving a certain direction and the MACD is moving in the opposite direction it's called divergence which can signal a reversal. A bullish divergence forms when the price action plots a lower low on the chart, but the MACD plots a higher low. You can use either the histogram or the MACD and signal line to draw your divergence lines. Keep the divergence cheat sheet handy for reference when you're first getting started.

You can see the place where the MACD crosses the red signal line downwards the price action had a downturn, and where the MACD curves upward over the red signal line the price action had an uptrend. As soon as the blue line starts to curve that's when you want to nail your buy orders.

You could form an entire strategy around buying and selling MACD crossings alone. Watch for MACD crosses, and keep an eye out for divergences. Use the MACD indicator in combination with other indicators for added confirmation.

To find the MACD indicator click on the indicators tab and type MACD in the search bar. You'll see the MACD appear in the section under the price action.

Relative Strength Index

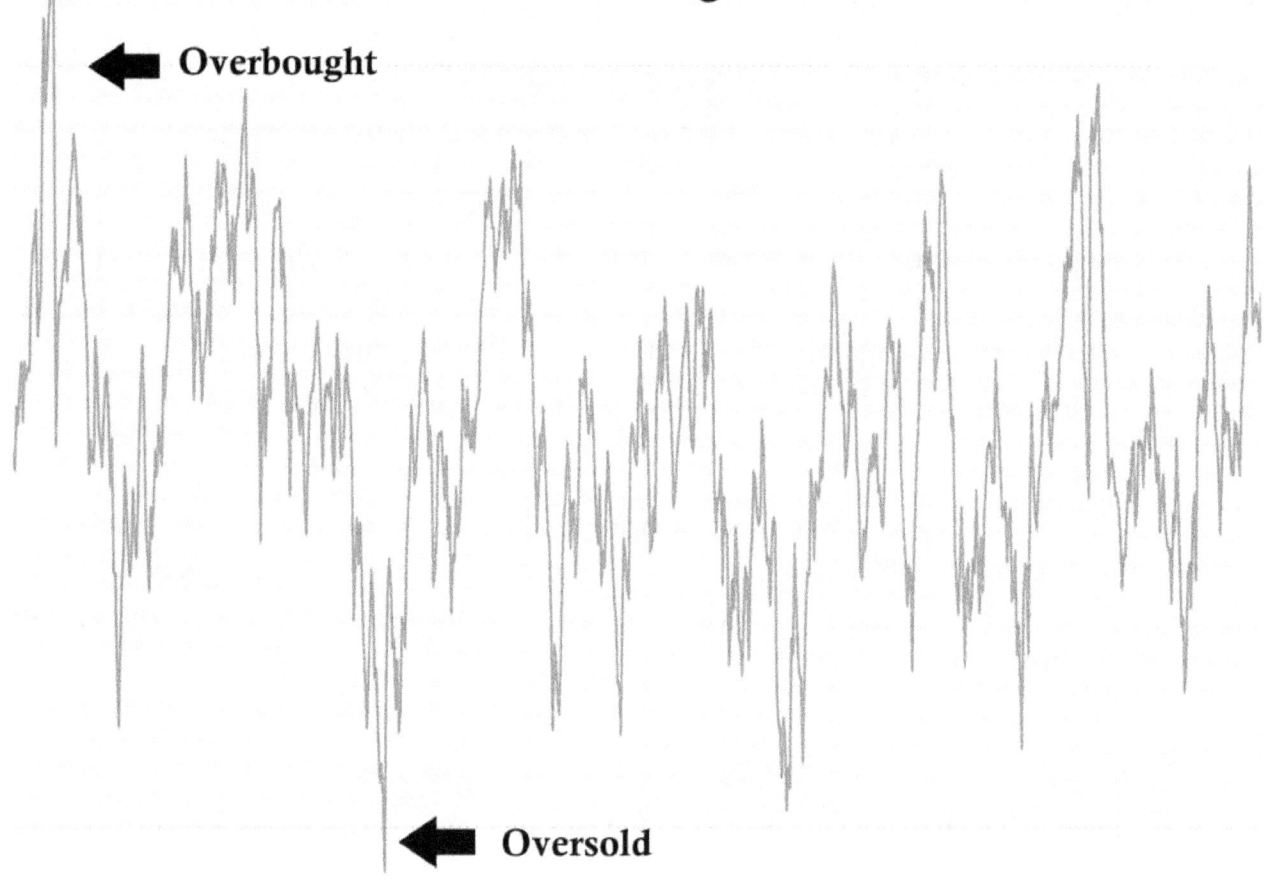

The relative strength index (RSI) is a momentum oscillator developed in 1978 by J. Welles Wilder Jr. It's one of the most popular indicators that helps traders determine if an asset is overbought or oversold. It's also a leading indicator so you receive the signals you need quickly.

The RSI is typically used on a 14-day timeframe and ranges on a scale from 1 to 100. As the number of bullish candle closes increase the RSI rises, and the RSI will decrease as the number of bearish candle closes increase. A high RSI reading means the price action has had a significant upward movement over a given period. A lower reading means a significant downward movement. An RSI reading above 70 means the market is overbought at the moment and an RSI reading below 30 means the market is oversold. When the reading reaches either of these levels it means a reversal is imminent. Traders view the RSI value of 50 to be support and resistance similar to the zero line on the MACD. Whenever the RSI crosses 50 it indicates bullish territory has been entered and the momentum is rising, and vice versa if it crosses below 50 into bearish territory. Keep in mind that during strong trends the RSI can stay pegged at the top or bottom for an extended period of time.

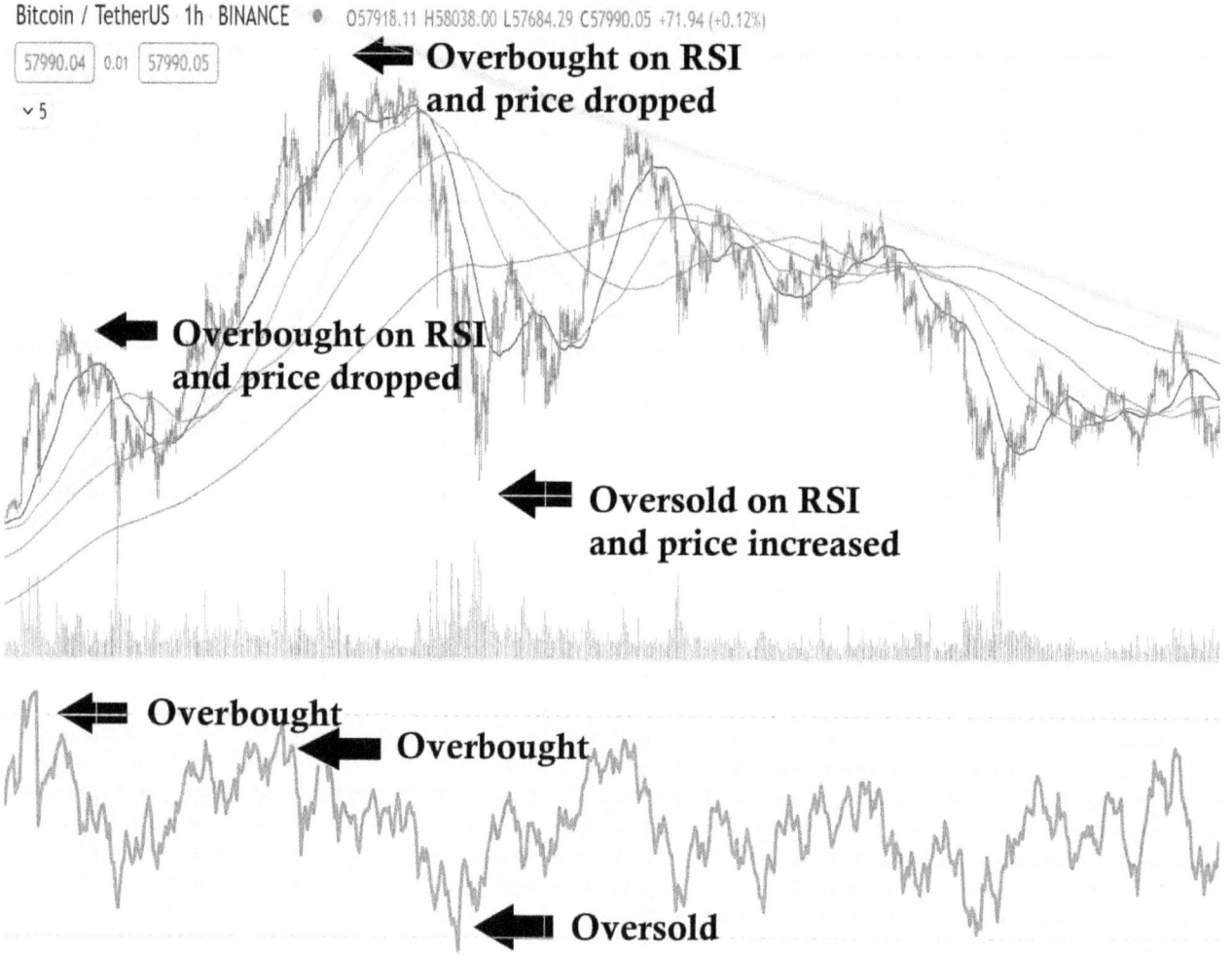

Just like the MACD, sometimes you will notice divergences where the price action doesn't match the RSI. Here you can see where the price action increased significantly, but there is divergence in the MACD and RSI indicators. The strength of the trend has decreased, and after the second peak you can see the price dropped.

Here are some different examples of divergences. To the untrained eye it would appear bitcoin was headed in the right direction. However, there was bearish divergence on the RSI indicator which was a signal that the price action was heading down even though it was going up at the time. The price action put in a higher high, but the RSI put in a lower high as indicated in red. After the price action made a higher high, traders took profits and bitcoin began consolidating. We begin to see signs of a turnaround when exaggerated bullish divergence appears as indicated in blue. The price action made a lower low, but the RSI had an equal low/double bottom signaling a trend change. Then, we see bullish divergence. The RSI makes a higher high while the price makes a lower low. This signals the trend is changing and the price is heading upward. However, it is important to note that it is always "possible" divergence until the move actually plays out and is confirmed.

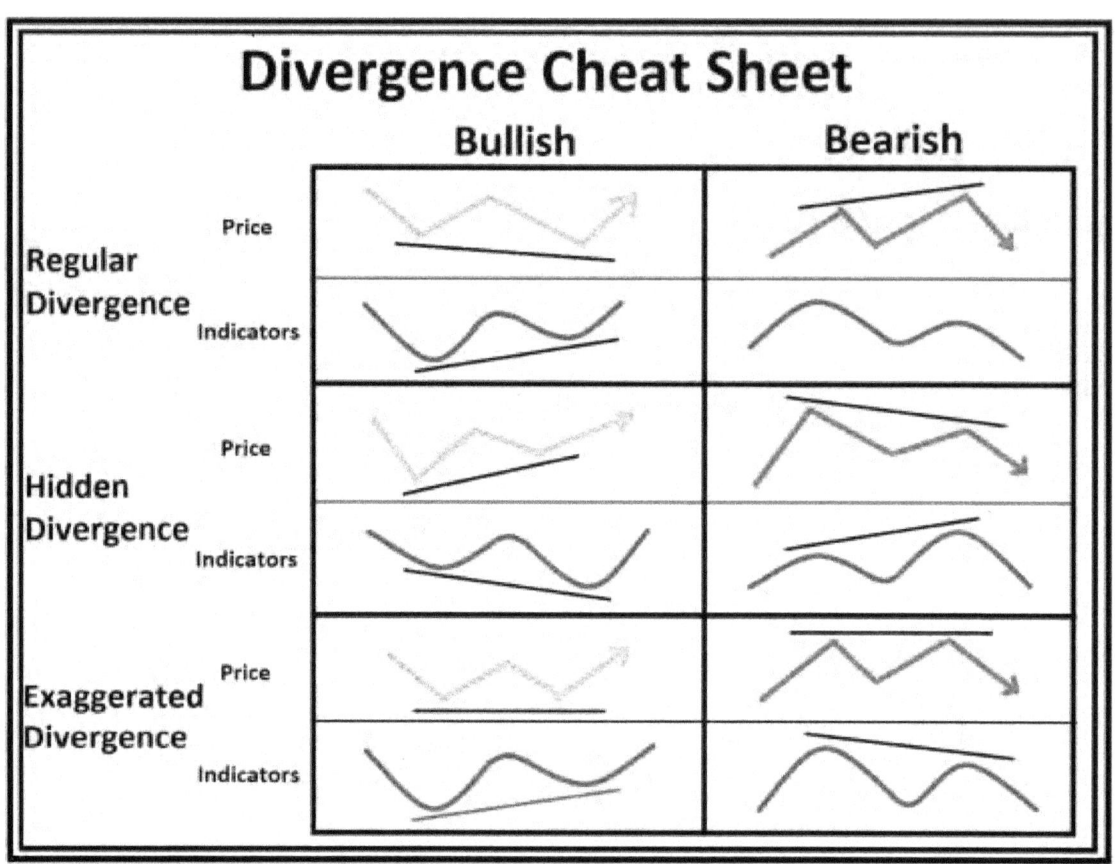

Keep this chart handy or draw it on your whiteboard so you have it in front of you.

To add the RSI to your chart click on the indicators tab and type relative strength index in the search bar.

I like to change the color of the RSI too. I like using green or yellow the most because it's the easiest to see. Click on settings next to where it says RSI on your chart. It looks like a little gear. Change the color to your preference and make it as bright as possible.

Bollinger Bands

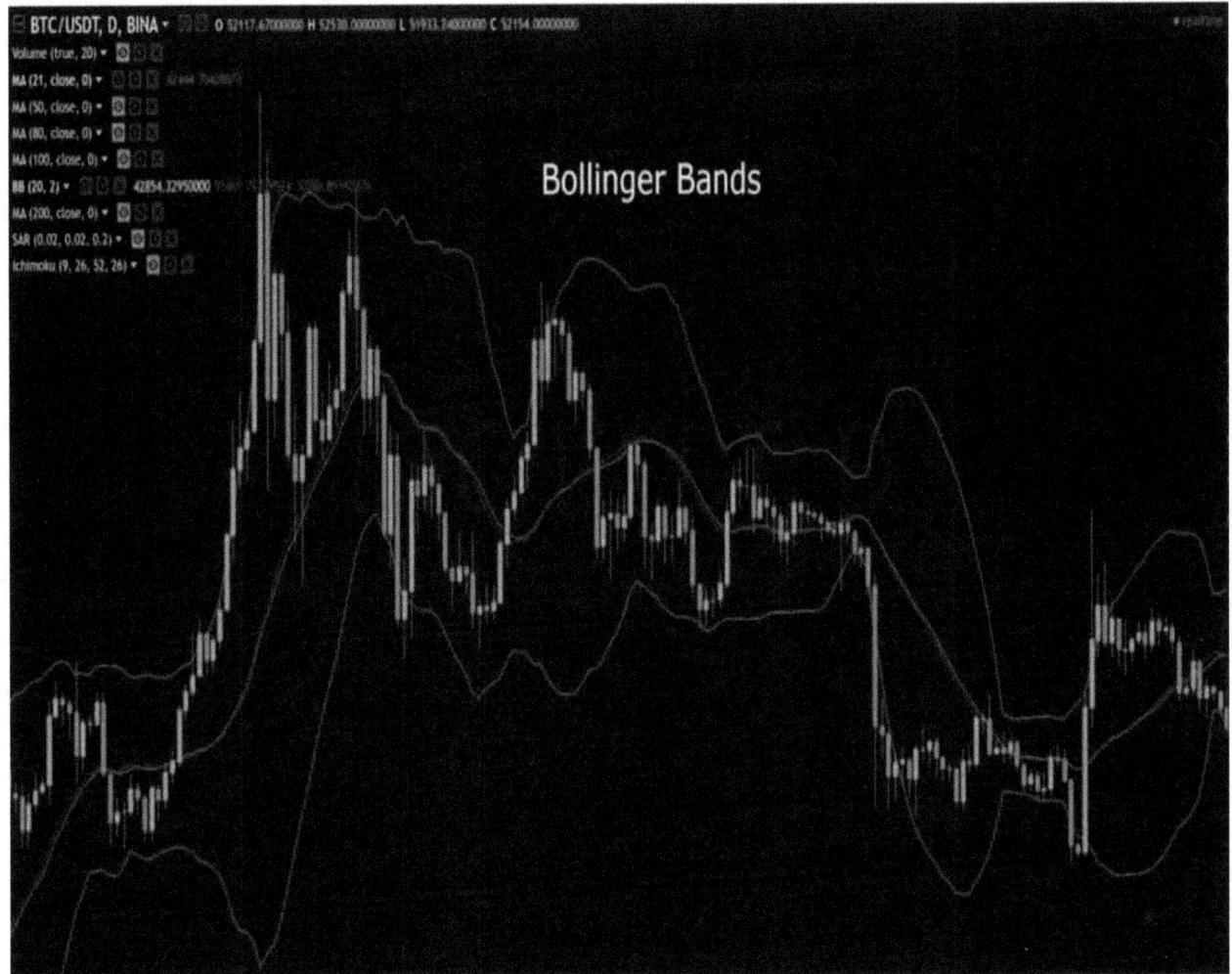

Moving averages are very useful, but they tend to give false signals in volatile markets. By applying what's called an envelope to a moving average, traders found some of these false signals could be avoided. Lines were added 5% above and below the moving average to form envelopes in order to prevent the false signals. They were called envelopes because they enveloped the moving average. A buy or sell signal would not be given unless the price moved outside of these newly added envelope lines.

There were a couple drawbacks to the envelope method which eventually led to the creation of the Keltner Channel in 1960. In his book "How to Make Money in Commodities," Chester Keltner laid out the idea of Keltner bands using a different way to calculate the bands around the moving average. Instead of using the closing prices to find the moving average he used the average of the high, low, and closing prices. He set the width of the envelope to a 10 day simple moving average of the daily range to arrive at what's called the average true range.

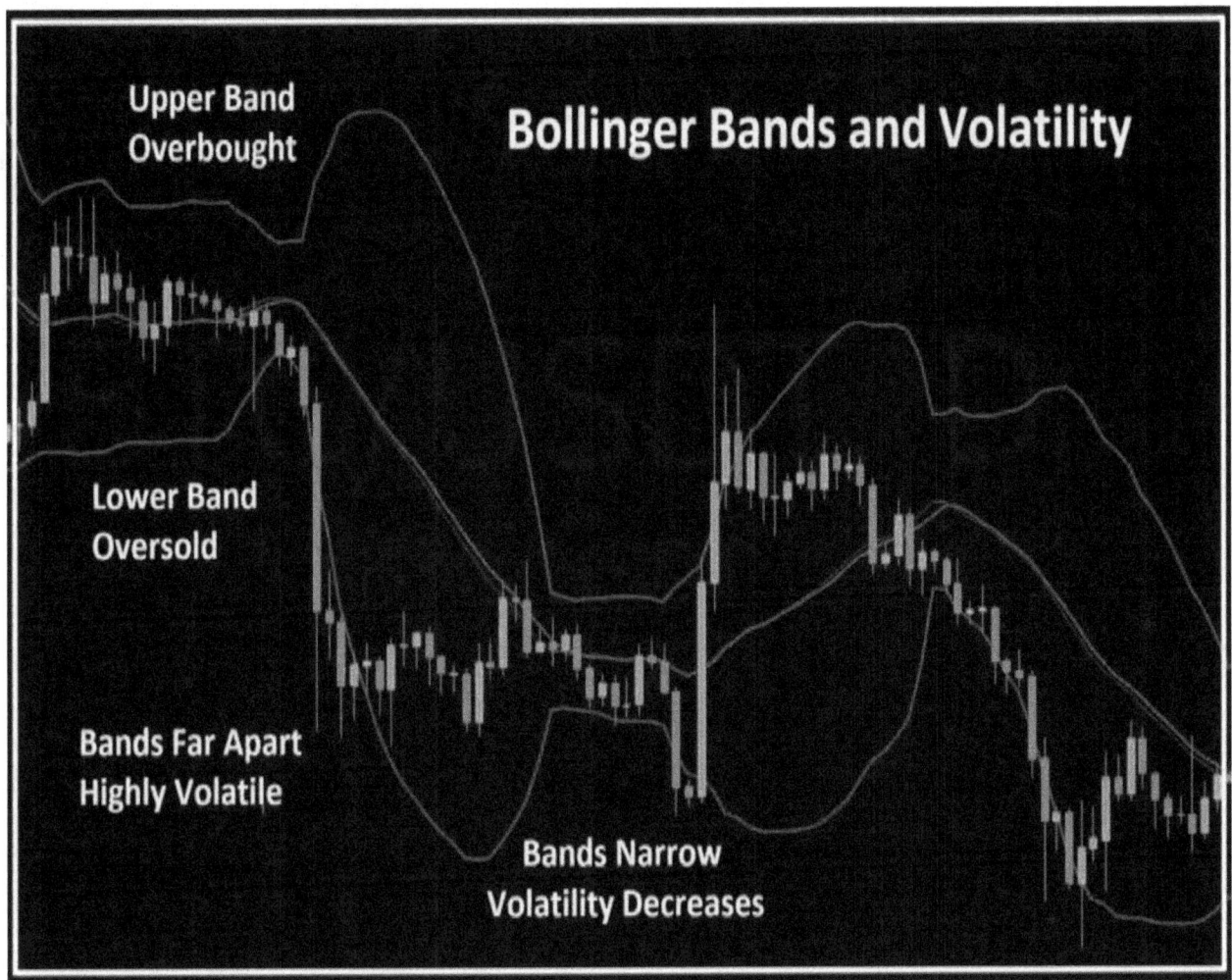

Eventually in the 1980's, a man named John Bollinger further improved upon the idea of the Keltner channel and developed what are called Bollinger Bands®. Bollinger Bands® use the popular method of standard deviation to calculate the outer bands. Standard deviation is a mathematical formula that's used to measure volatility. This was a much more accurate method to account for adjustments due to volatility swings. The moving average can be either an exponential moving average or a simple moving average.

Traders use the width of the bands to evaluate current volatility. Price reaching the outer band usually signals a reversal because when the price reaches the upper band it is considered to be overbought and when the price reaches the bottom band it's considered to be oversold. If the price action is able to breakout and stay outside the bands it shows trend strength.

In strong up trends the price will usually fluctuate between the upper band and the moving average, and in strong downtrends the price will stay between the bottom band and below the moving average. Whenever the price crosses over and closes above the moving average it is considered to be a bullish trend reversal. A cross below the moving average signals a bearish trend reversal.

The wider the bands are the more volatility in the market. When the bands come closes together there is less volatility. When the bands come close together around the moving average it's called a squeeze. It shows low volatility for a period of time which means a big move is coming soon. As always, use the Bollinger bands in combination with other indicators for confirmation.

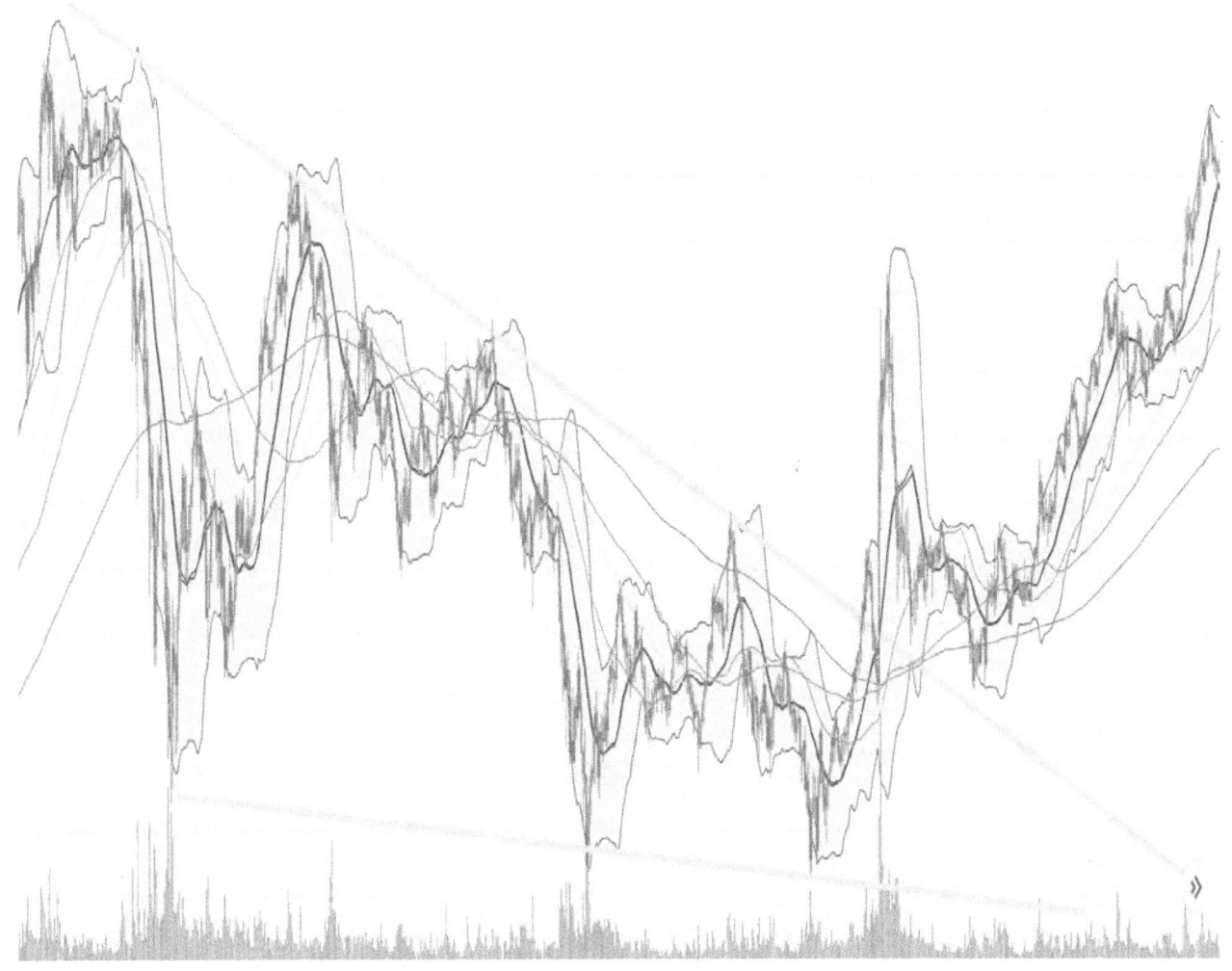

Here you can see where the Bollinger Bands® respected this triangle pattern before the price broke out and went to new highs. You can also see where the price action was squeezed at times followed by subsequent price spikes.

Watch for the bands to curve up or down. This could be an early indication as to which direction the price is heading.

Market Volume

Underneath the price candles at the bottom are the volume bars. Volume measures the amount of buy and sell orders in a period of time. Green bars indicate more buy orders than sell orders and red bars indicate more sell orders than buy orders.

Volume is probably the most important tool you can use when trading because it shows how much an asset was traded over a period of time. It's used to determine the balance between supply and demand, and indicates the force behind a trend. Whenever you see a large amount of volume it means there is a high interest in a coin at it's current price, while low volume means there is a low interest in a coin at it's current price, and more people are selling than buying.

The volume moving average(the light blue shaded area) is good to use too because it shows if the volume is trending upwards or downwards. You can see in the example above where the volume increased until the price started falling. Investors took profits after the big run up in price.

If a coin is moving out of a pattern or retesting, but doesn't have much volume you might as well not even buy it because it usually won't go up very much. You always want a strong force behind the trend you are hoping to capitalize on. Make sure you check the volume before you enter a position.

Watch for when the price makes new highs while the volume drops. When this happens it's called volume divergence, and this can sometimes be a reversal signal.

Volume Profile Visible Range

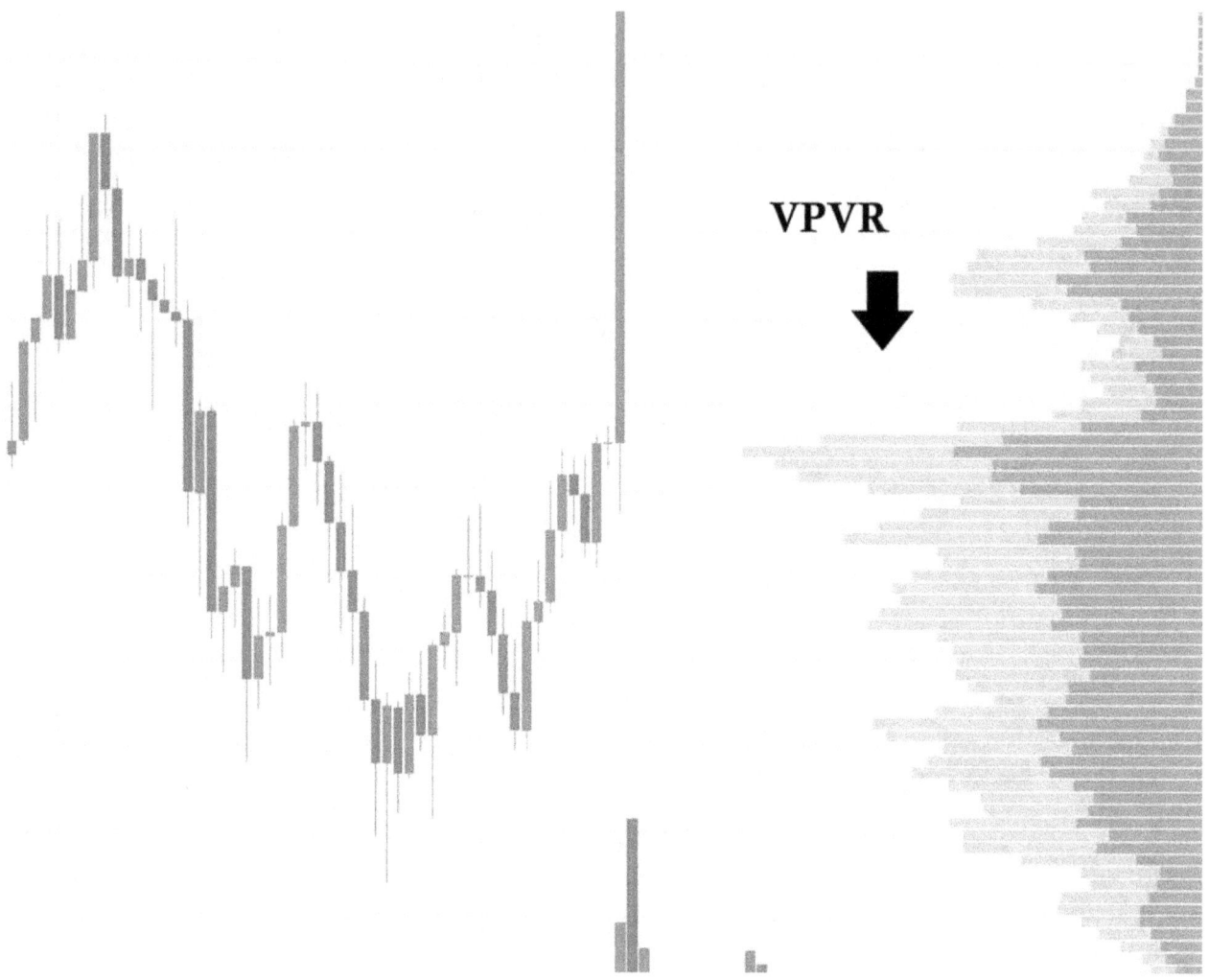

Volume shows traders how much an asset was traded during a period of time. The volume profile visible range (VPVR) is a leading indicator that shows how much an asset is being traded at different price levels. It's one of the most useful tools a trader can use.

The VPVR let's traders know the state of the current market, help identify areas where volatility can be expected, and can help traders identify levels of support and resistance. It can also help traders to determine entries, exits, and stop-losses.

How does it work?
The VPVR plots the information on the side of the chart next to the price action in the form of horizontal bars. The longer the horizontal bar, aka node, the more volume/transactions that occurred at that price point. This essentially tells a trader what the supply and demand is at specific prices.

Allow me to explain in further detail. The bars that stick out furthest to the left are called High Volume Nodes (HVNs). They show where there is higher than average volume at certain prices. These areas serve as areas of support and resistance. If the price is above a large VPVR bar it is seen as support, if it's below it's seen as resistance.

The smaller bars you see in the picture are called Low Volume Nodes (LVNs). They show where there is lower than average volume at various price levels.

Seventy percent of the volume is located in what's known as the value area. The highest price in this area is called the value area high, and the lowest price in this area is called the value area low.

The largest node in in the volume profile is called the point of control (POC). It is the price level with the highest traded volume. Traders view the POC as key support due to the large amount of positions opened at this price. Because orders are constantly being placed the position of the POC can change over time.

The areas where there are large gaps in between the HVNs are called clearance areas. Clearance areas provide little to no resistance due to the lack of sell orders at these price levels, so the price action can easily shoot right up through them. The same goes if the price is falling through a clearance zone. If there are little to no buy orders the price action will usually fall straight through to the next HVN where it finds support.

To find the VPVR in Tradingview you'll need to click in the indicators tab and type VPVR in the search bar. Keep in mind that since this is a highly sought after tool Tradingview requires a pro membership to use it. To use the VPVR In Coinigy you'll need the beta version of coinigy.

To find the VPVR in Coinigy, click on the blue link in the top right hand section of the chart on the left side of settings. This will take you to Coinigy's beta version. Here you'll want to click on boards tab.

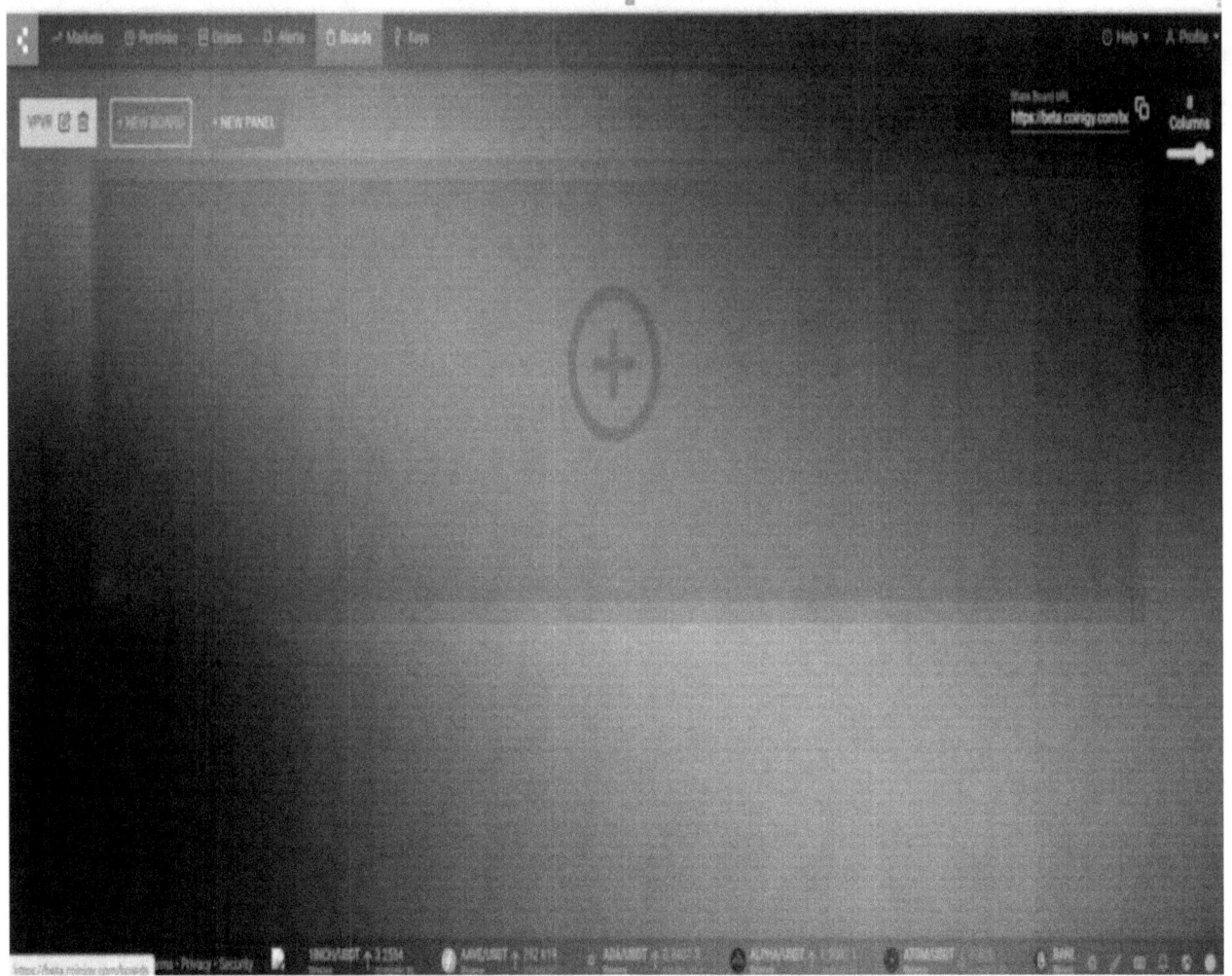

Next, click the button that says + NEW PANEL, or you can click on the plus sign in the middle of the screen to add a new panel.

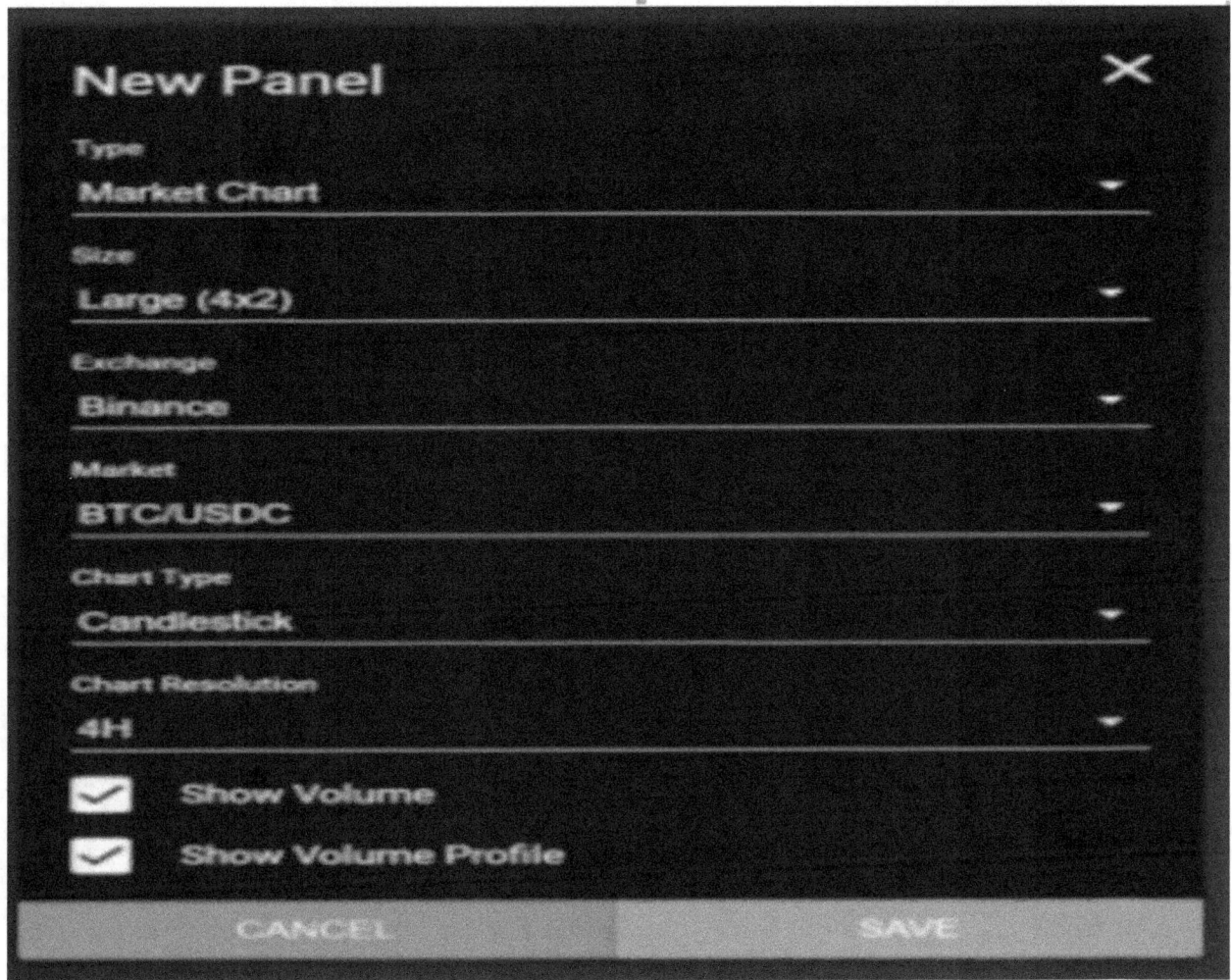

In this section you will need to fill in each blank section to complete the panel. For the type select market chart. I chose the large size so it's easier to see. Binance is the exchange I'm currently using so I will select Binance as the exchange. You should choose whichever exchange you're using so the numbers are accurate. I will choose the BTC/USDC chart to view the VPVR on. Chart type is candlestick, and we'll go with the four hour chart resolution. Make sure to check the show volume profile before you click save.

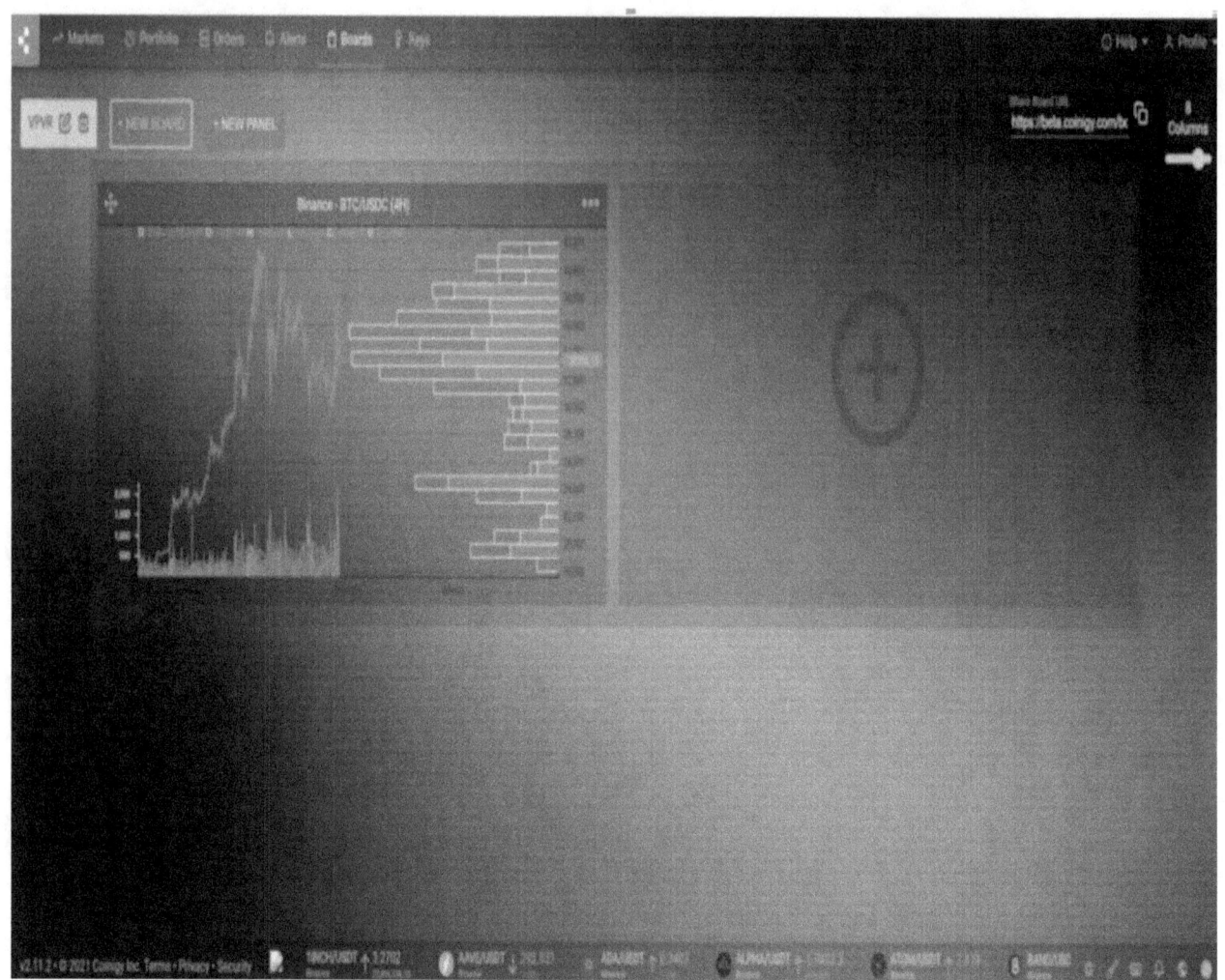

The end result will look like this if you chose the same settings.

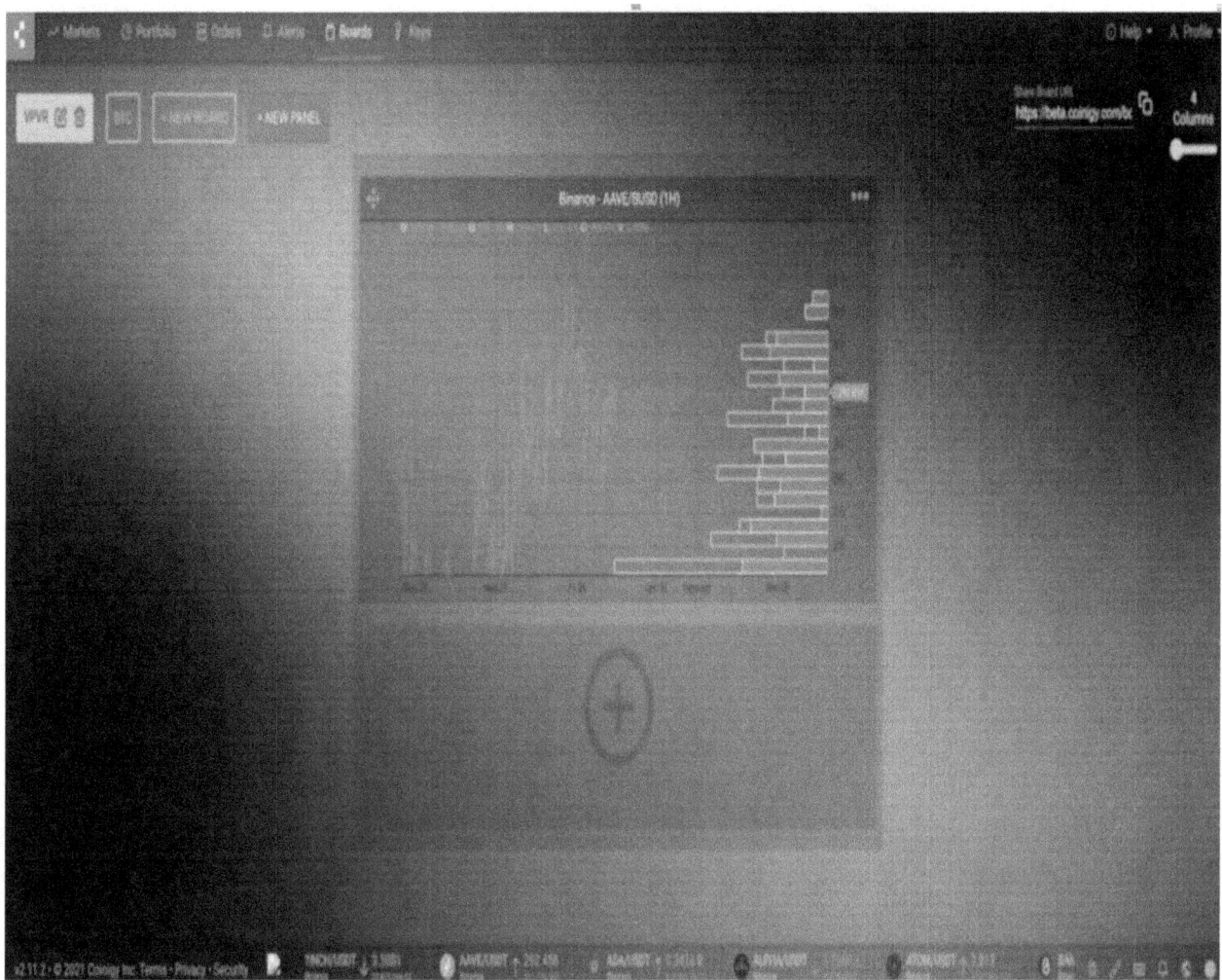

You can lower the number of columns in the top right hand side of the screen.

Fibonacci Retracement Tool

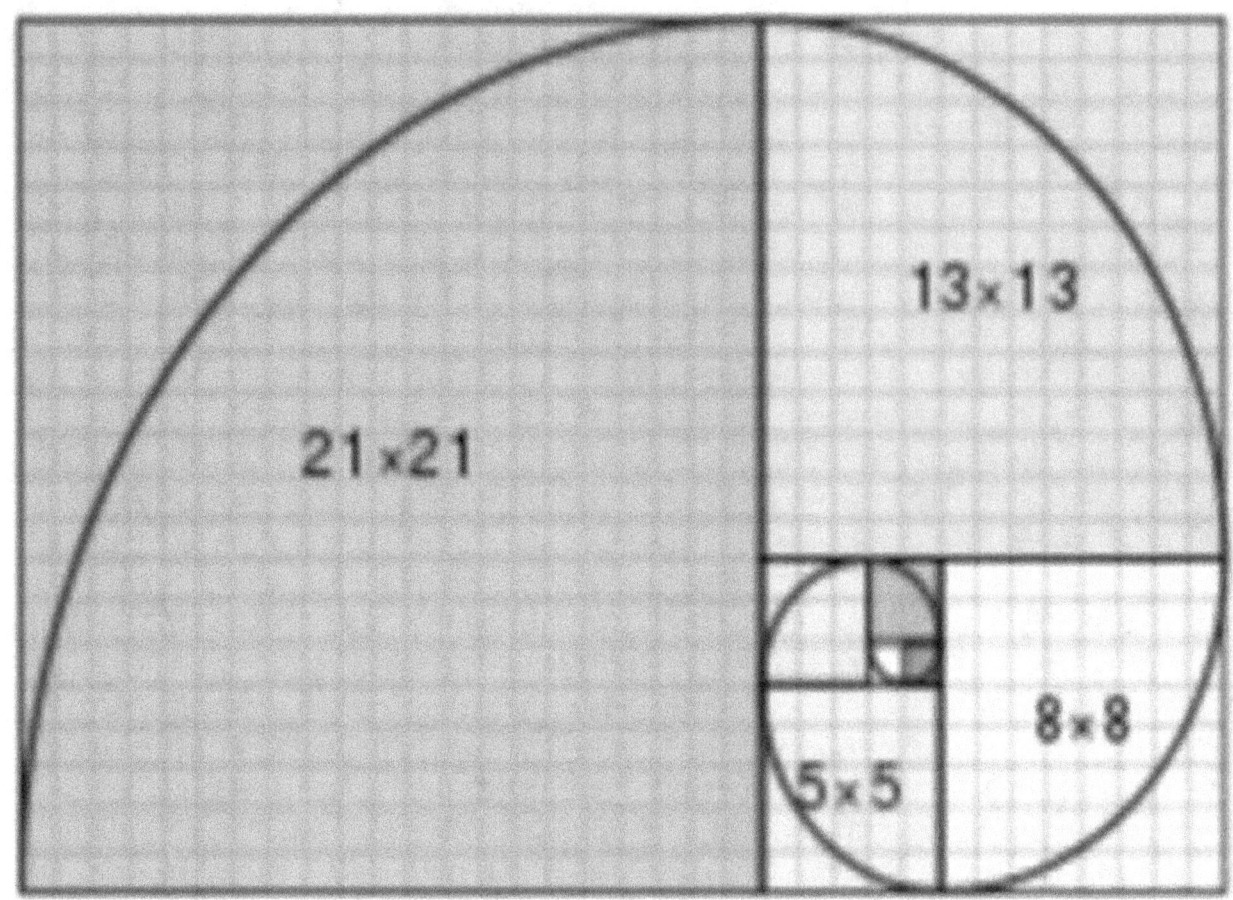

The Fibonacci retracement tool helps traders identify support and resistance levels where they can place buy, sell, and stop-loss orders. This tool really comes in handy when you're trying to find an entry while the price of an asset is falling after a recent run up. The Fibonacci retracement tool can give you an idea how far the price is going to fall so you can time your entry.

The concept comes from a man named Leonardo Bonacci. Leonardo Bonacci, whose nickname was Fibonacci, was an Italian mathematician who developed a system that took the place of the previously used Roman numeral system. His system improved business calculation capabilities which led to the exponential growth of accounting and banking in Europe.

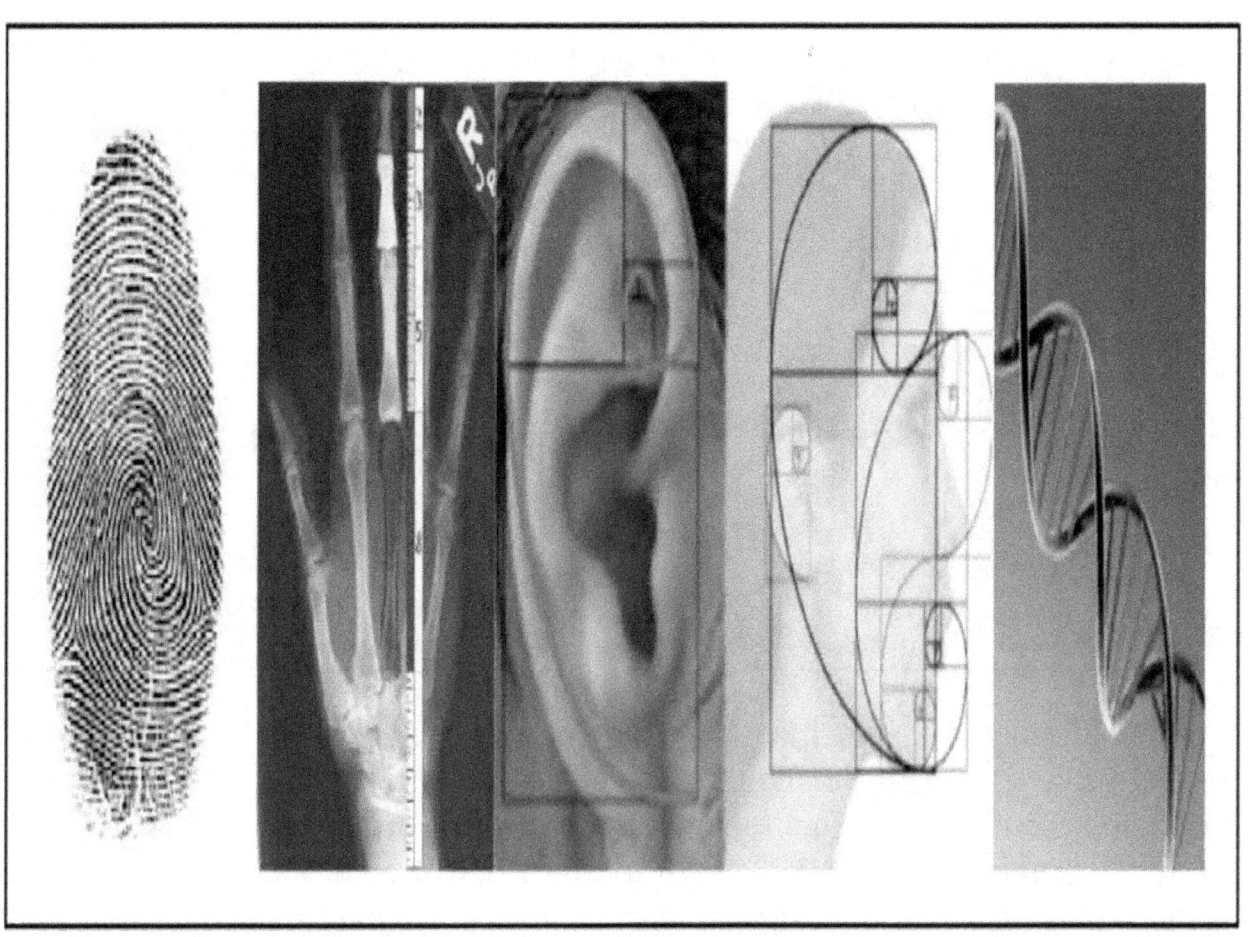

This ratio of numbers became known as the Fibonacci sequence, otherwise known as the Golden Ratio, or God's ratio.

0112358132134558914423337761098715972584418167 65

Interestingly, the Fibonacci sequence patterns can be found everywhere in nature, as well as, human creations like music, art, and architecture. This pattern is found in the human hand, fingerprints, sea shells, flowers, even our DNA structure. It's also found in human structures like the layout of the Great Pyramids, the structure of the pyramids, famous paintings like Leonardo da Vinci's Mona Lisa and Vincent Van Gogh's Starry Night. There is evidence that suggests that famous musical composers like Mozart and Beethoven used the Fibonacci sequence in the structure of their compositions, and modern day artists use it to this day.

The Fibonacci levels that are used in trading are 23.6%, 38.2%, 50%, 61.8%, 78.6%, and 100%. The 50% level is not officially a Fibonacci ratio, but stems from Dow's Theory which says assets often retrace half of their prior movement. These levels are important because they are psychological barriers that repeat in the market. They are places where traders anticipate a bounce off resistance or support. It works because there are so many other traders that use it that think it works. You can use it to determine entries, determine stop loss levels, or set price targets.

The most important level in the Fibonacci retracement tool is the .618, also known as, the Golden Mean Level.

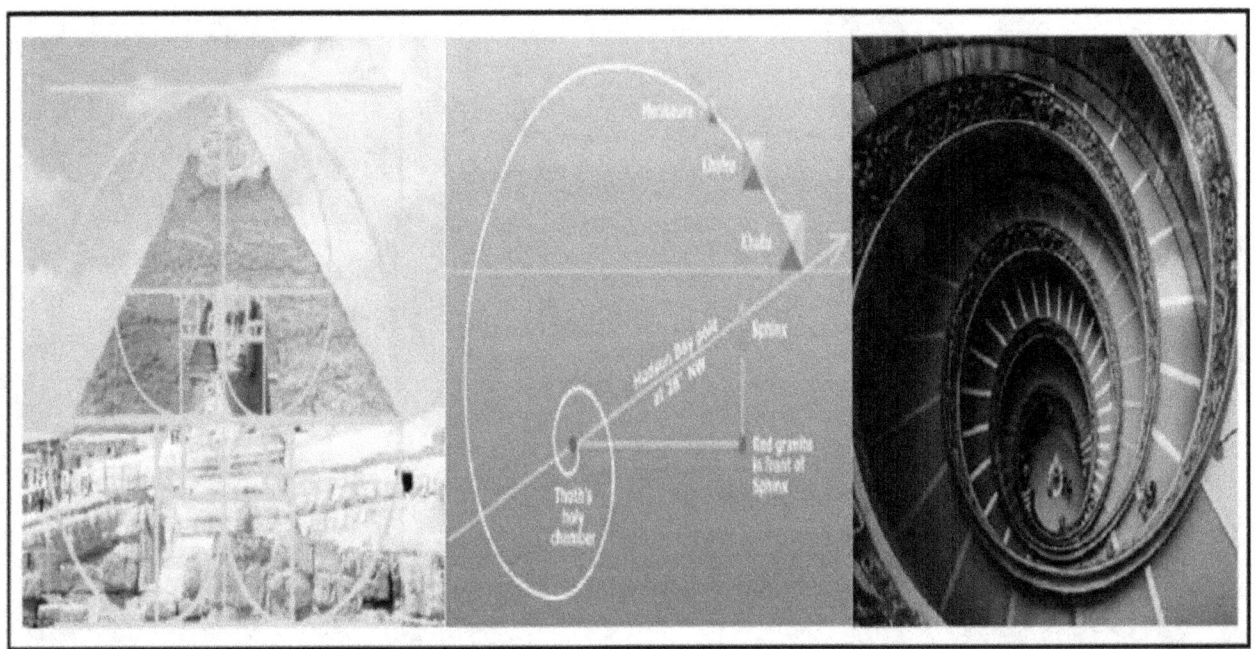

    This indicator is best used after a run up in price to ascertain where the price will fall. By selecting two price levels, a recent low and recent high after a run up, you get the two points of reference the tool needs to give you an accurate reading.

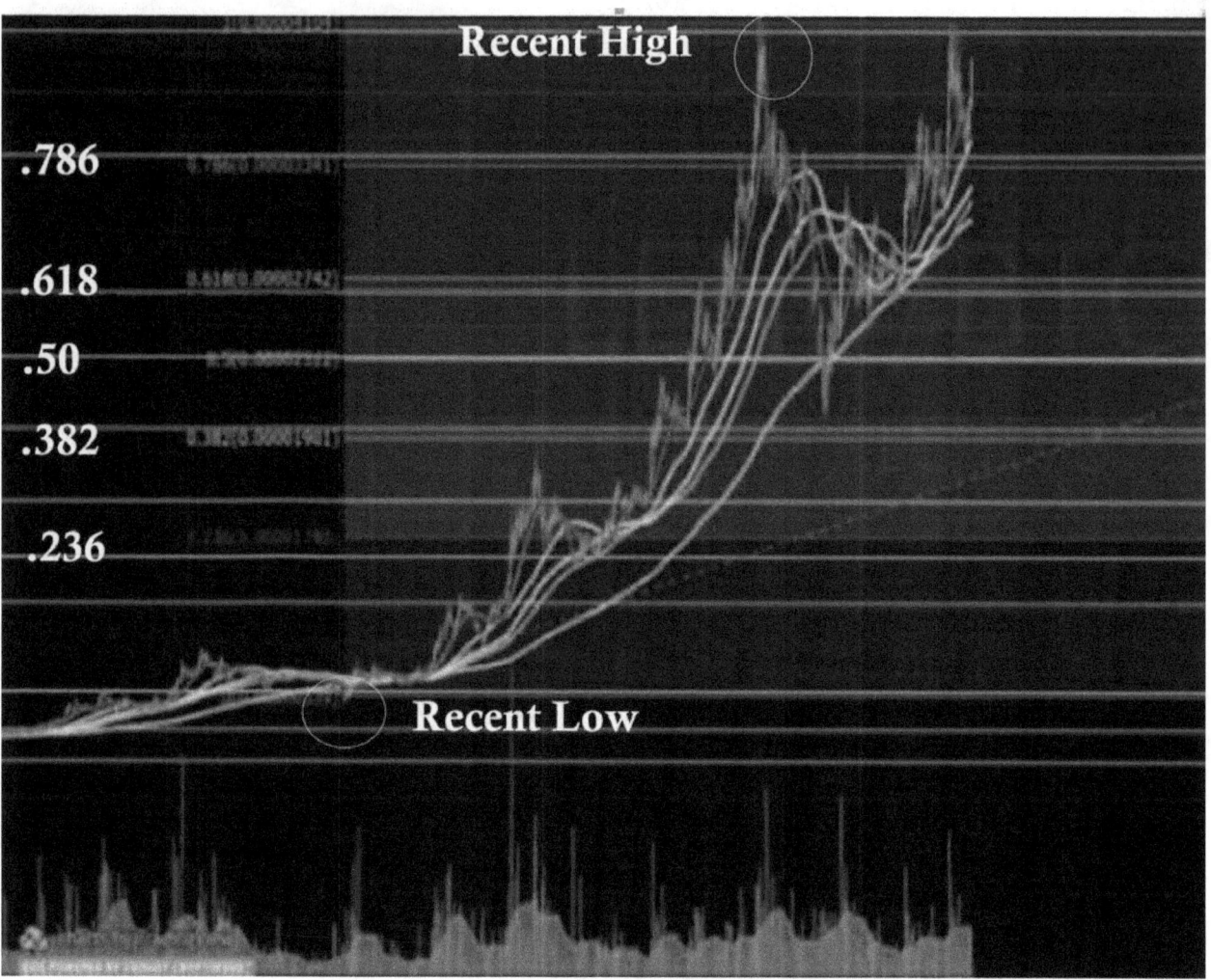

In this example, you can see how my white resistance lines are very close to matching up with the Fibonacci levels. I selected the wick of the recent low and the wick of the recent high. You can use the candlesticks or the wicks, whichever works best for the chart. You want the lowest and highest points. The price action bounced around the .50 mark and the .618 served as strong support here.

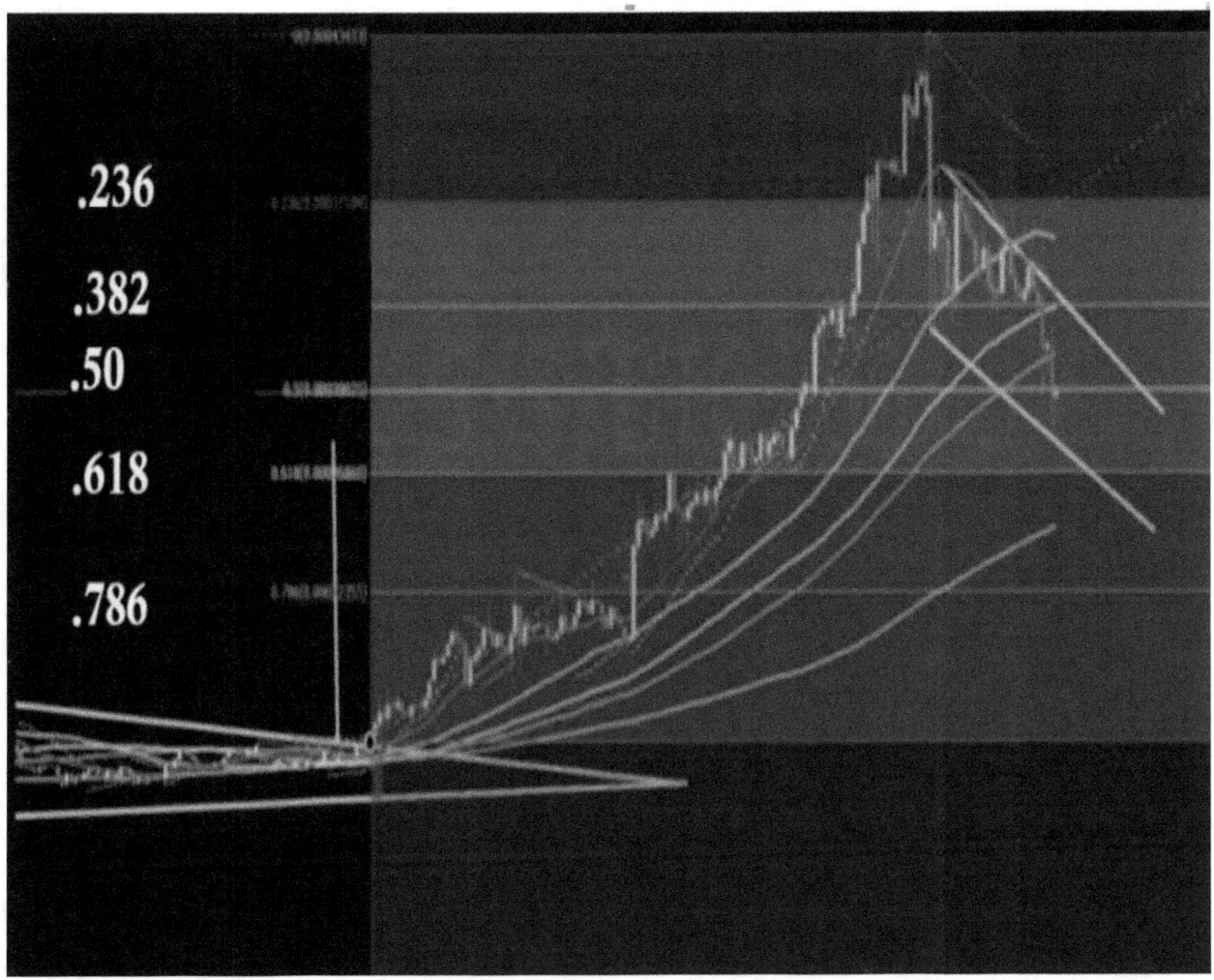

In this example, I chose the point at which SXP broke out of a triangle pattern and the top of the wick of the run up before it retraced. The support and resistance points line up almost perfectly with the falling channel. Now I can either buy at the .50, buy at the .618, scale into the trade and place an order for the .50 and another order to buy at the .618, or I can buy some at the .50 and some more when it breaks out of the falling channel. Trading is a lot like chess you have to think two and three steps ahead.

Fibonacci levels aren't 100% accurate, and should be used in combination with other indicators for confirmation. I love to use it to nail entries between the .50 and the .618 after a retracement. The .50 and .618 is the sweet spot.

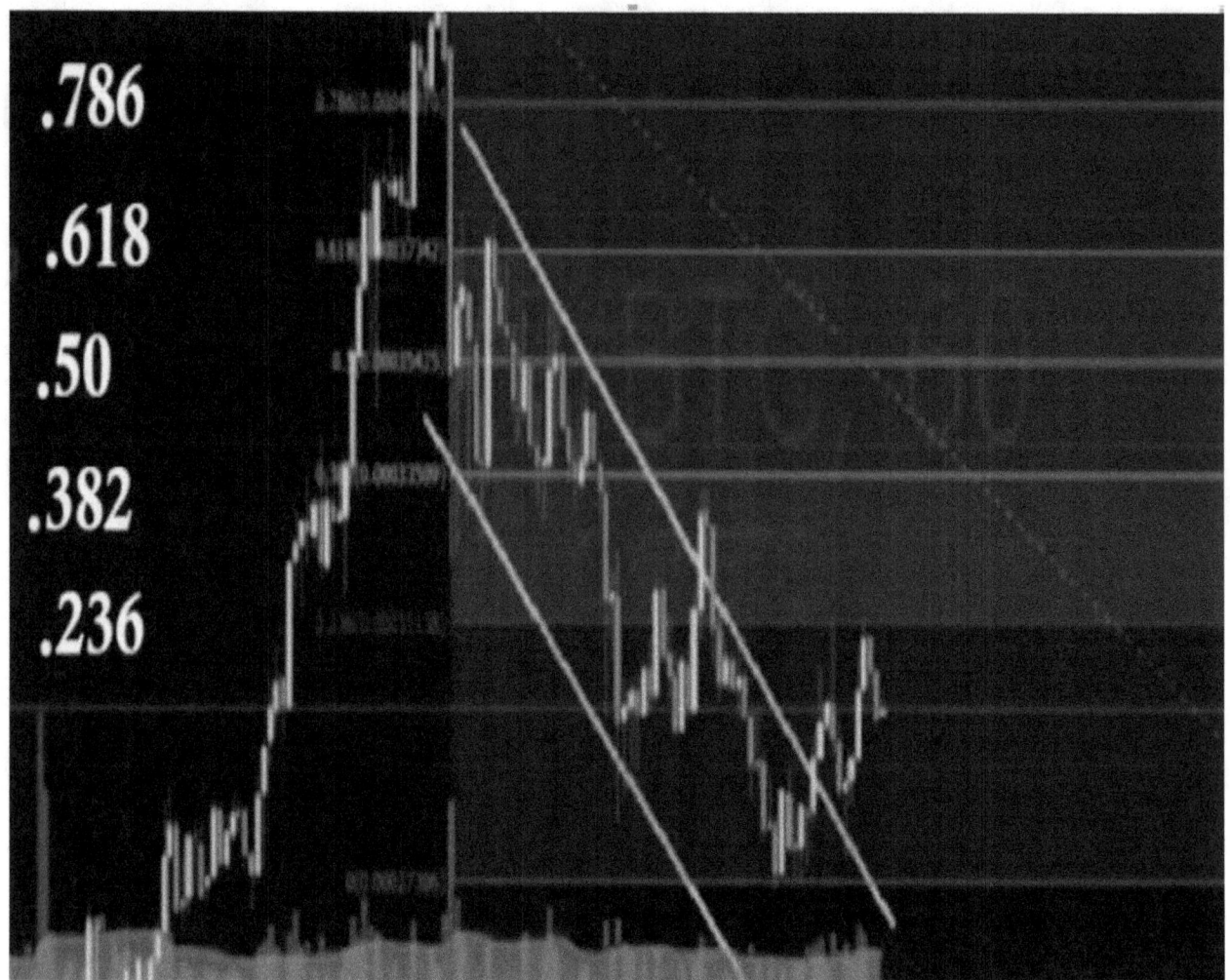

If you go from the bottom to the top you can see levels of support the price action will potentially bounce off of and go to new highs. If you go from the top to the bottom you can identify levels of resistance. This is where you can set your take profit levels in the next run up. You could choose to take 25% profit at the .382, 25% at the .50, 25% at the .618, and let the remaining 25% ride while moving my stop loss up along the way to support levels. Just make sure to set your take profit levels just before the Fibonacci levels because there are a lot of others out there using this tool, including institutional buyers, and they're going to set *their* sell levels at the Fibonacci retracement levels. This is why they become levels of resistance. Don't be greedy! Lock in profits when you get the chance before someone else takes your profit from you.

To find the Fibonacci retracement tool in Tradingview find the toolbar on the left hand side of the screen, and click on the 4th option down. Scroll down to find Fib Retracement.

Fibonacci Extension Tool

The Fibonacci extension tool is used by traders to find hidden areas of resistance to use as take profit targets when there is no previous price history as a reference to draw resistance lines. It's also used to estimate how far the price will go after a pullback. The Fibonacci extension tool uses Fibonacci ratios just like the Fibonacci retracement tool. The difference is the extension tool gives you an idea how far the price will go up and the retracement tool gives you an idea how far the price will go down.

To use the Fibonacci extension tool you need to select three points of reference: the start of the impulse, the end of the impulse, and the end of the retracement. After your three points are selected it will show the Fibonacci extension lines on your chart. The lines offer places of potential resistance where it will be difficult for the price action to break through. This is why investors use the extension levels to determine where they will take profits. These levels are susceptible to price reversal.

Fibonacci extensions are projections greater than 100%. The most important Fibonacci extension levels are the 100, 123.6%, 138.2%, 150%, 161.8%, 200%, and 261.8%. One easy way to remember Fibonacci extension levels is by adding 100 to each of the regular Fibonacci retracement levels:

23.6 + 100 = 123.6%
38.2 + 100 = 138.2%

50 + 100 = 150%
61.8 + 100 = 161.8%

Add another 200 to the most important Fibonacci extension number the 61.8 to arrive at the 261.8 level. You can change the levels to whatever you want, but these are the recommended Fibonacci extension levels in a strong uptrend. As a rule of thumb the 50, 61.8, or 78.6 Fibonacci retracement will usually hit resistance at the 161.8 extension level. A 38.2 Fibonacci retracement will usually hit resistance around the 138.2 extension level and so on.

These levels are the percentage of the impulse move added on to the end of the retracement. The 100% is calculated by taking 100% of the impulse move and adding it to the retracement. The 138.2% level is calculated by taking 138.2% of this impulse move and adding it to the retracement. You can do the same for the rest of the Fibonacci extension levels.

If the Fibonacci extension tool you're using doesn't have these levels you will need to add them manually. In Tradingview right click on one of your Fibonacci extension points and click on settings. From there you will be able to change all the levels to what you want.

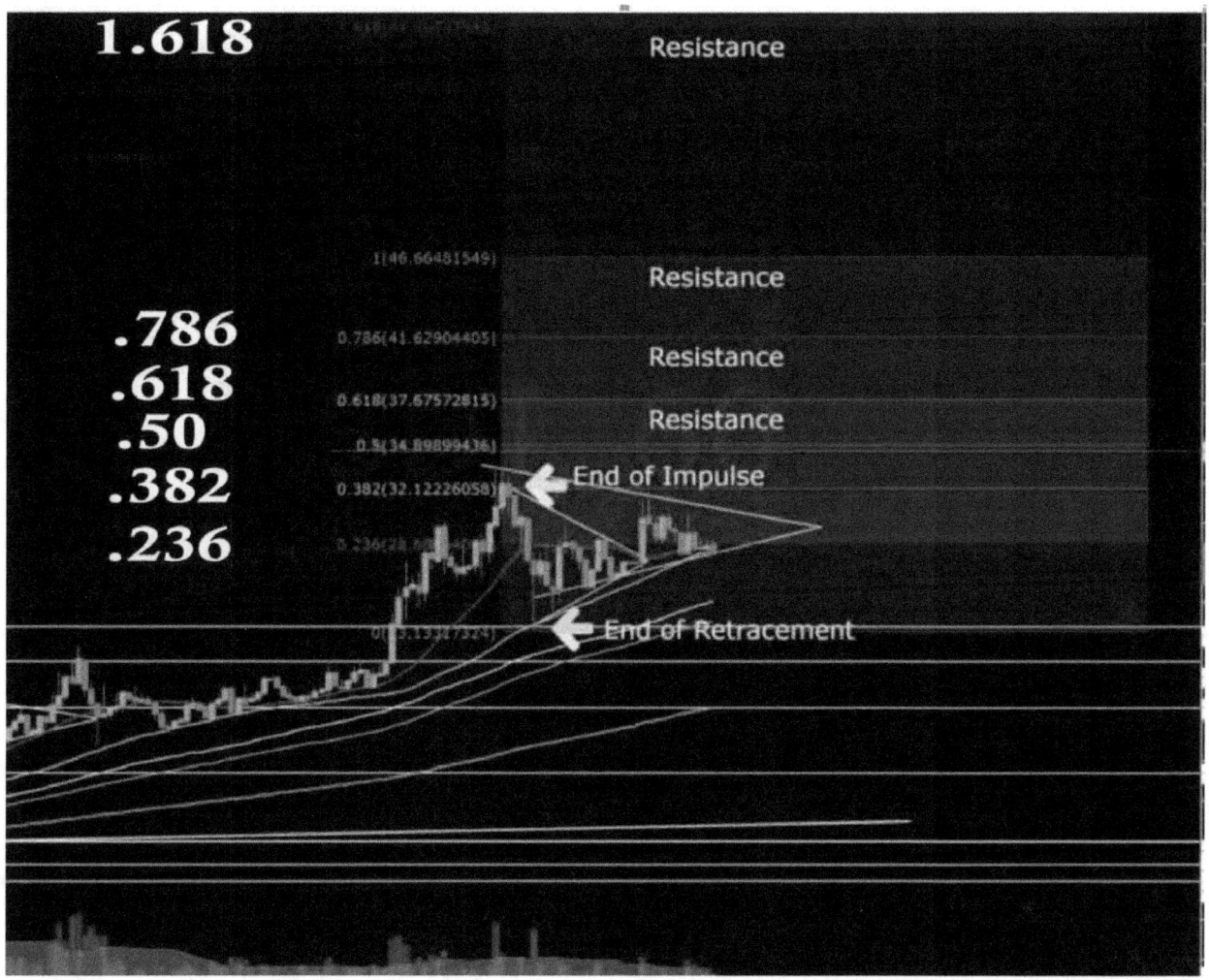

In the example above you can see where the extension tool gave us our possible areas of resistance. If drawn correctly it should line up or at least be close to lining up to some of your existing support and resistance levels if we have any.

You can also use the Fibonacci extension tool for support levels. To use the Fibonacci extension tool this way you will select the same three points of reference as we did before: the start of the impulse, the end of the impulse, and the end of the retracement.

In order to find out which Fibonacci extension level to set your profit target at you will need to combine it with support and resistance levels, trendlines, and moving averages for added confirmation. As with any indicator or tool this is just a guide. Always use other information as confirmation. I usually look to take profits around the 100% and 1.618% levels.

To find the Fibonacci extension tool in Tradingview find the toolbar on the left hand side of the screen, click on the 4th option down. Click on Trend Based Fib Extension tool.

Candlestick trading

In this section I will go over some of the most common candlestick reversal and continuation patterns. Knowing how to identify common candlestick patterns will help you better nail your entries and exits, and let you know when the trend is going to continue or reverse. You can use line charts, but I prefer candlesticks charts because they provide more information for a trader. Line charts just take the open and close prices in the time frame you selected, and plots them on the chart. Once you become familiar with common candlestick patterns you will be able to read them like a book.

Thomas Bulkowski is one of the world's leading authorities on chart patterns. His book, Encyclopedia of Candlestick Charts, details how to identify 103 candlestick chart patterns and their statistics of success. Bulkowski used around 4.7 million candlesticks in his research to determine the probabilities of success for each candlestick pattern, and I have found them to be very accurate.

The statistics I use in this chapter come from Thomas Bulkowski's Encyclopedia of Candlestick Charts book, and I would highly recommend you read it. I've listened to many people on YouTube and other social media talk about candlestick patterns, and the information they provided was sometimes incorrect. There are some misconceptions about how some of the patterns perform, so I want to review some of the most common patterns that you should be aware of.

Here's a list of the most common patterns I look for:

Doji

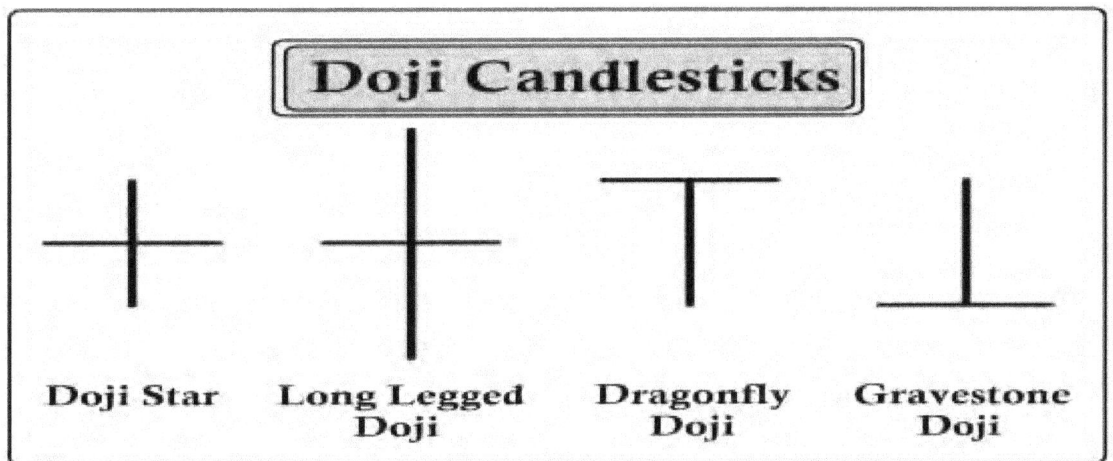

A Doji candlestick is where the opening and closing prices are the same or close to the same. A doji candle is one of the most popular reversal patterns. However, in a bull market most of the time the price action continues upward. Always wait for the next candle to confirm if the trend is continuing or reversing.

The doji candle shows the bulls and bears have battled it out and the result was a draw. Doji candlesticks are a sign of indecision and can *sometimes* be a reversal signal.

Long legged doji has a 51% chance of continuation in a bull market.
Dragonfly 50% chance of reversal
Gravestone 51% chance of reversal

A doji star isn't a good reversal indicator in a bull market. In a bull market a doji star shows continuation 69% of the time. Look out for a doji near the edge of a price channel because it could potentially indicate a bearish correction.

Hammer & Hanging Man

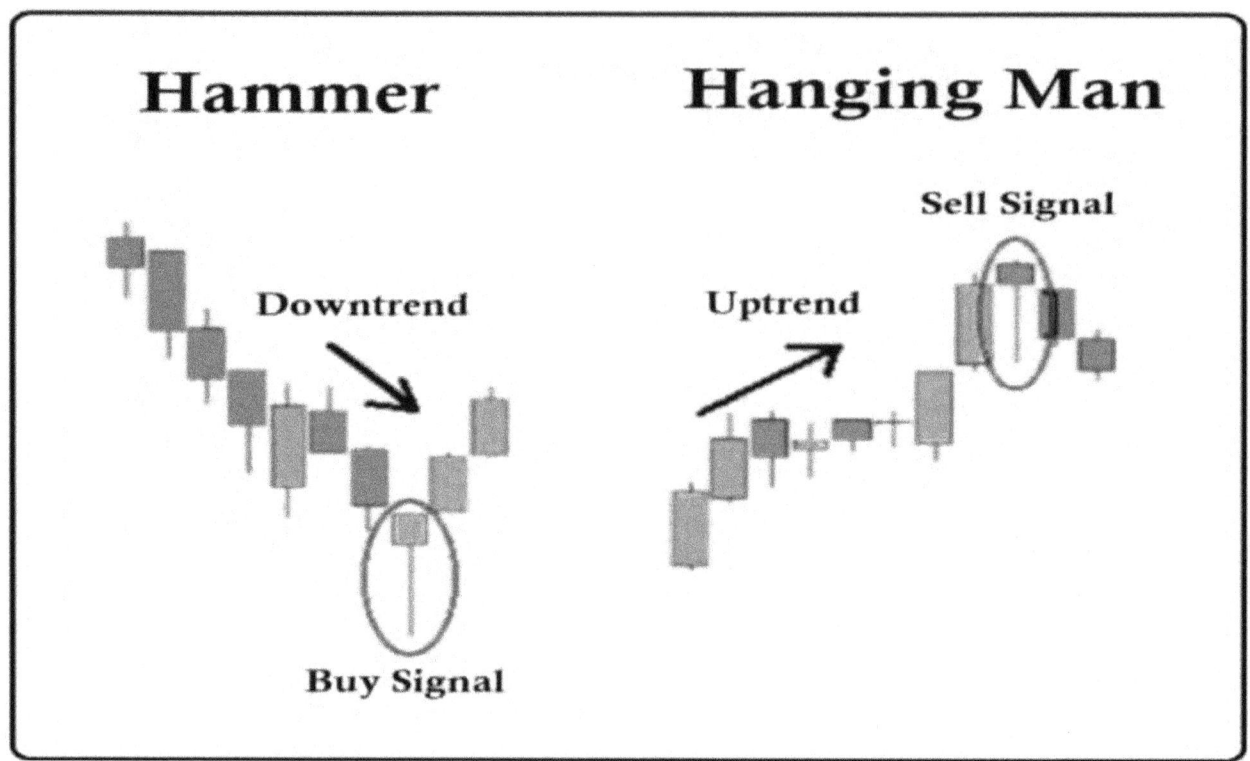

Hammer candlesticks can be found at the end of a downtrend and signals a bullish reversal. The long wick at the bottom tells us that at one point the bears were winning the battle, then the bulls took over and pushed the price back up showing a bullish trend. The lower wick should be at least two times longer than the body. Indicators will show oversold. A hammer will break the downtrend 60% of the time in a bull market.

A hanging man, or inverted hammer, candlestick looks like a hammer too. The only difference is a hanging man can be found at the end of a bullish pattern and indicates a bearish reversal. Indicators will show overbought. In a bull market, however, the hanging man actually acts as a continuation 59% of the time.

Inverted Hammer & Shooting Star

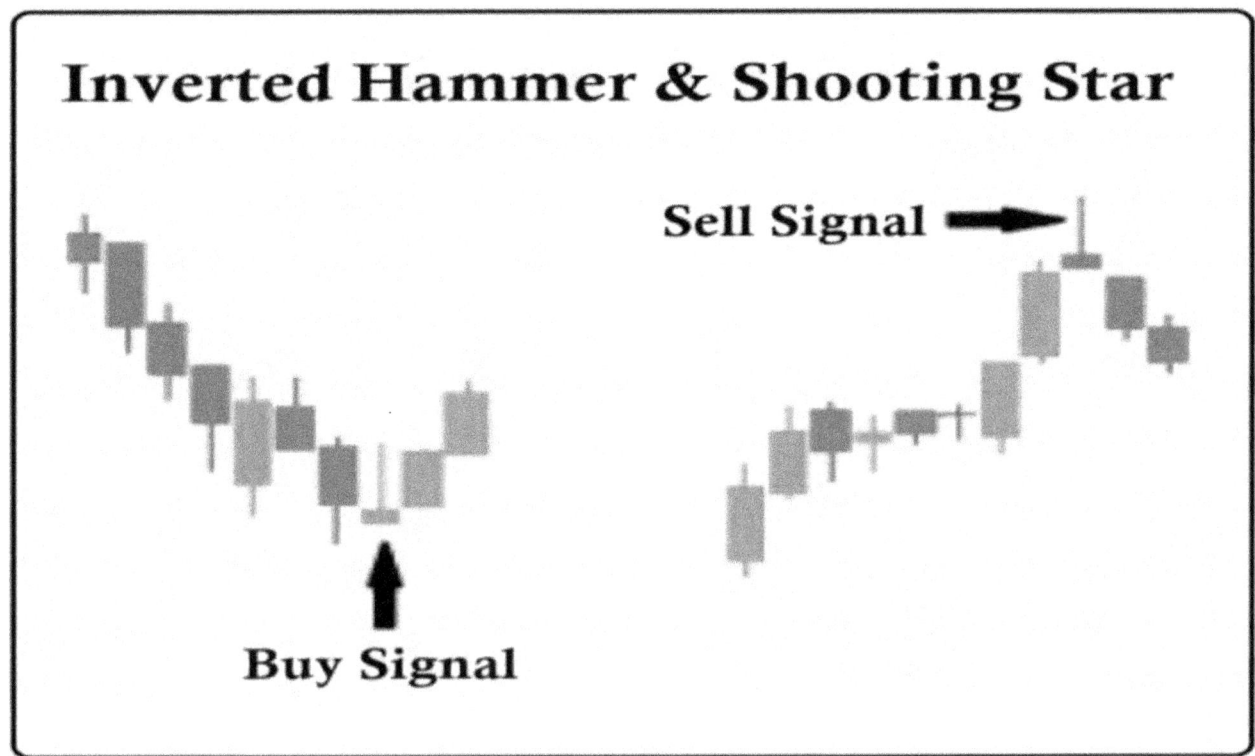

An inverted hammer looks like a hammer turned upside down. It can be found at the end of a downtrend, and can signal a bullish reversal. Bulkowski's statistics show it actually works as a continuation 65% of the time versus a reversal in a bull market. The pattern works best in a bull market when the price action is trending upward. Look for the inverted hammer in a temporary pullback. Don't rely on this pattern when the price action is in a downtrend.

A shooting star looks just like an inverted hammer, but it's found at the end of an uptrend. It shows the bulls drove up the price, but the bears took over and pulled the price down leaving a long wick behind. A bearish reversal will follow 59% of the time in a bull market.

Bullish & Bearish Engulfing Patterns

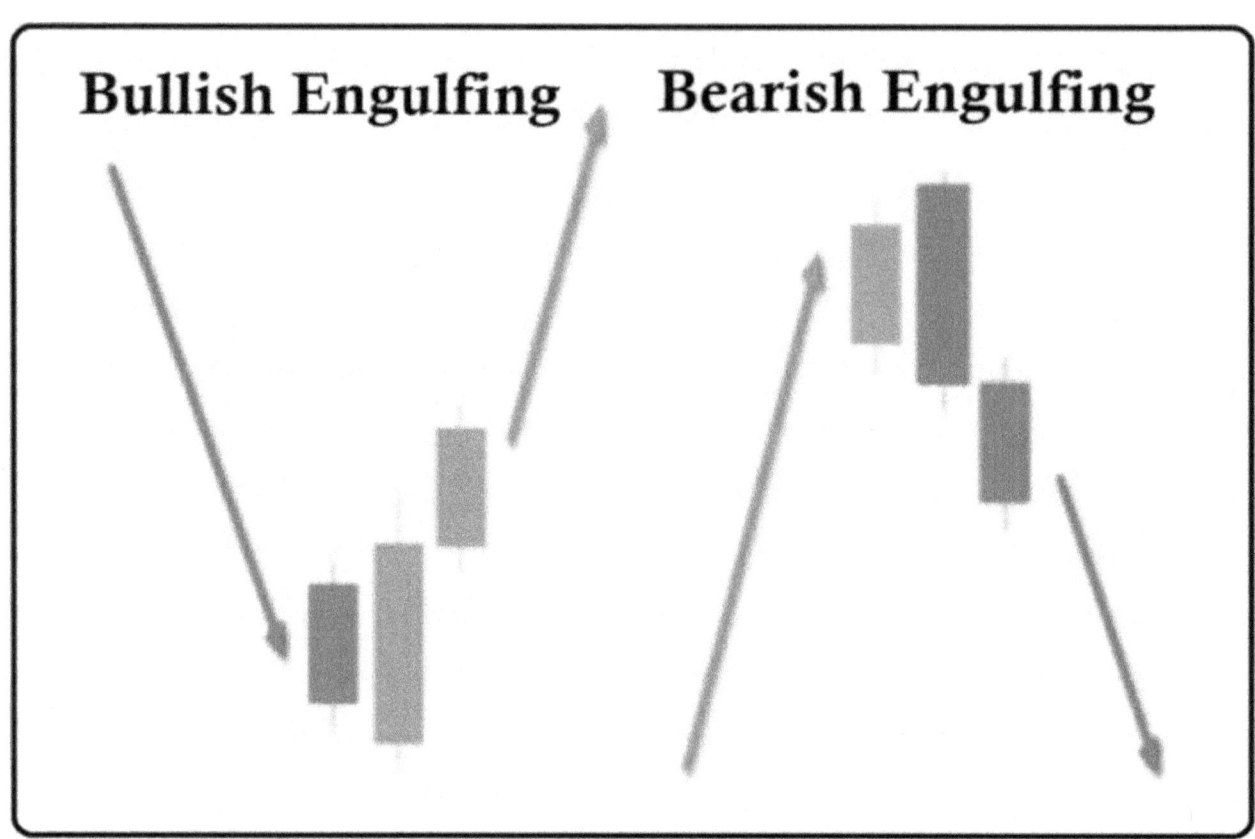

Engulfing patterns are reversal signals. They consist of two candles and the body of the second candle must completely "engulf" or cover the body of the first candle. A bullish engulfing pattern will reverse 63% of the time in a bull market, and a bearish engulfing pattern will reverse 79% of the time in a bull market. This number increases to 95% with confirmation.

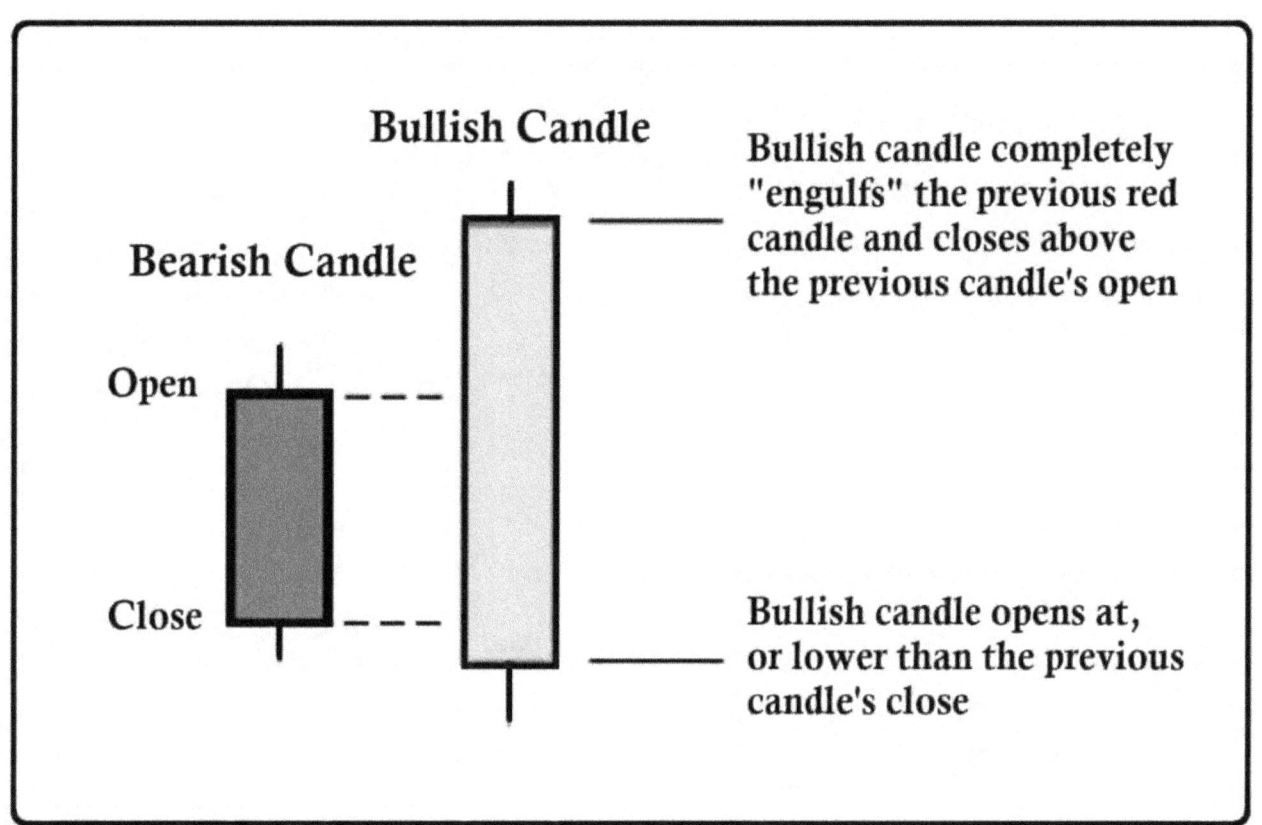

Piercing Line & Dark Cloud Cover

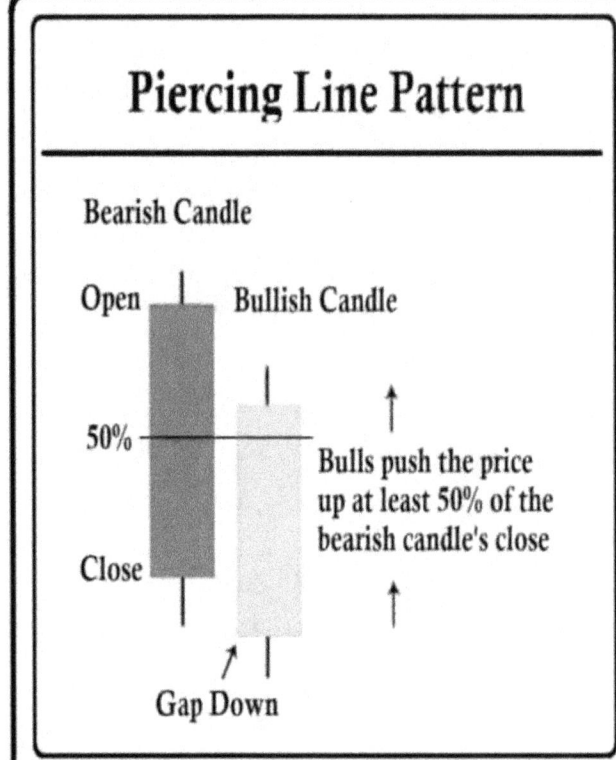 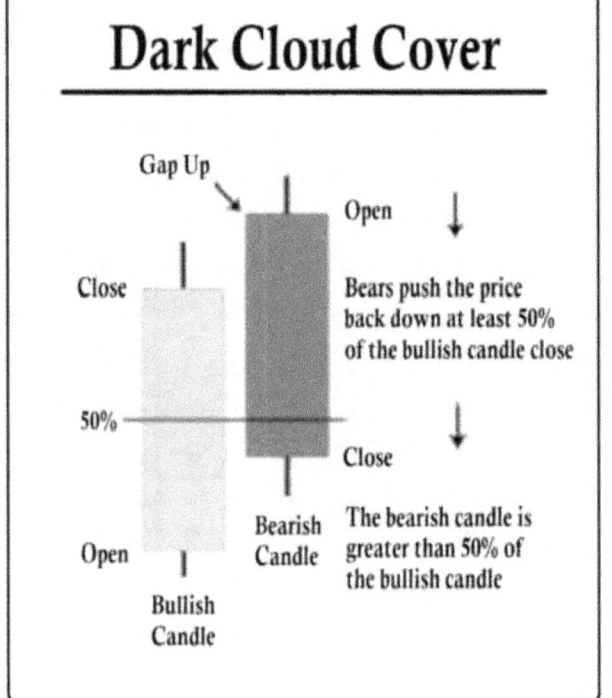

The piercing line & dark cloud cover reversal signals are very similar to the engulfing patterns except the second candlestick doesn't completely engulf the body of the first.

You can find piercing line patterns in a downtrend, and they serve as bullish reversal patterns 64% of the time in a bull market. A large red candle is followed by a candle that opens below the previous candle's close, but the bulls step in and drive the price up. The candle closes above the halfway point of the previous candle's body.

Dark cloud cover patterns are found in uptrends. A long red candle opens above the previous green candle close, but falls below the middle of the body of the previous green candle. There is a 60% chance of a break to the downside in a bull market when you see a dark cloud cover pattern. Wait for confirmation and it goes up to 80%.

Harami

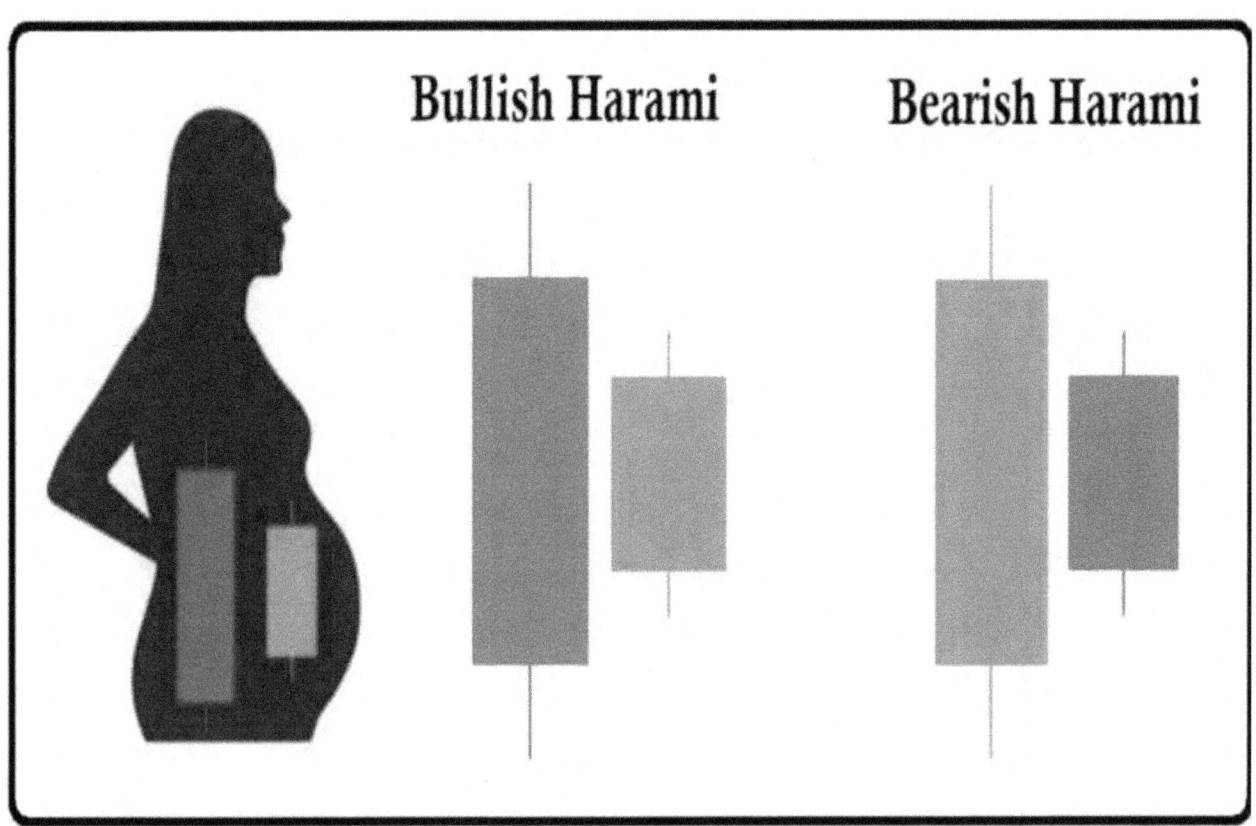

The word harami comes from an old Japanese word meaning pregnant. Harami patterns consist of two candles of opposite color and signal a trend change. The bullish harami works best as a reversal of a temporary pullback in a primary uptrend. It only has a 51% chance of reversal in a bull market though. A bearish harami acts as continuation pattern 53% of the time in a bull market.

Three Inside Up

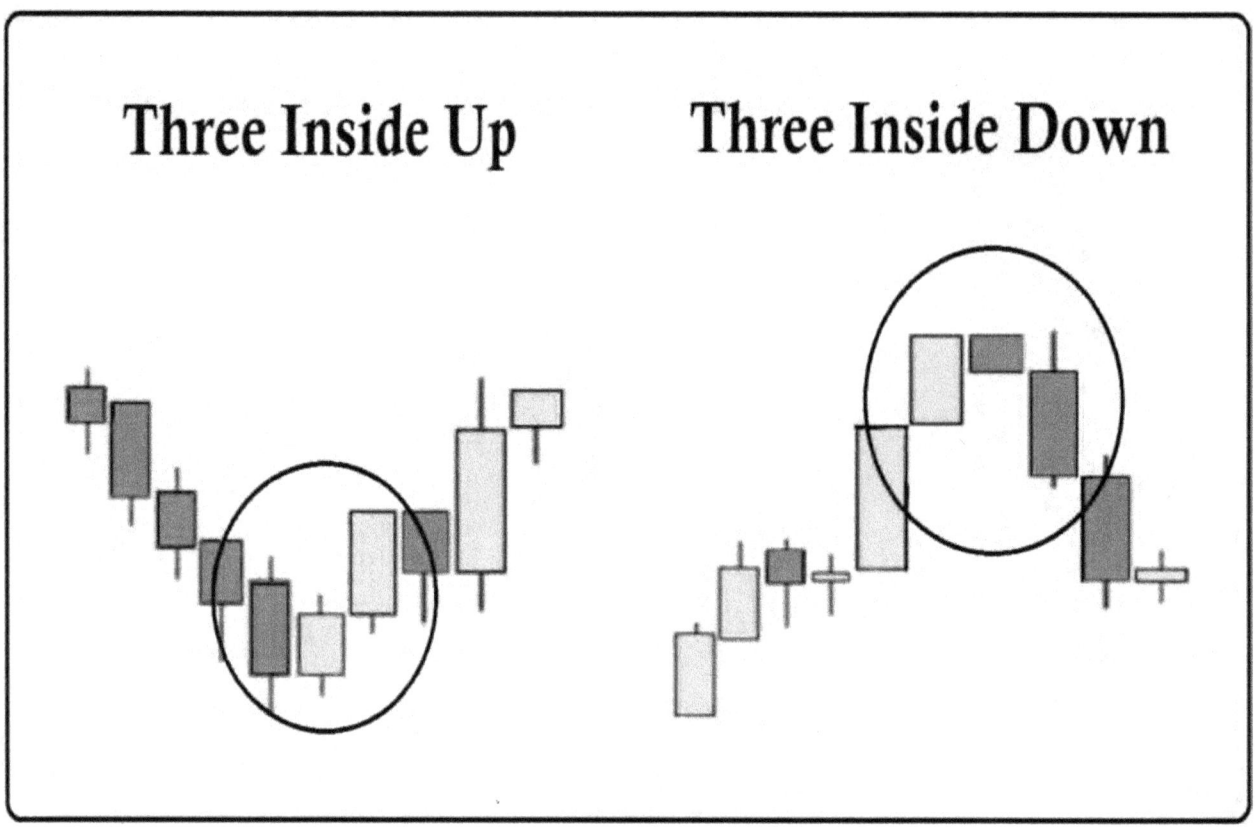

A three inside up pattern is a bullish harami pattern that has been confirmed. A long green candle after the bullish harami closes higher confirming the trend is headed upward. You can rely on this pattern 65% of the time in a bull market. 87% with confirmation.

Three Inside Down

The three inside down pattern is a confirmation of the bearish harami. A long red candle after the bearish harami closes lowerer confirming the trend is headed downward. You can rely on this pattern 60% of the time in a bull market. 84% with confirmation.

Morning Star & Evening Star

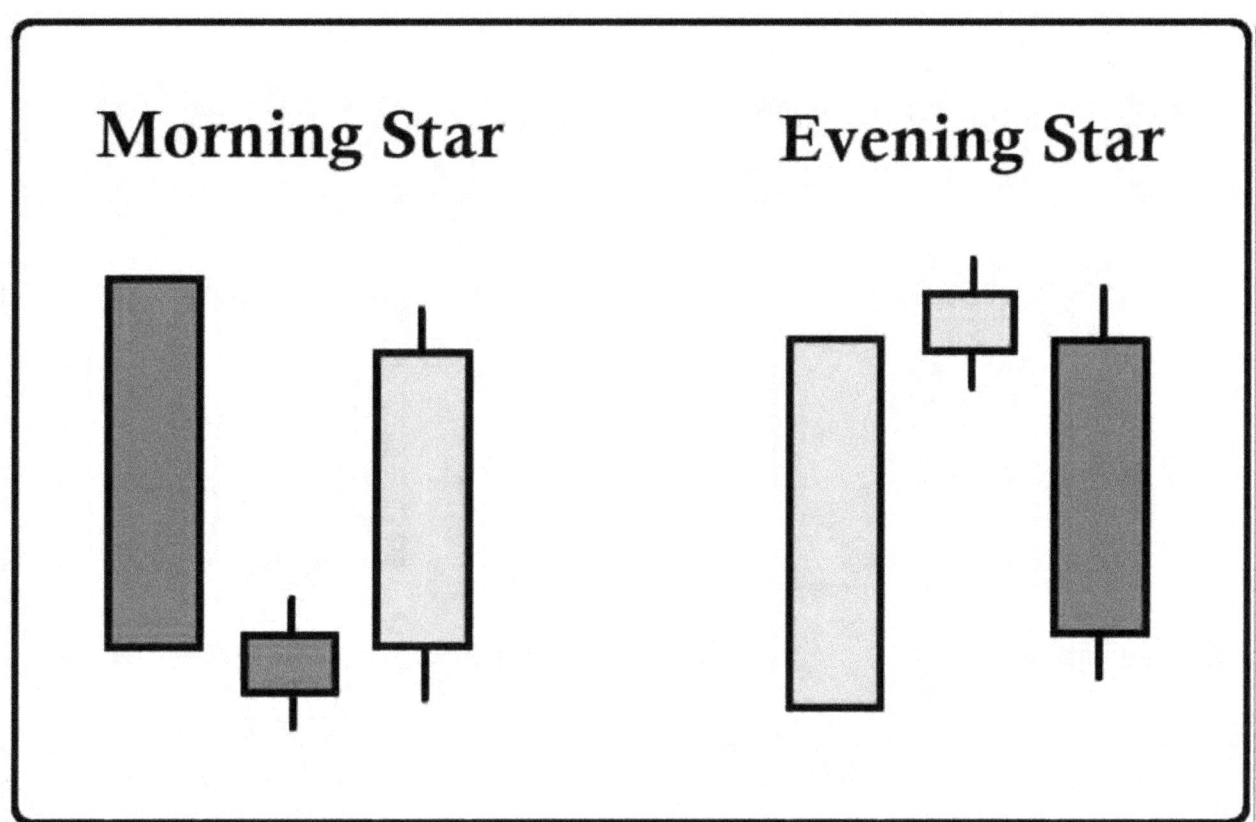

A morning star is a three candle pattern that begins with a candle that's strongly down. The second candle's body is small and shouldn't touch the first candle's body. During the third candle the bulls start dominating.

An Evening Star pattern is the opposite of a morning Star pattern. The first candle is a large bullish candle in this scenario. The second candle's body, the small green doji, shouldn't touch the first candle's body.(change picture) During the third candle the bears take over and push the price action strongly down. According to Bulkowski there is a 72% chance the price action will break to the downside when this pattern plays out.

The star represents indecision by bulls in the morning star and bears in the evening star. Just remember morning up and evening down.

Abandoned Baby

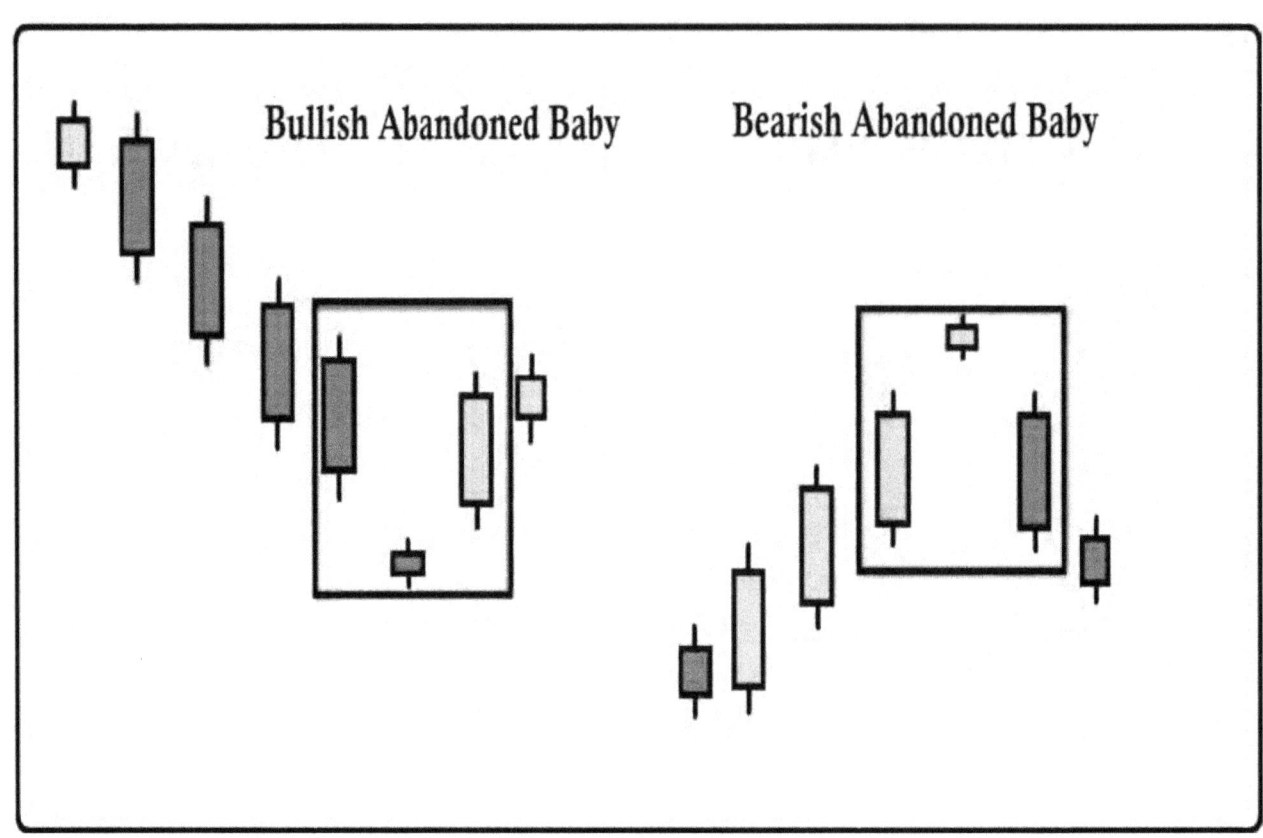

Watch out for a similar pattern called the abandoned baby. The only difference is the doji candle at the bottom won't touch the previous red candle. Just like the morning star pattern this is a bullish reversal pattern. Bulkowski says there is a 70% chance of reversal with this pattern, and a 69% chance of reversal with the bearish abandoned baby in a bull market.

Three White Soldiers & Three Black Crows

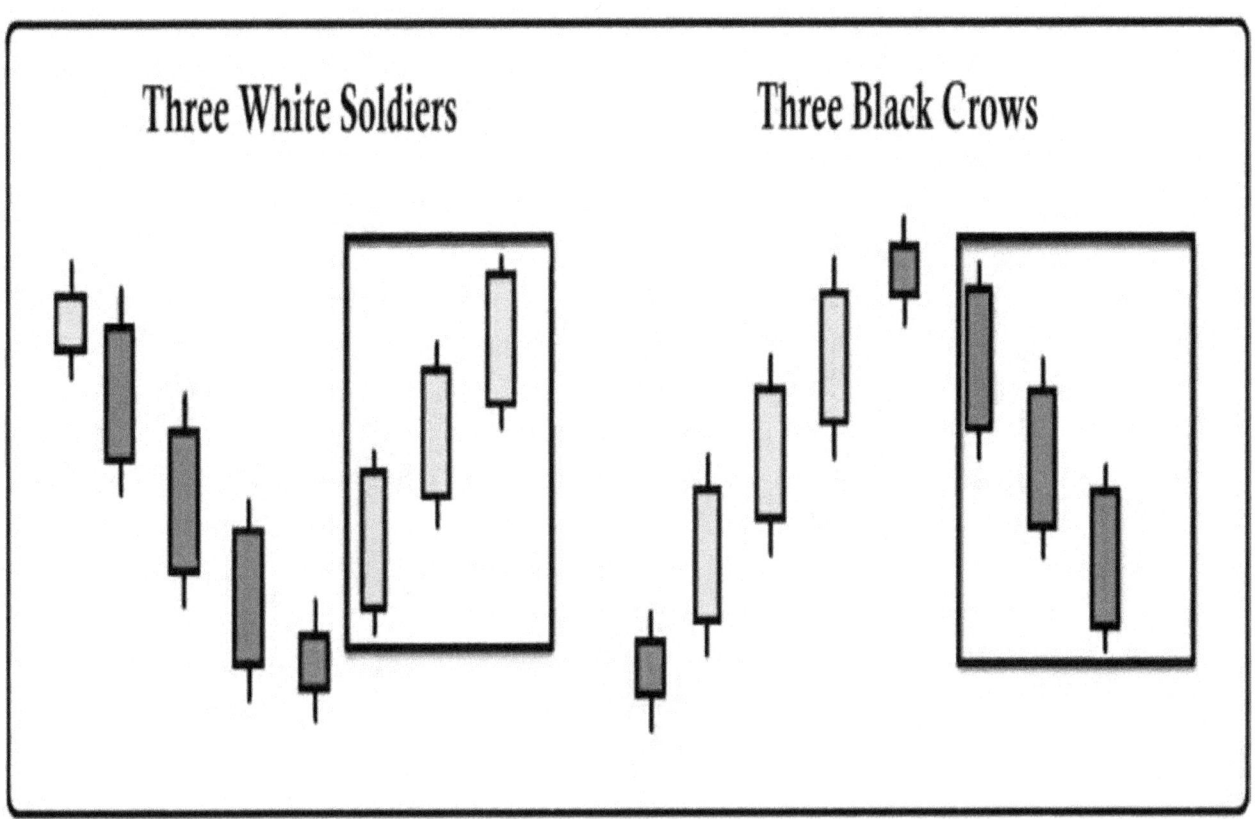

The Three White Soldiers consist of three large green candles just after a downtrend driving the price action up. Three large green candles clearly show the trend has changed from bearish to bullish and the price action will most likely continue upwards. Each candle should open in the body of the previous candle and close higher to be considered a valid pattern. Odds of a bullish reversal with this pattern is around 82%

Three Black Crows

The Three Black Crows pattern is just the opposite of the Three White Soldiers. The pattern begins at the end of an uptrend. It shows the sellers have taken control for the moment and the bullish trend has now become bearish. The price falls throughout this three candle pattern before the uptrend is resumed. Three black crow pattern acts as bearish reversal 78% of the time.

Above the stomach

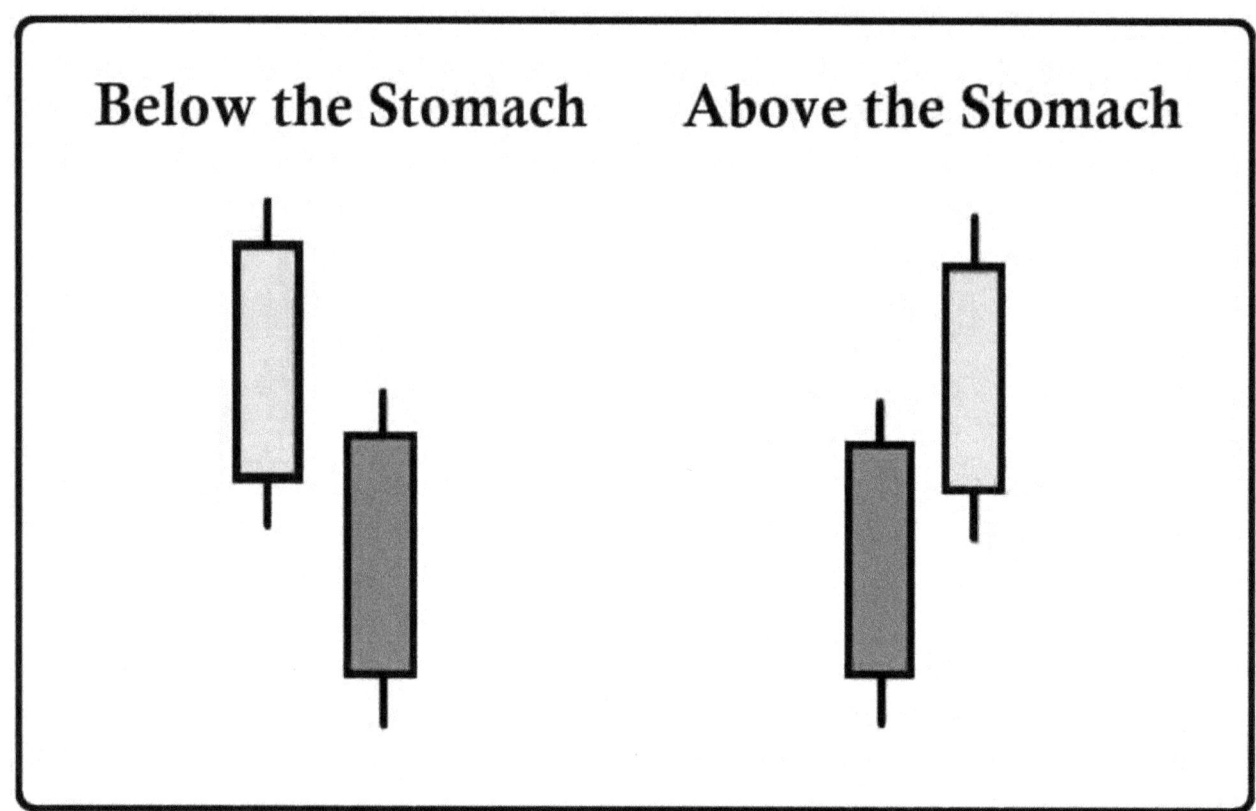

An above the stomach pattern is a two candle pattern where the price opens and closes above the stomach of the previous candle in a downturn. The price action has to open and close at or above the middle of the previous candle's body to be considered a valid pattern. There is a 66% chance of reversal in bull market. The chance of reversal increases to around 88% when you wait for confirmation of the following candle to close higher.

Below the stomach

A below the stomach pattern is where the price action is in an uptrend and then the trend suddenly changes. The next candle opens below the stomach of the previous candle's body and continues to the downside. This pattern bearish reversal 60% of the time. If you wait for confirmation the odds increase to 86%.

Belt hold

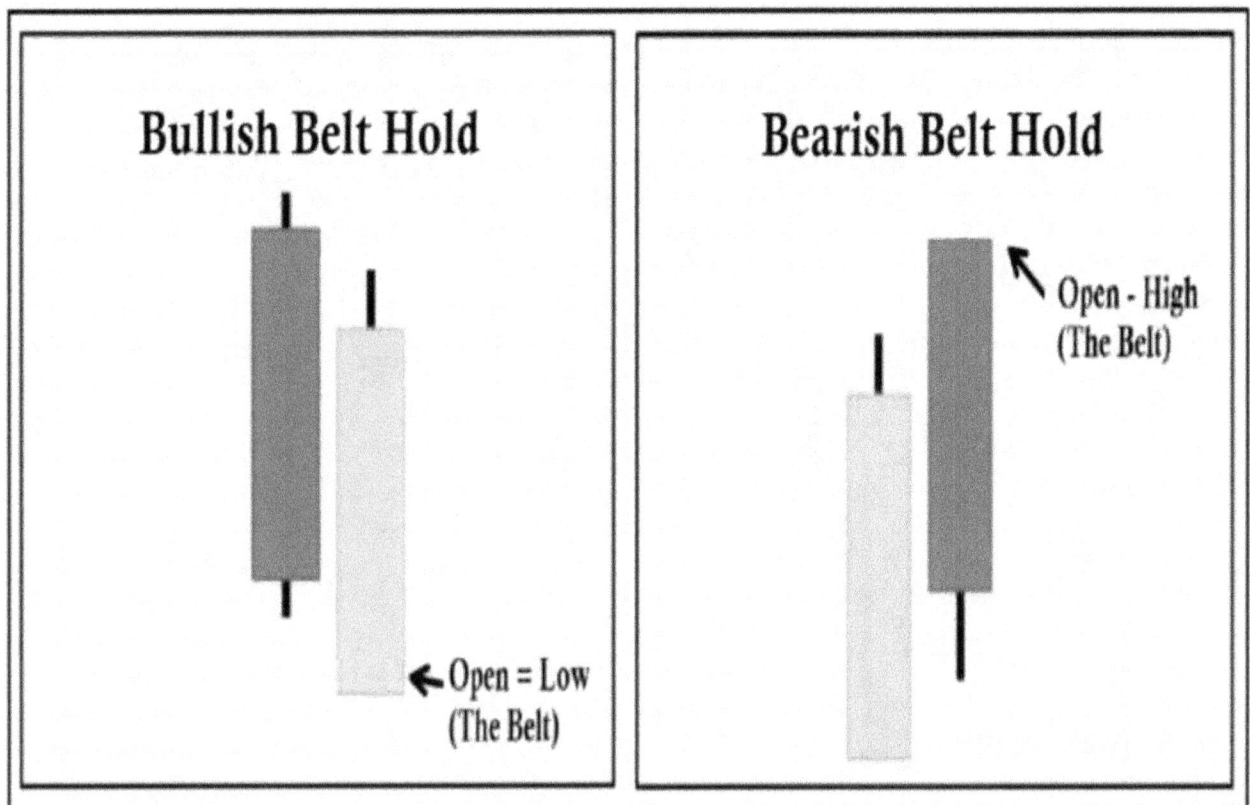

Bullish Belt Hold
You can find the bullish belt hold at the end of a bearish trend. The price opens at the low for the day increasing to somewhere near the high leaving a tall green candle behind. 71% chance bullish reversal in bull market.

Bearish Belt Hold
Bearish, After an uptrend the price opens at the high and closes near the low. 68% chance bearish reversal in a bull market with the bearish belt hold. Wait for confirmation and the chance of reversal goes up to 95%.

Advance Block

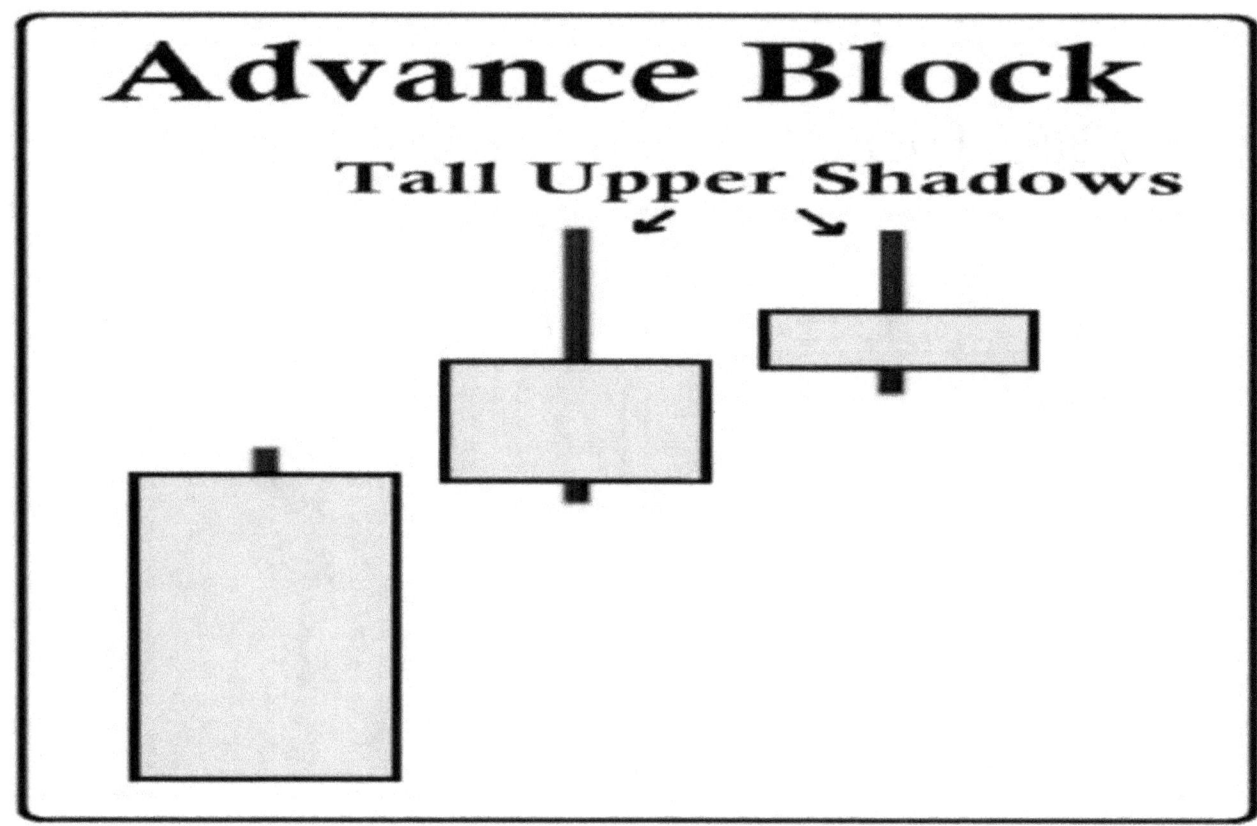

Bulls take over the price action in three consecutive candles beginning with a large green candle. The candle bodies in this pattern get smaller while the wicks get taller signaling a possible reversal. In a bull market this pattern acts as a continuation 64% of the time.

Deliberation

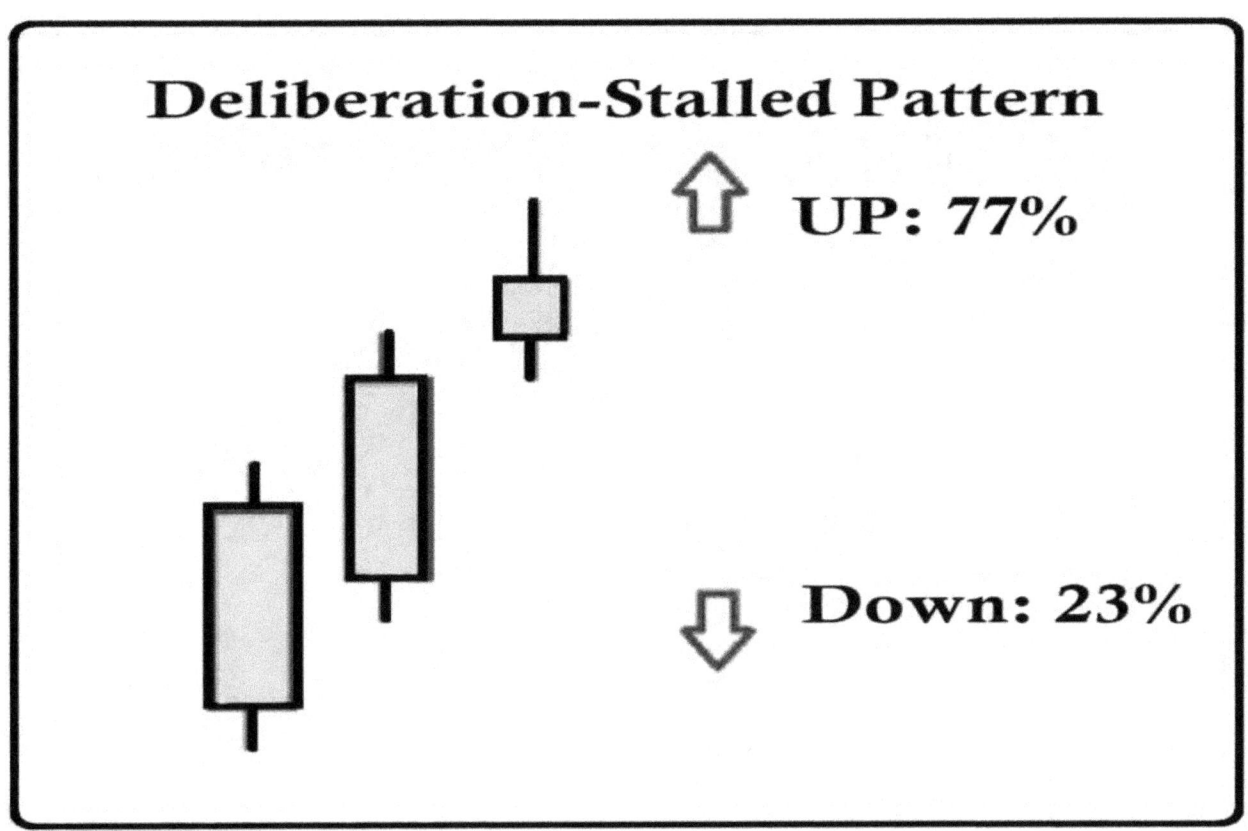

A deliberation pattern is a three candlestick pattern that begins in an uptrend. Bulls push up the price in the first two large candles before battling it out with the bears on the third. The body of the third candle is much smaller as the price hangs in deliberation signaling a possible reversal, but no need to worry because in a bull market the price will continue to the upside 77% of the time.

Mat Hold

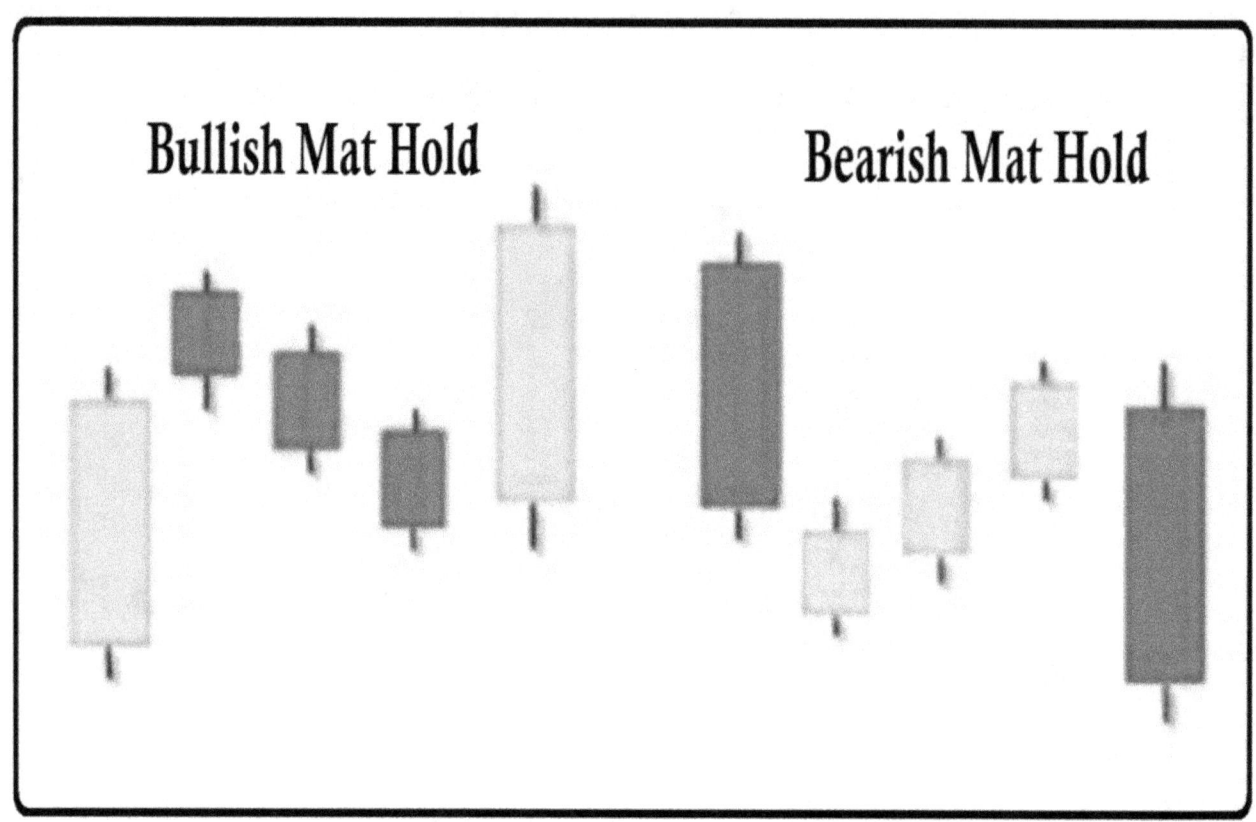

Mat hold patterns appear during an uptrend and acts as a bullish continuation 78% of the time. It's a five candle pattern and according to Bulkowski the first candle is a tall green one followed by three small red candles(the middle one can be green), followed by another tall green candle. You will see a gap between second candle and the first and it will close higher. The gap is what separates the Mat hold from the rising three methods pattern.

Rising three methods

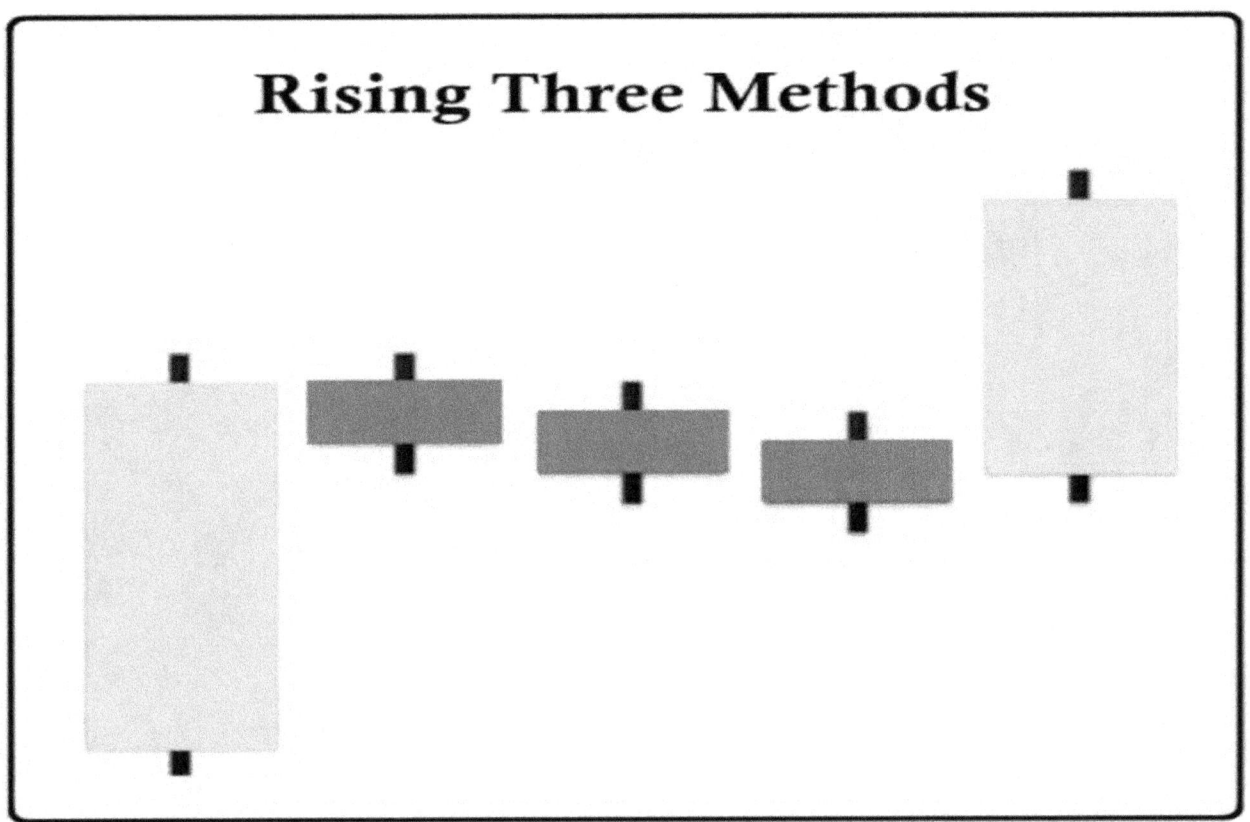

The rising three methods pattern appears during an uptrend and acts as a bullish continuation 74% of the time. Just like the mat hold pattern it is a five candlestick pattern. As I mentioned before the difference between the two is there is no gap between the second candle and the first.

Three Line Strike

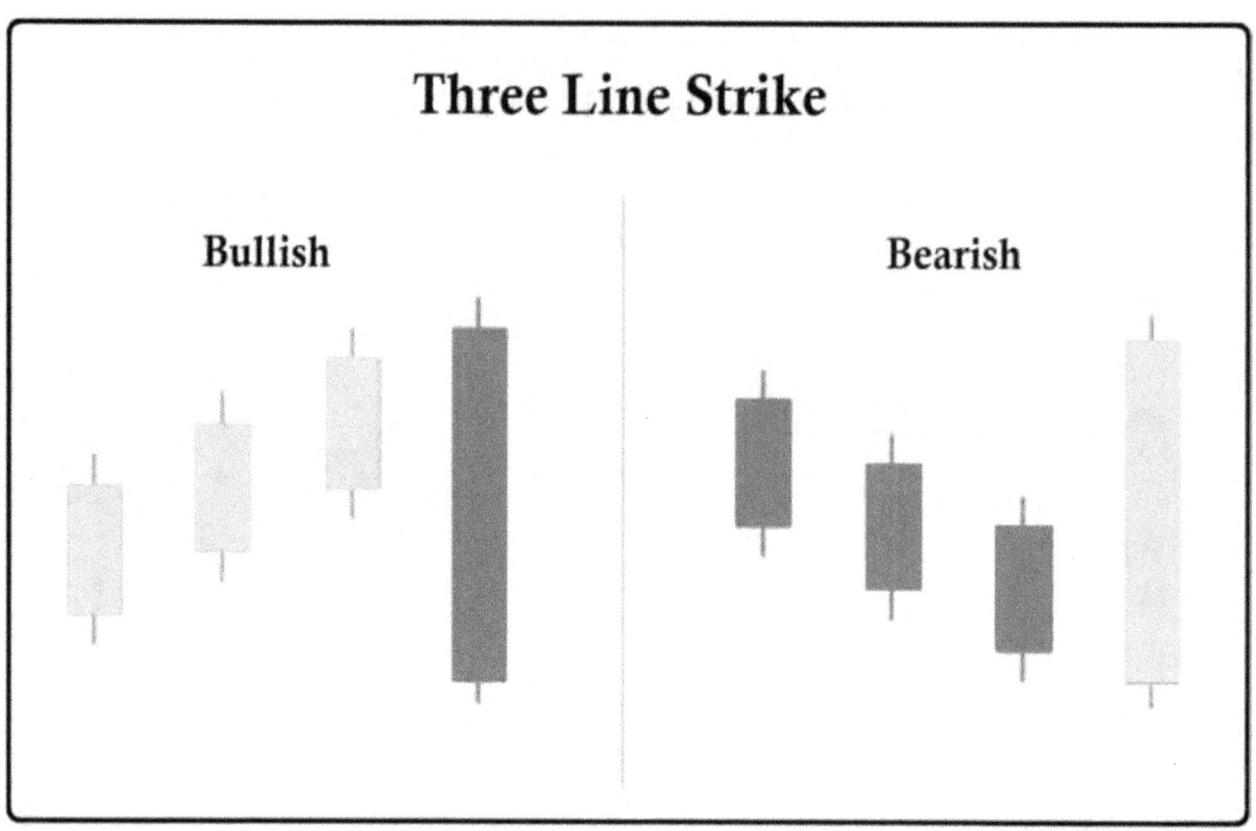

Bullish, In spite of it being a rare pattern it performs well showing a bearish reversal 65% of the time. This 4 candle pattern is found at the end of an uptrend starting with three green candles, each closing higher than the other, followed by a large red candle that engulfs the others. Confirmation increases the success rate to 92%.

Bearish, The three line strike is found at the end of a pullback, and acts as a bullish reversal 84% of the time. Each of the three red candles close lower until the bulls step in with a large green candle that engulfs the other three and reverses the trend. Wait for confirmation and the reversal rate jumps to 97%.

Three Outside Up

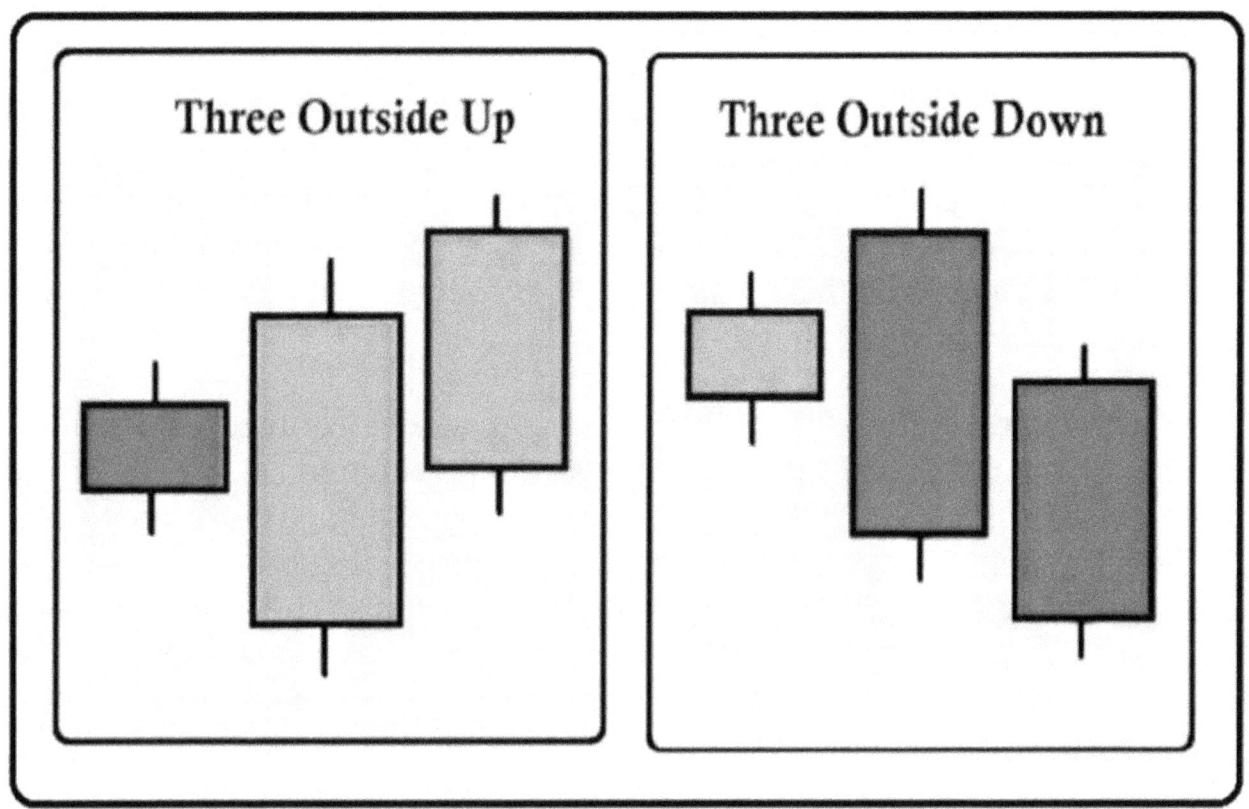

A three outside down pattern is basically a confirmation of a bullish engulfing candle. The confirmation candle must close higher than the engulfing candle to be considered a valid pattern. Bullish reversal 75% of the time. 93% with confirmation.

Three Outside Down

A three outside down pattern is confirmation of a bearish engulfing candle. The confirmation candle must close lower than the engulfing candle to be considered a valid pattern. In a bull market this pattern will reverse to the downside 69% of the time. 90% with confirmation.

Identifying Common Patterns

As a beginner you'll want to familiarize yourself with some of the common patterns that repeat on the charts and how they perform. The two types of patterns are continuation patterns and reversal patterns. Continuation patterns signal to a trader that the trend is going to continue in the same direction. Reversal patterns signal to a trader that the price action may be due for a reverse in price soon. Knowing which direction the price is headed is essential for any trader.

Thomas Bulkowski also wrote another book called Encyclopedia of Chart Patterns. In a similar fashion to his Encyclopedia of Candlestick Patterns book, Bulkowski analyses over 38,500 chart patterns in his second edition to provide solid probabilities of performance. The probabilities I have listed here were extracted from his book. I highly encourage you to obtain a copy of his book for greater detail into these patterns.

The common bull patterns I'm going to cover are: symmetrical triangles, ascending triangles, bull flags, pennants, double bottom, cup and handle, falling wedge, triangles, and inverse head and shoulders. The common bear patterns I'm going to cover in this chapter are: descending triangles, head and shoulders, double top, rising wedge, drawing patterns, and channels. Let's take a look at these common patterns and learn how we can trade them.

Triangle Patterns

There are three types of triangle patterns: symmetrical, ascending, and descending. These are usually continuation patterns, but rarely can be reversal patterns. Look for the price to continue upwards during up trends and continue downwards in downtrends.

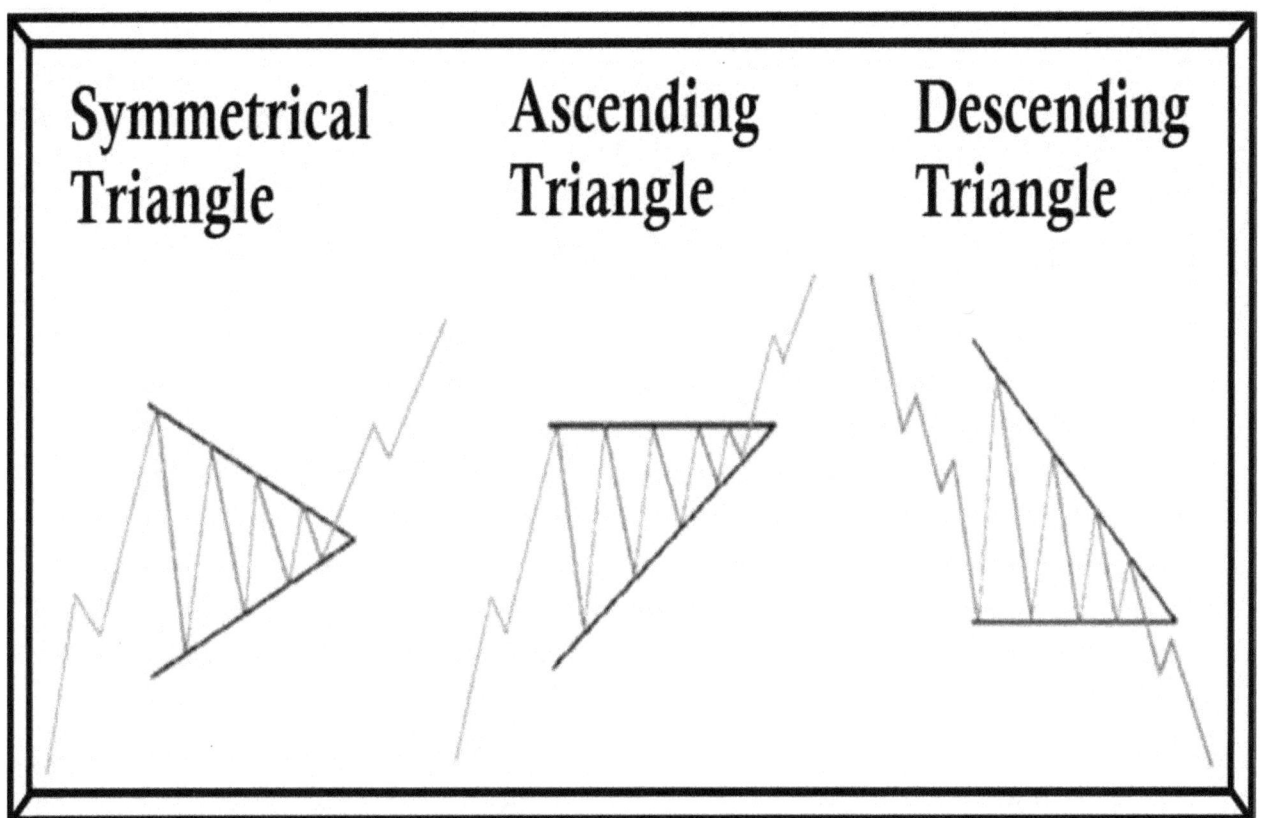

When you draw a triangle there needs to be at least two swing highs and two swing lows. You'll want to draw your triangles along the top and bottom of the price action connecting as many points as possible. The more points connected the more valid the pattern, and the higher the time frame to more valid the pattern. The price might make a couple more swings within the triangle before breaking out. Adjust the lines of your triangle to accommodate the new price swings.

Symmetrical triangles are continuation patterns that follow the prevailing trend 54% of the time. Ascending triangles are bullish patterns that breakout to the upside about 70% of the time. Descending triangles are bearish patterns that breakout to the downside around 70% of the time.

When drawing triangles and wedges you want at least 2 touches on each side for a valid pattern, but 3 is better. The more touches you have the more confirmation you have that your pattern is correct. You want them to be spread out along the trend line and not be clustered together. Longer time frames are more likely to give valid lines.

When drawing them you want to connect as many high points with other high points as possible and you will do the same with the lows. On the VET chart below I had at least 5 touches on the top and four touches on the bottom to form this pattern. After I confirmed the pattern I bought by the bottom trendline. VET eventually broke out of the pattern and then came back down to retest the breakout level before moving up to new highs. Normally these descending triangles break to the downside 70% of the time, but this one decided to do the opposite. Remember, always use multiple methods of confirmation. In this situation the 200 day moving average held as support and the price responded.

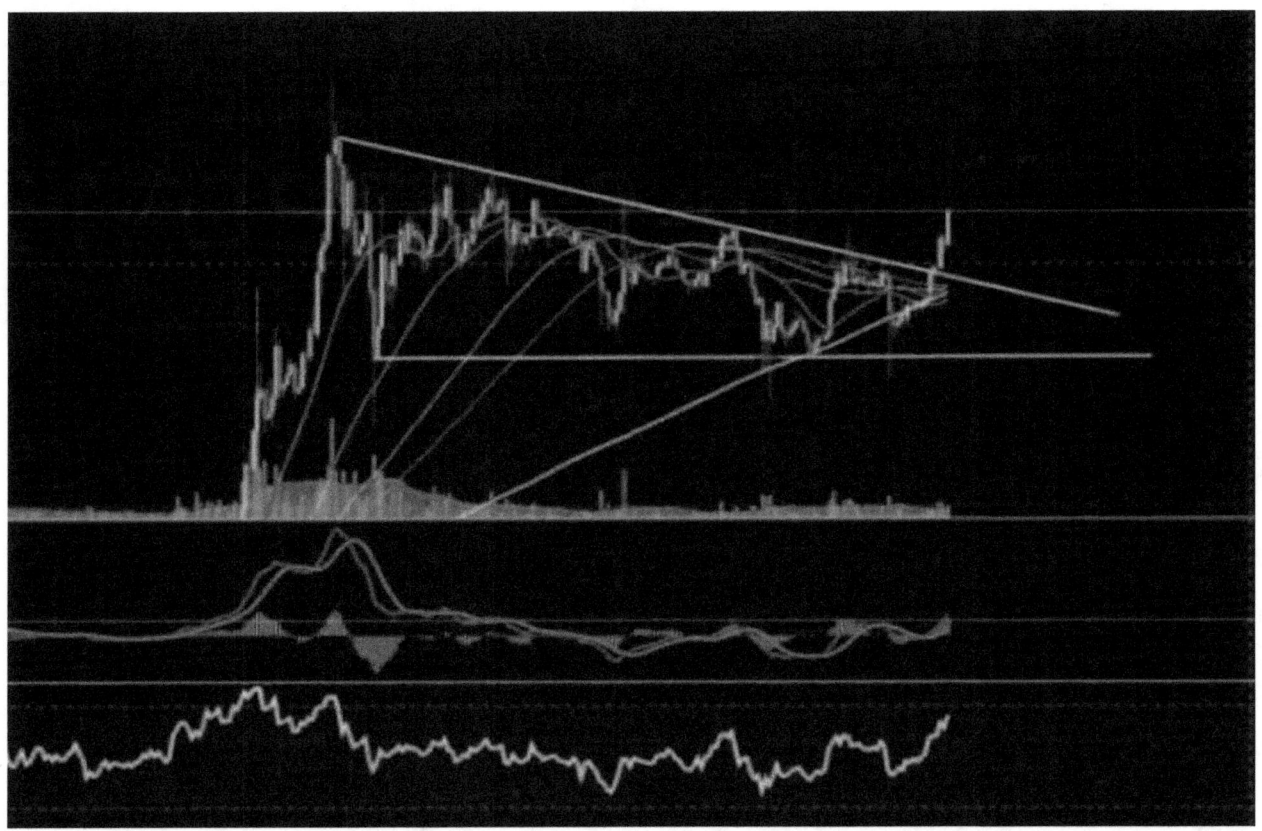

You can draw your trend lines with the wicks, or you can use the candle bodies. You can use either or as long as you're not using wicks on one side and candles on the other. Use one or the other. I like to use candle bodies because that's where most of the action took place.

Use the one hour, four hour, and daily time frames to draw your trend lines. Shorter time frames often reveal smaller patterns within the larger daily and four hour patterns. The smaller patterns can give you an indication of where the price will move within the larger pattern.

If you want to buy a breakout you'll want to wait until a candle body closes outside the top of the triangle pattern with volume. Not a wick, a candle body must close outside the pattern on the hourly time frame or higher. The higher the time frame the more valid the pattern. You want to set your stop loss somewhere back inside the triangle pattern. I like to leave a little room in case the price action comes back down and retests the breakout. Sometimes a wick can come down and stop you out before the price takes off so be careful. Retests are usually very safe opportunities to jump into a trade.

This is where the most seasoned traders will jump in.

You could also front run this pattern and buy at the bottom of the triangle. In this case you would want to set your stop loss just outside of the triangle pattern on the bottom side. Whichever method you choose make sure your indicators confirm your move. You want to look at each trade like a court case. You want to look at the bullish side of the case and the bearish side of the case before you make an educated decision to move forward.

The length of the opening of the triangle is your target. You can usually bet on the price action reaching 70% of your target.

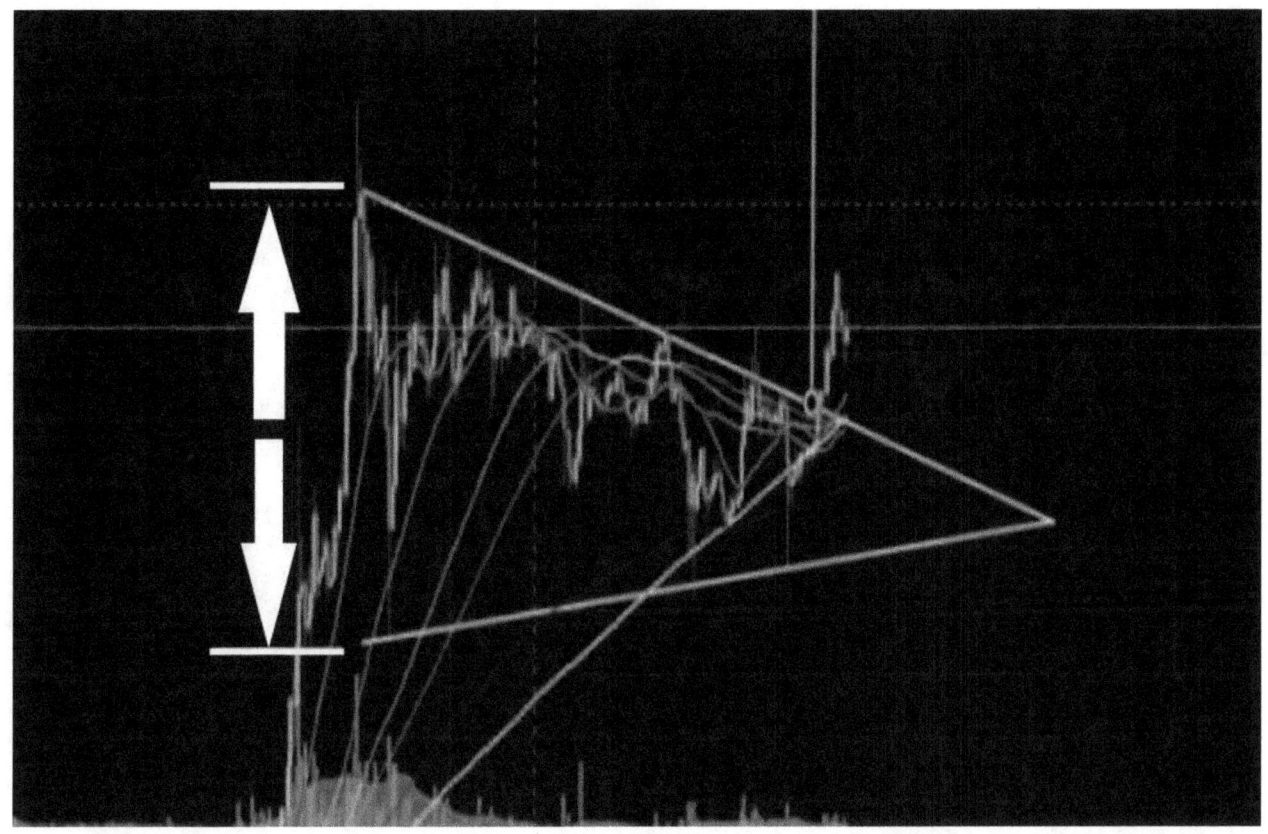

Keep an eye out for these triangle patterns, and when you see them start to form draw your trend lines around it. Find out what the price would need to be in order for it to break out of the pattern and set an alert for that price. This way you don't have to keep watching the chart. You'll be notified when the price gets there.

Continuation Patterns

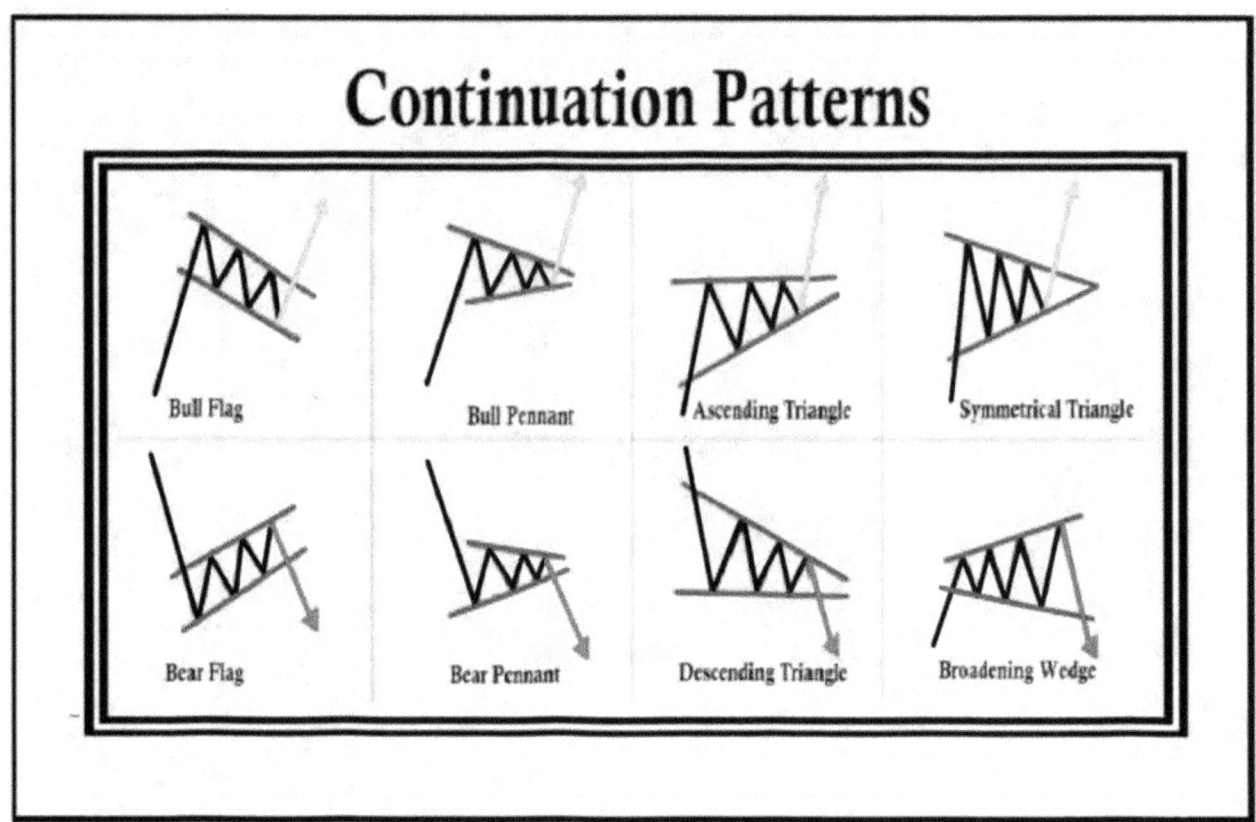

Flag patterns are very similar to pennant patterns. The only difference is that a flag pattern doesn't come to a point at the end like a pennant does. They are created when there is a significant movement, known as the flagpole, followed by a short period of consolidation. The converging lines create a pennant shape. These are continuation patterns like symmetrical and ascending triangles. Price consistently reaches higher lows and lower highs, creating two converging trend lines that form a cone type shape.

The pennant includes a flagpole at the beginning of the pattern, which is not present in the formation of the triangle. The flagpole is a very important characteristic of the flag and pennant, and is created when price suddenly shoots up or dives down dramatically in the direction of the current trend, forming an almost vertical line. At the same time heavy volume pours into the market and the price moves rapidly with the current trend. The price movement begins to slow down forming the body of the pennant. When the price movement slows down and moves sideways this allows the indicators to cool off before the price breaks out again. Flag and pennant patterns are short term continuation patterns.

Cup and Handle

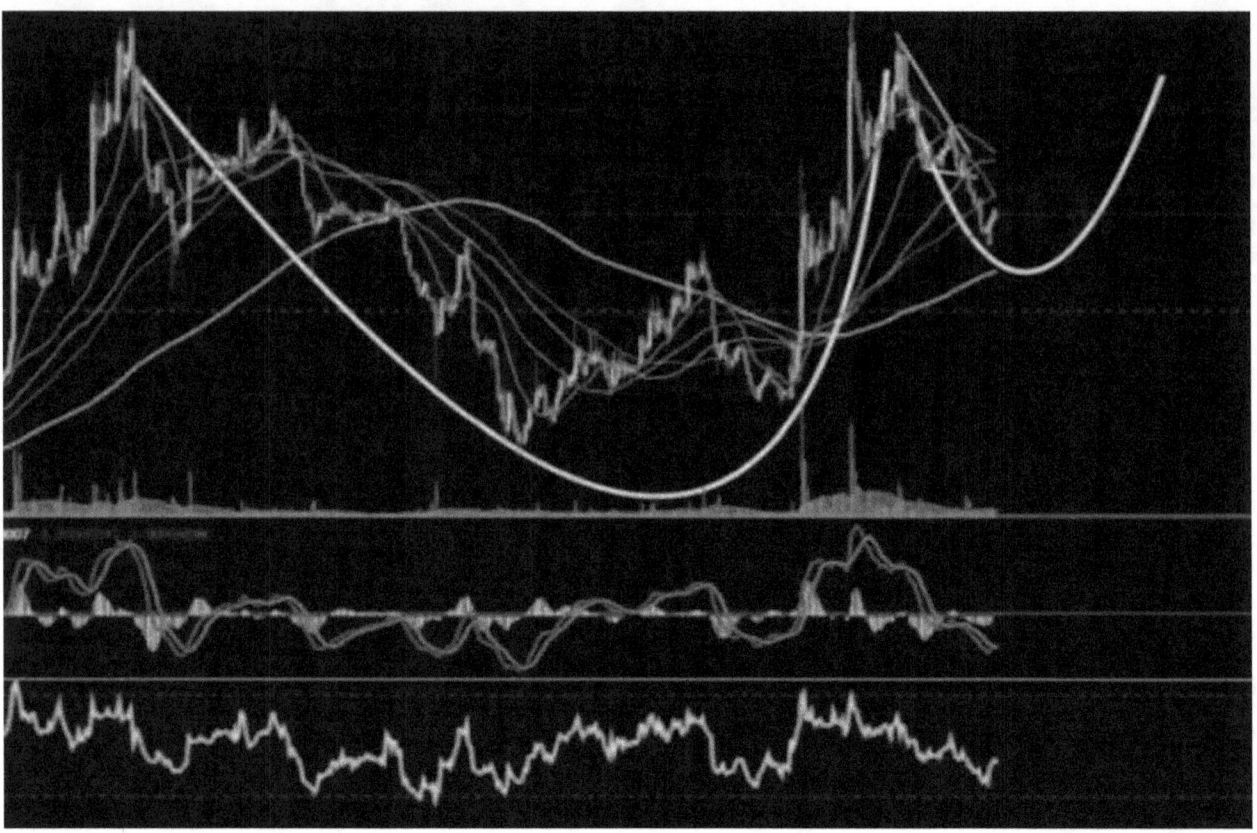

The cup and handle is a bullish continuation pattern that gets its name from the obvious pattern it forms. There is a large dip in price which forms the cup, and a smaller dip no deeper than 50% that forms afterwards is the handle. Ideally you want to buy at the bottom of the cup or the bottom of the handle, but you can also buy when the price action breaks out of the opening of the cup.

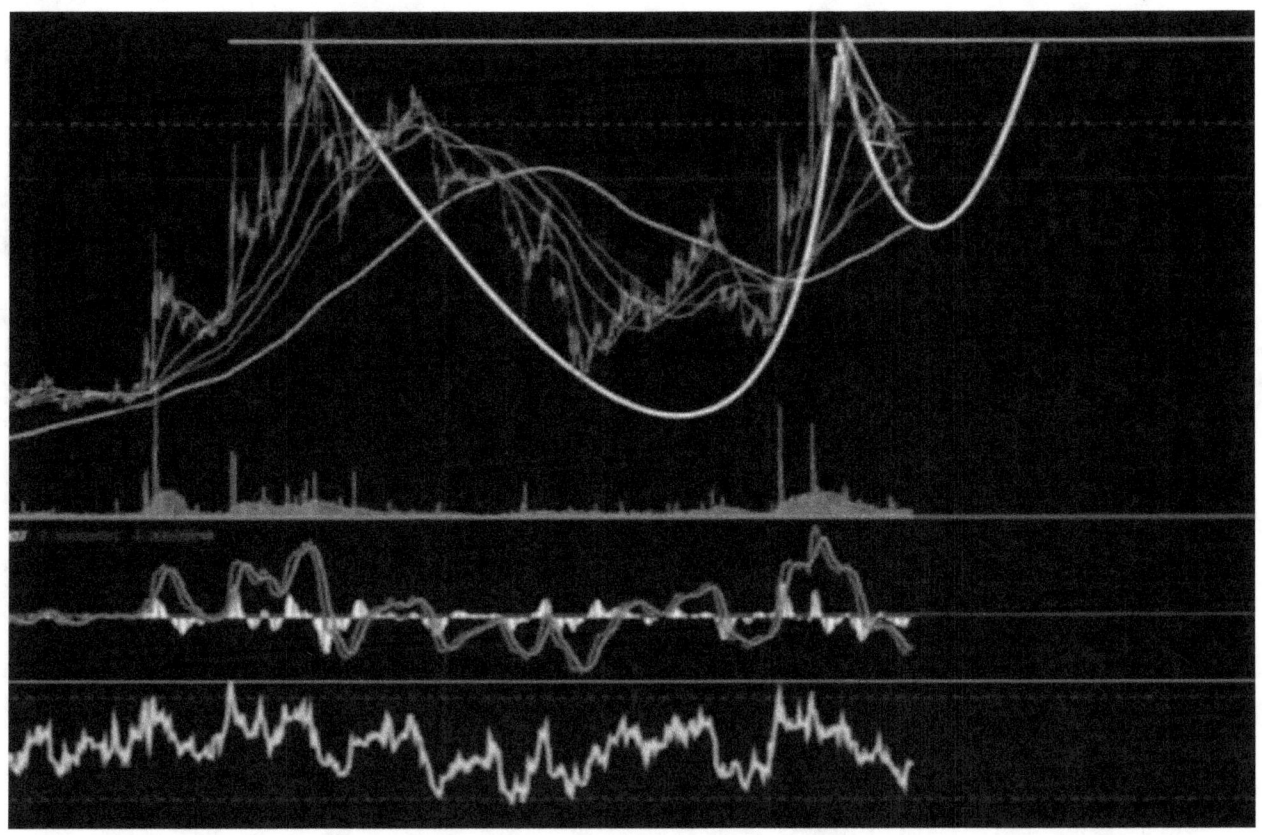

Your first target is the distance between the bottom of the cup and the neckline.

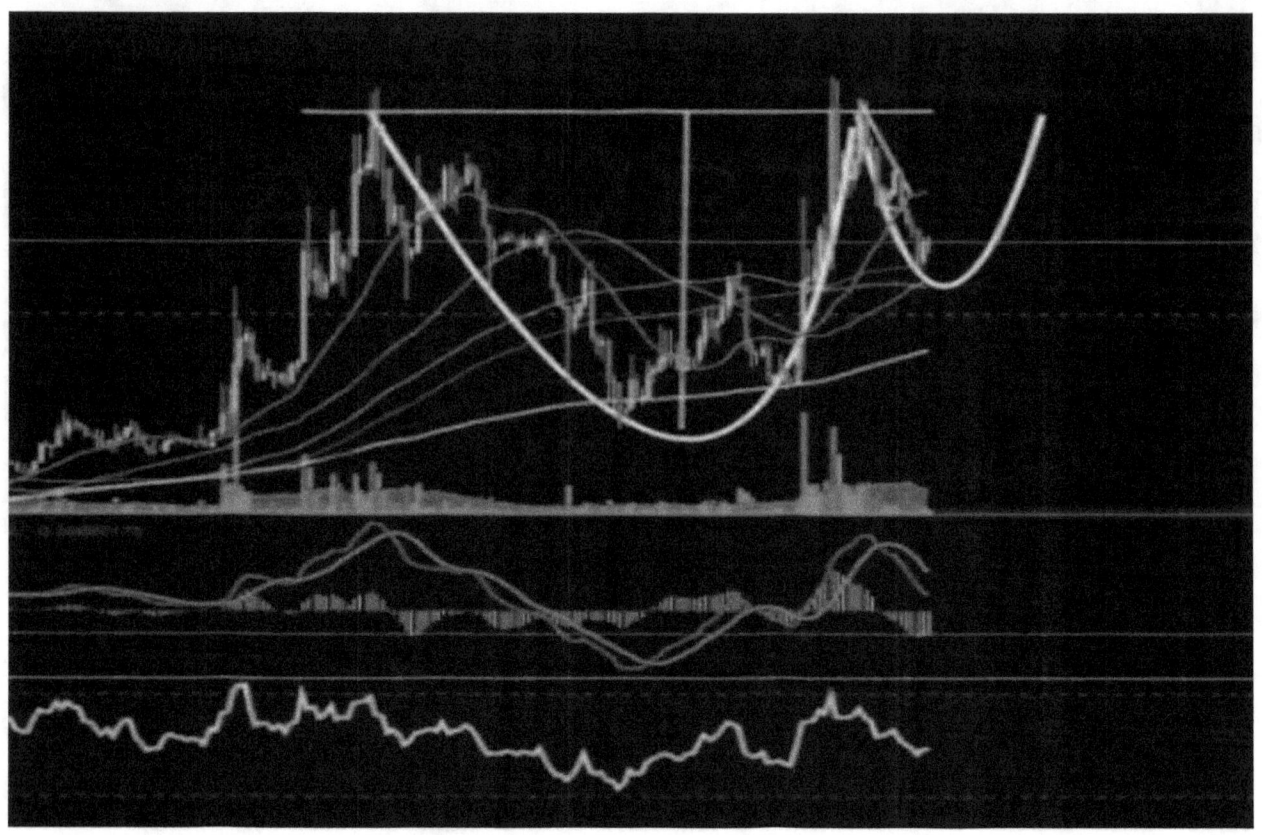

Put your target on top of the neckline. The price action could go beyond this target, but this is the measured move for now.

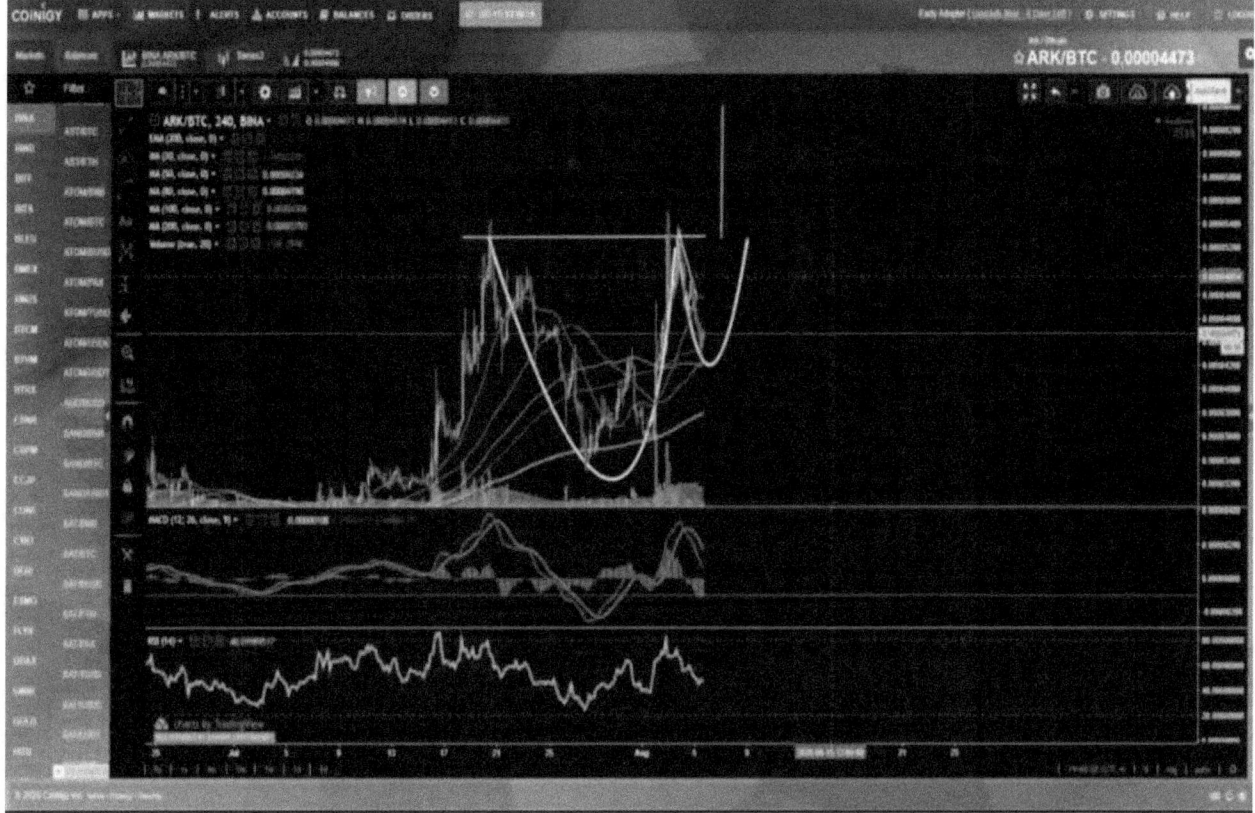

Reversal Patterns

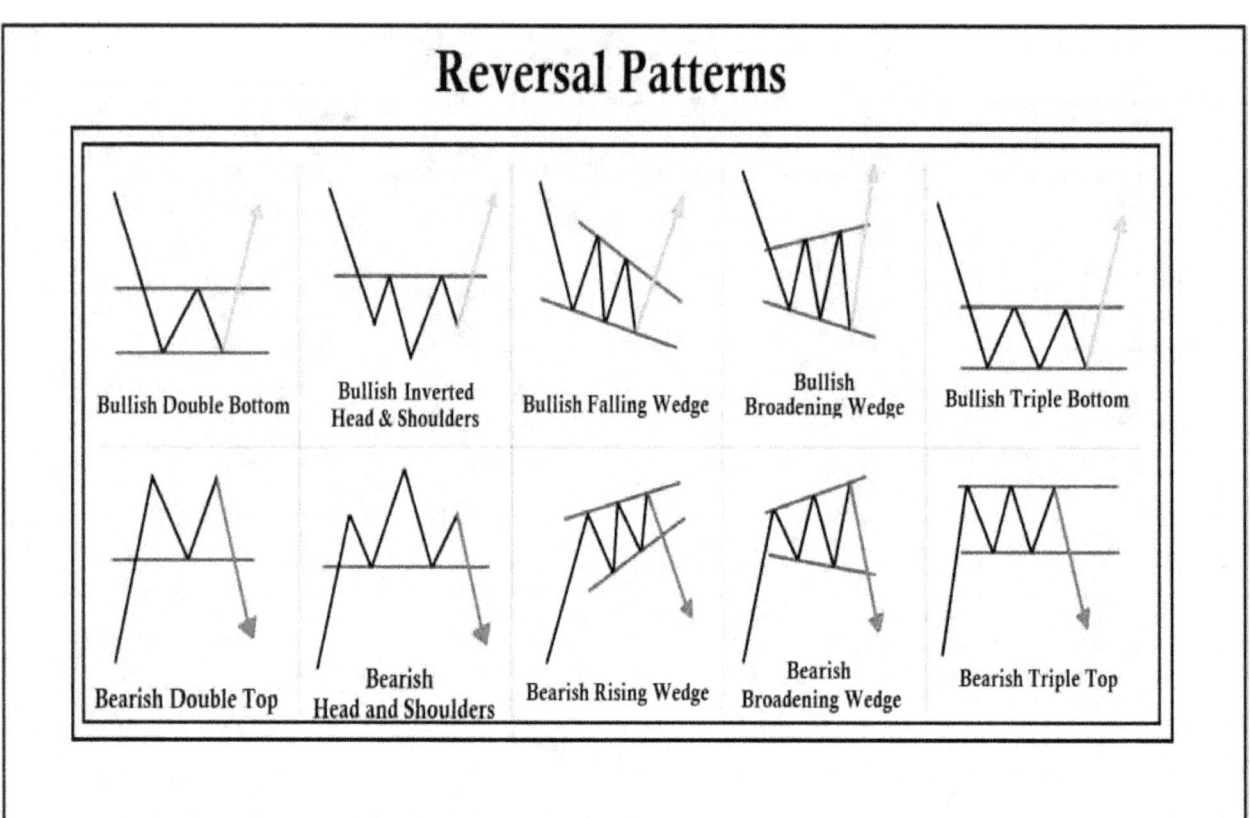

Rounded Patterns

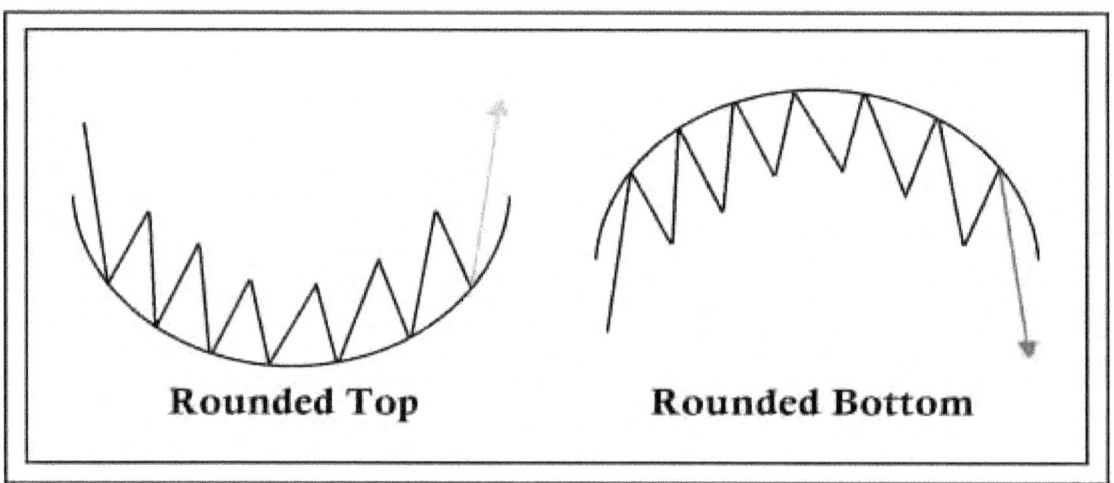

Rounded patterns are similar to the cup and handle, but without the handle. Rounded tops are bearish reversal patterns and rounded bottoms are bullish reversal patterns. Also like the cup and handle you want to buy the breakout of the neckline, and the first target is the distance between the furthest point at the bottom and the neckline.

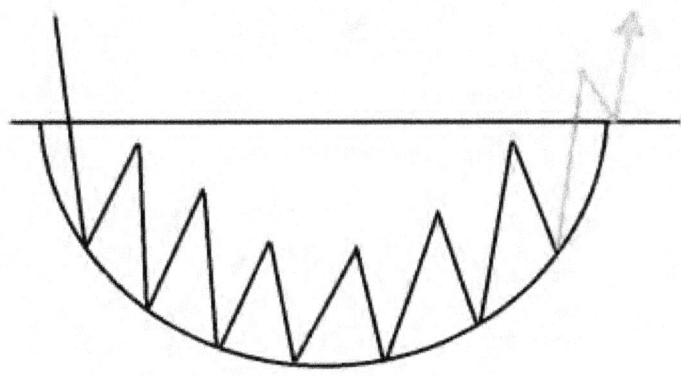

Double & Triple bottoms and tops

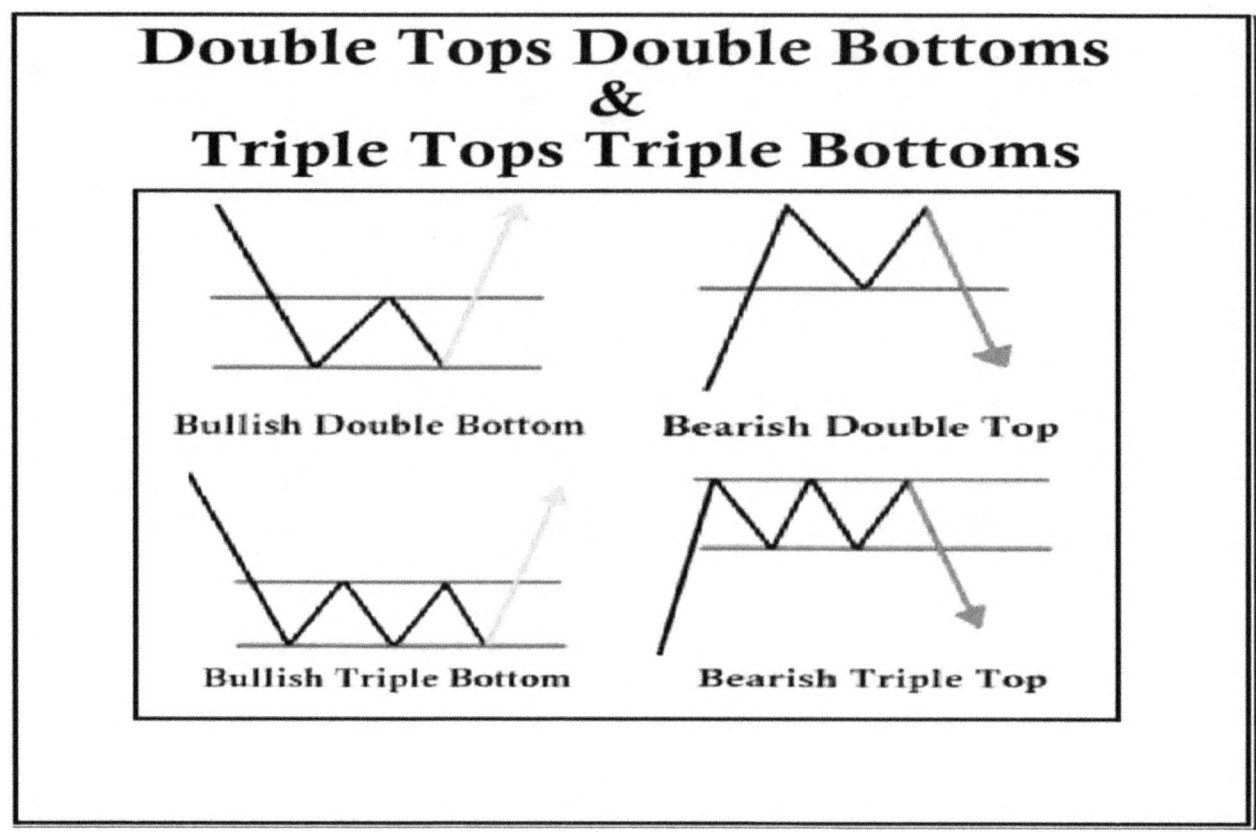

The double and triple bottom & top patterns are reversal patterns. The double and triple bottom is a predictor of a reversal to the upside following a long downtrend. The bottoms don't have to be on the same exact price line, they just have to be at or around the same price level. The double and triple top patterns are bearish reversal patterns that are seen following a long uptrend.

It's best to buy double and triple bottoms at, you guessed it, the bottom, but if you don't catch it in time you'll want to buy the breakout of the neckline at the top. A good time to sell a double top or triple top is when the price action breaks out of the neckline to the downside. Your first target is the distance between the bottom and the neckline.

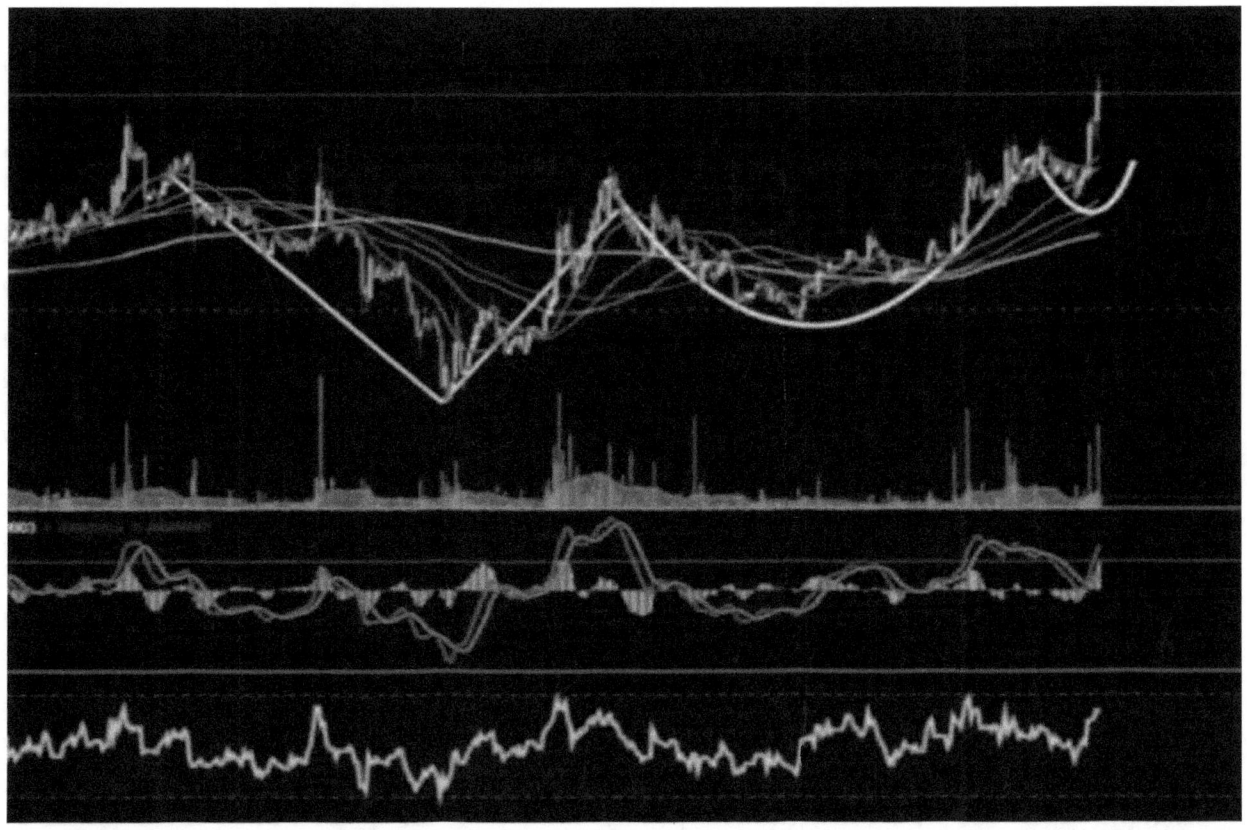

This is an example of an Adam and Eve double bottom. The only difference between a double bottom and an Adam and Eve double bottom is one bottom comes to a point which is the Adam part of the pattern. This one came down to form a cup and handle before breaking out of the neckline.

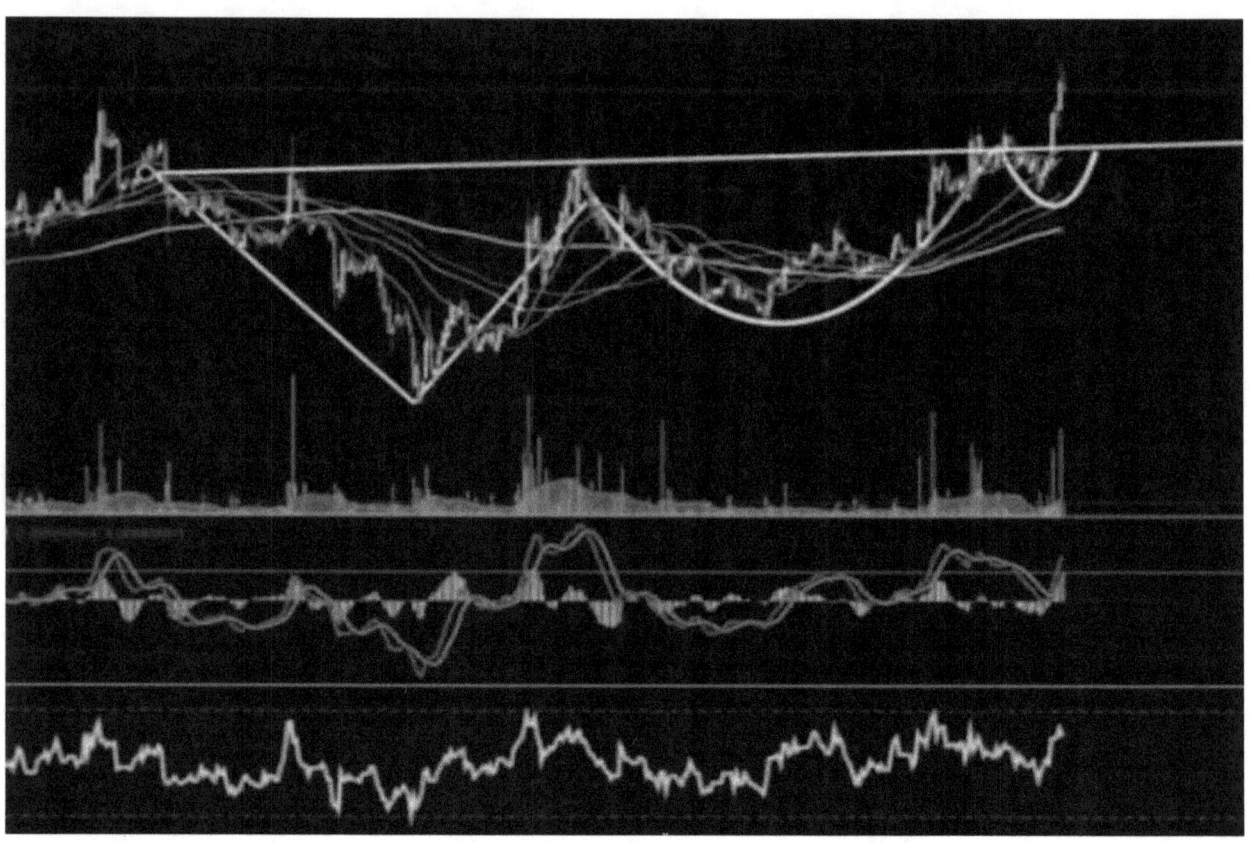

Buy the breakout or retest of the neckline if you miss the bottom.

Head & Shoulders and Inverse Head & Shoulders

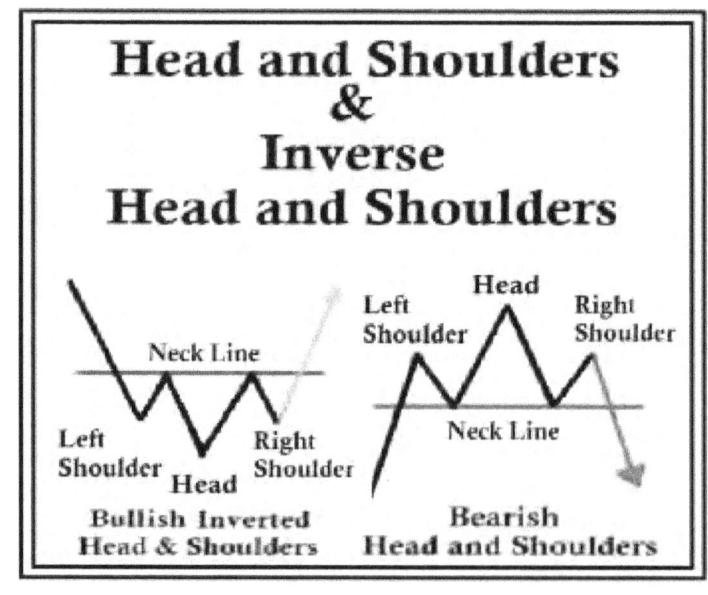

Head & Shoulders and Inverse Head & Shoulders patterns are common reversal patterns. The inverse head & shoulders pattern is a bullish reversal pattern. To trade this pattern you want to buy when the price breaks out of the neckline or wait for the price action to retest the neckline for entry.

The head & shoulders pattern is a bearish reversal pattern. You'll want to place your stop-loss just below the neckline on this one.

The patterns don't have to line up perfectly. They can be sloping. They can also have more than two shoulders. When this happens the patterns are known as complex head and shoulders or complex inverse head and shoulders.

Broadening Wedge

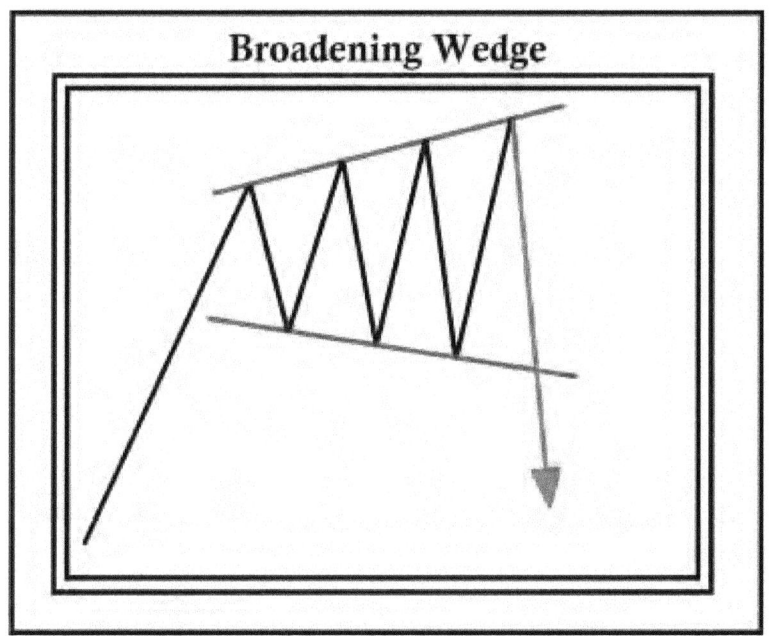

Keep an eye out for broadening formations. Broadening formations occur when investors disagree about the price of a security over a short period of time. Buyers buy at increasingly higher prices, while sellers repeatedly take profits. This creates a series of temporary higher peaks in price and temporary lower lows. When you connect these highs and lows, the trend lines form a widening pattern that looks like a reverse symmetrical triangle.

Broadening wedge formations are bearish patterns that break to the downside 76% of the time. Most of the time you will find them at the end of a rising price trend before the price reverses.

Rising Wedge

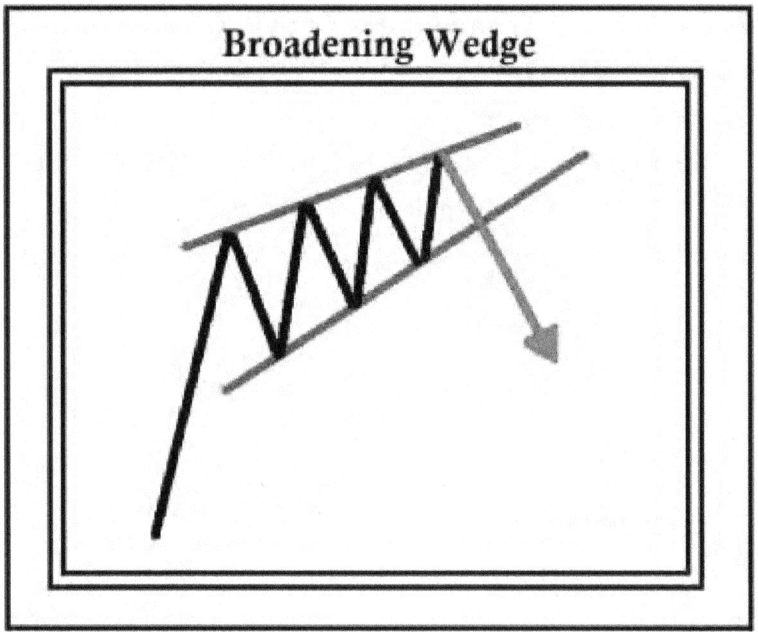

Another reversal pattern is the rising wedge. This pattern occurs when the upward buying pressure slowly dwindles out before breaking to the downside. These patterns break to the downside 68% of the time according to Bulkowski.

Rising wedges have a high probability of breaking to the downside, but in a bull market if this pattern breaks to the upside watch out because the price action can go parabolic.

The Parabolic Curve

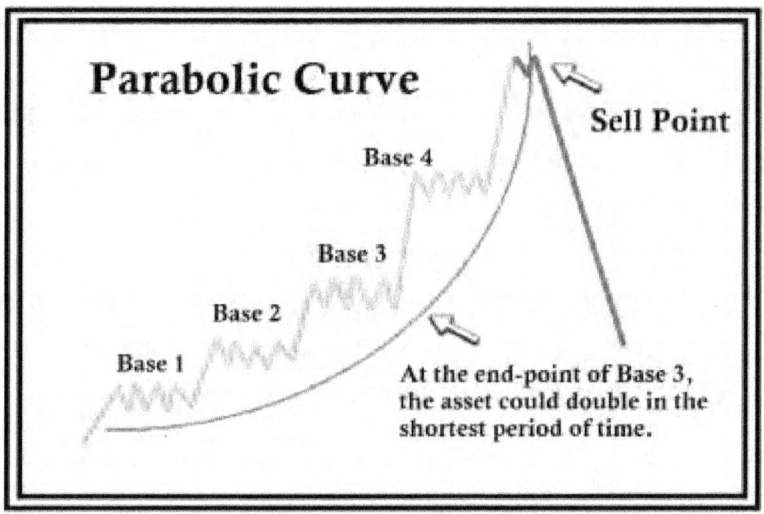

The parabolic curve occurs when irrational buying causes a steep rise in price which forms a parabolic arc. As an asset begins its parabolic rise traders think it's never going to end so they rush to buy. The price continues to rise with short pauses in between. During the pauses you will see the price action form patterns like bull flags and bull pennants along the way, so if you miss the initial move you can just buy the breakout of one of these smaller patterns.

In the last stages of a parabolic arc the price action moves rapidly in a vertical direction. Traders continue to buy in because of their fear of missing out on this massive price increase driving the price up even further. Towards the top of the arc buyers become exhausted and sellers begin to take profits. A quick sell off follows creating a panic, and the price reverses dramatically until the price finds a bottom usually at the .618 Fibonacci level or below.

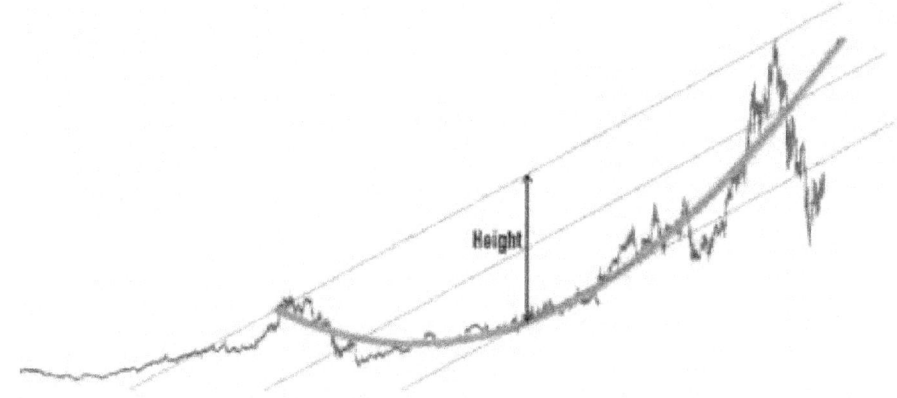

You can draw a channel connecting the top and bottom of the parabolic curve pattern to get an idea of where you should set your stop-loss, and when you can open a short position. When the price action falls and breaks the parabolic curve trendline that is your cue to sell.

Parabolic curve patterns can be excellent opportunities if you can enter a position at the right time and sell before the big sell off. Look for the price action to start to curve and around the halfway point is where I like to start looking for entry. You will begin to see higher highs and higher lows.

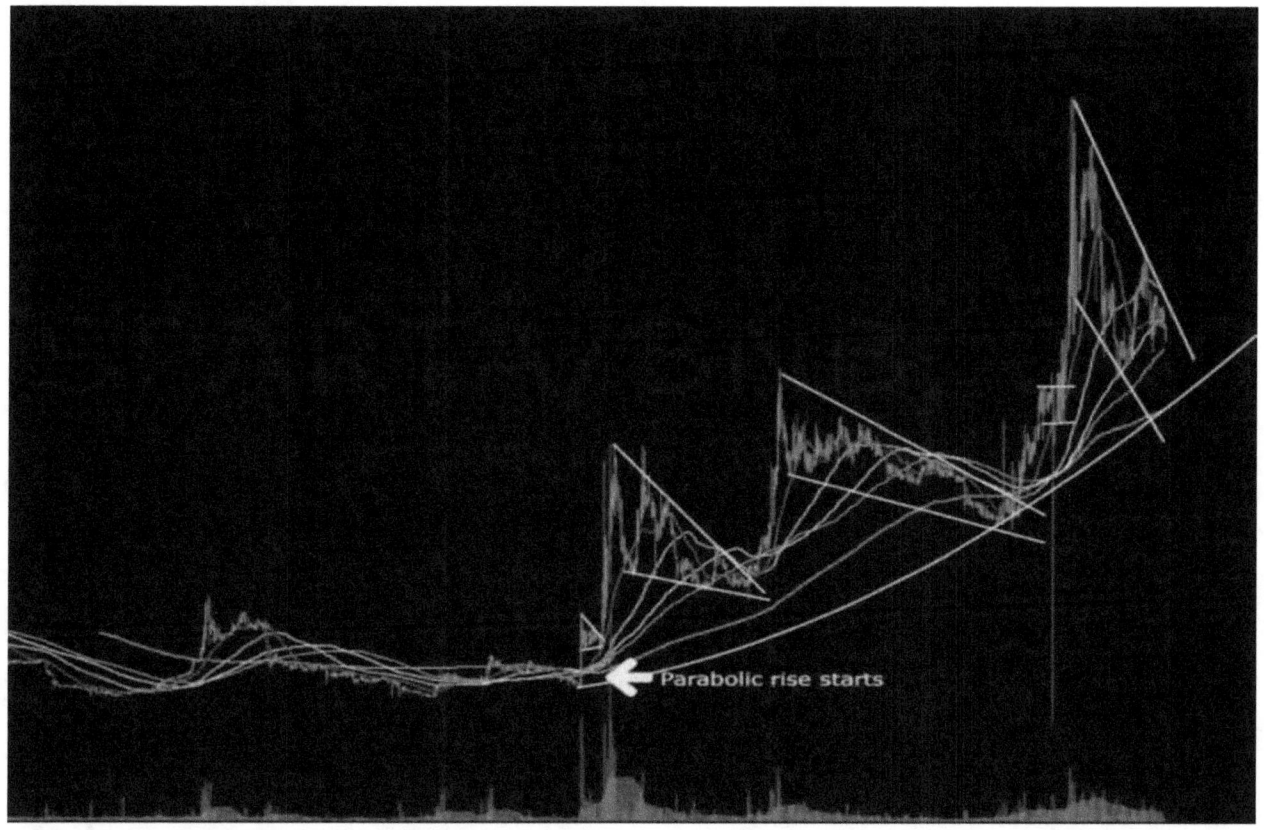

This Sparta setup formed a double bottom before crossing over the 200 day moving average and beginning the parabolic ascent. Notice the patterns the price action formed along the way.

No pattern can predict what the price action is going to do 100% of the time. However, if we combine these patterns with other signals and indications we can arrive at a fairly accurate estimate.

Buying the Breakout

"The secret to success know something nobody else knows." -

Aristotle

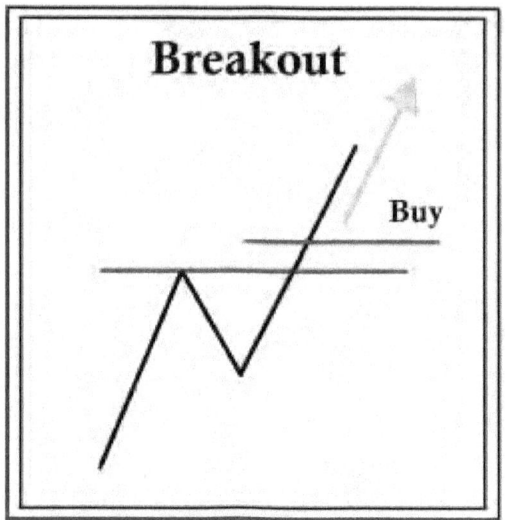

Breakout trading is when traders attempt to capitalize on a trend as soon as it begins. When the price action breaks from support or breaks out of resistance with volume explosive volatility and price surges can sometimes follow. The largest price surges come from reversal and continuation pattern breakouts such as triangles, channels, and falling wedges. Trading this way maximizes the gains of the trend and minimizes the risk making it an excellent strategy to use.

You can use this method to both long and short the market. Longing and shorting the market allows you to make money no matter which direct the market is moving. You want to focus on breakouts to the upside during up trends and breakouts to the downside during down trends. For this explanation though I will be focusing on long trades.

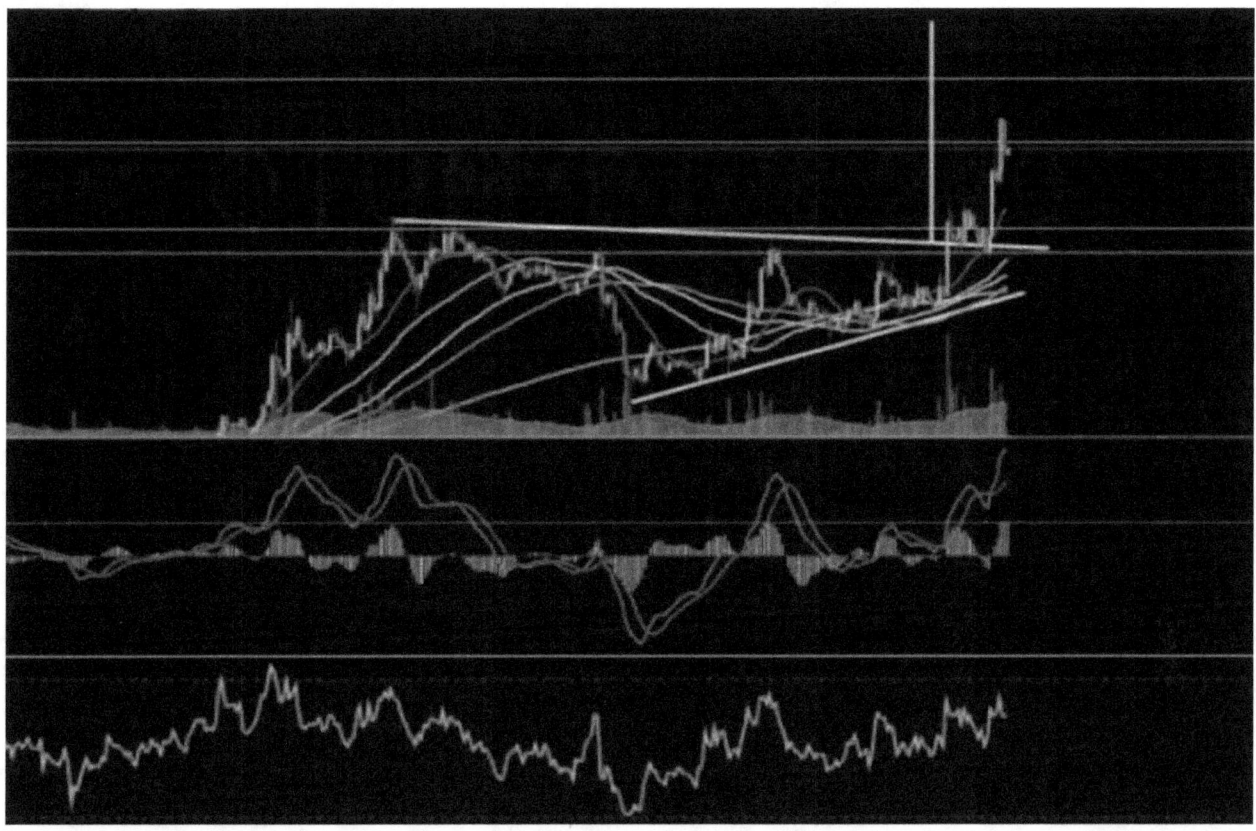

A breakout occurs when the price action moves outside of a support or resistance level with increased volume. The price action has fallen into a reversal or continuation pattern and is in the process of ranging back and forth. There needs to be at least two swing highs and two swing lows to be considered a valid pattern. Look for higher highs and higher lows as the price action moves towards the resistance. The price action then needs to move up above the trend line and have a candle close outside of the pattern to be considered a breakout. The higher the time frame the more confirmation of the breakout. When you're waiting for entry you want at least a one hour candle body to close outside of the trend line or pattern you're watching before you enter into a position. Any time frame less than that is highly susceptible to a fake out.

Pay attention to the volume. Volume is your guide when you're breakout trading. You want to see an above average amount of volume to confirm the breakout idea.

Also look for volume divergence. If the price is moving up, but the volume is moving down it could be a fake out. If you see the price action moving outside of a pattern but there isn't any volume it's probably going to be a fake out.

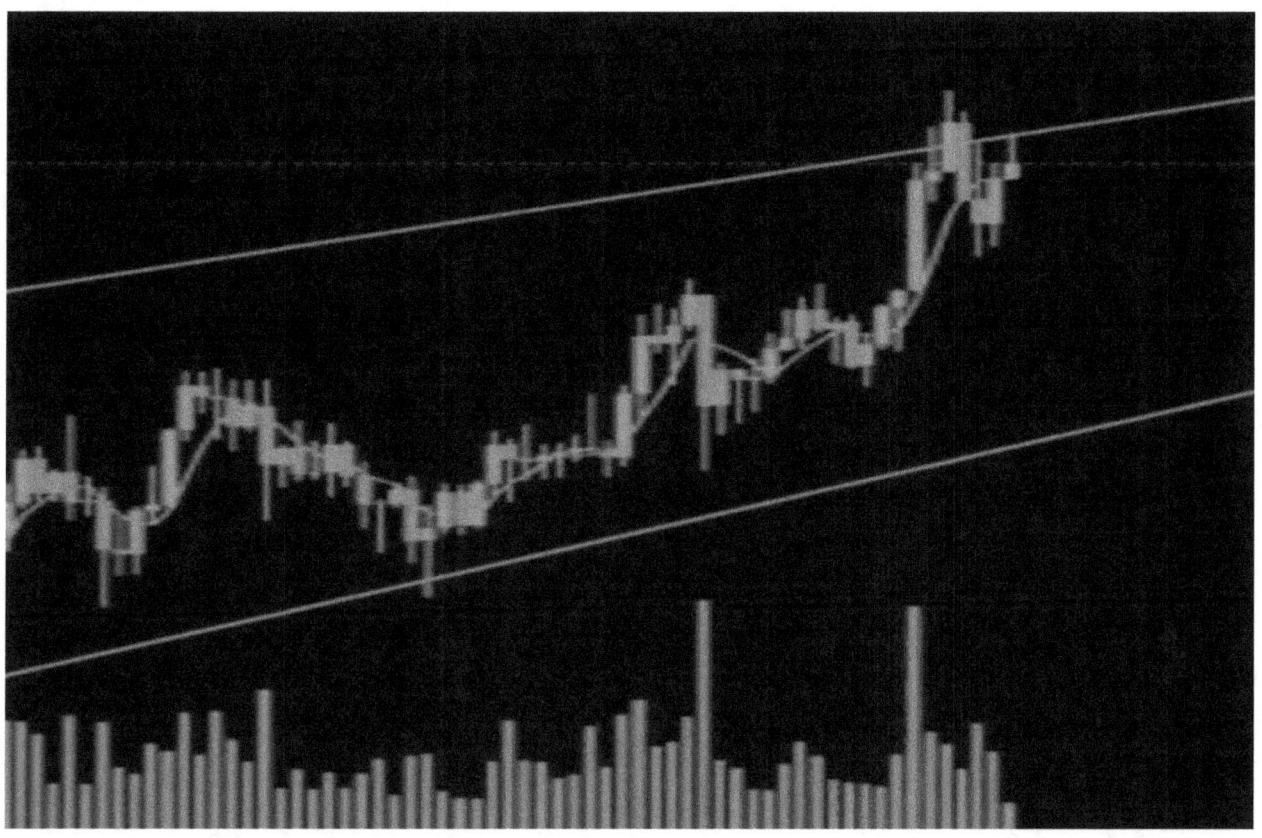

Fake outs occur when the price action breaks out of a pattern or level of resistance and then retraces back into the pattern. If you're getting faked out a lot chances are you're not waiting for a candle body to close in a one hour time frame or greater, or you're not waiting for above average volume and indicator confirmation.

Buying the breakout is like training wheels for a new trader. After you gain some experience and you're successful buying breakouts you should start buying the retests instead. A retest is when the previous resistance of the upper trend line of the pattern is turned into support before heading to new highs. Experienced traders will wait until then to enter their position. When they see volume increasing they have the confirmation needed to execute the trade.

Buying the retest is much safer than buying the breakout because there are less fake outs, but don't always happen in every set up. Sometimes the price will breakout of a trend line and just keep going without the retest. You'll have to determine how strong the uptrend is and if you're willing to lose the position waiting on the retest. If there are massive amounts of volume there may not even be a retest at all.

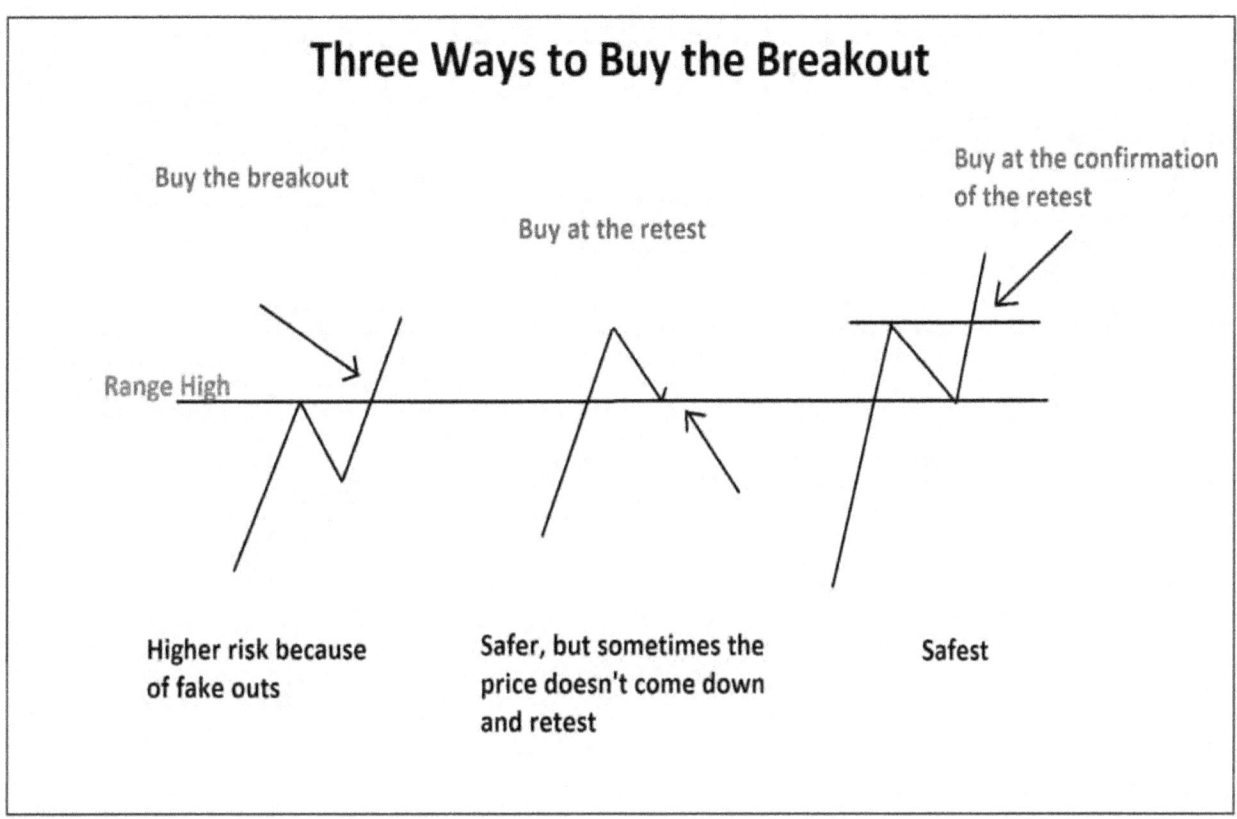

You can take this a step further if you want even more confirmation of the trend direction. You can wait until after the retest when the price action moves past the high of the breakout before it turned downwards to retest. This is the safest time possible to enter a position, but you miss a small portion of the price increase.

Determine what your strategy is going to be and then execute your plan. Your plan could be to buy 50% of the position at the breakout and the other 50% of your position on the retest, or you could buy 50% at the retest and 50% once you have confirmation. It all depends on your risk tolerance. Develop a plan that is comfortable for you.

In a bull market you can start to front run these patterns and buy even earlier than the breakout and retest. When you get good at buying the retests, start buying the third or forth touch at the bottom of the pattern with bullish divergence. This is an absolute game changer! Trading this way ensures that you maximize every bit of the upswing in price, and because the price hasn't taken off yet and you're able to identify the bullish divergence you'll be able to enter the position before most people know the price is going up. Then, set your stop loss slightly below the bottom trend line just in case the price action decides to dip. If you follow this process correctly you can easily 50x your portfolio throughout a bull run cycle.

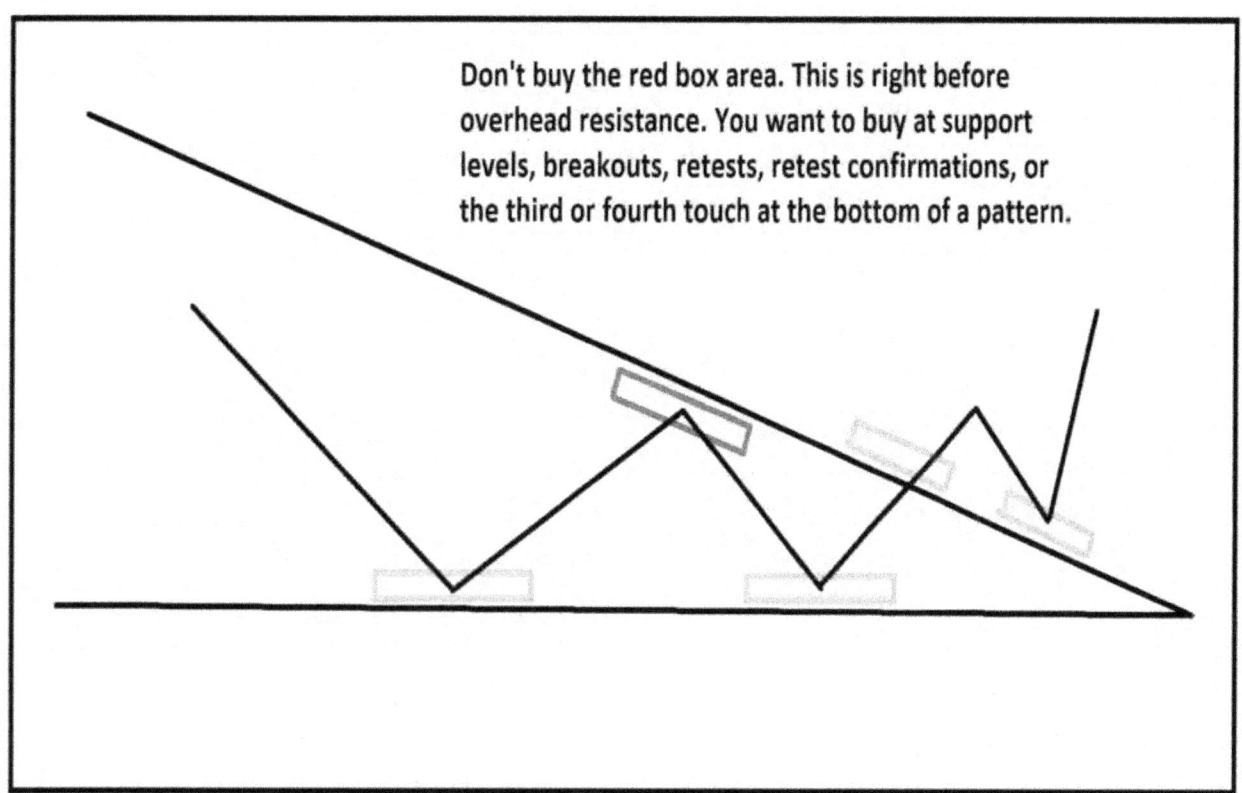

Never buy at the top of a pattern. You always want to buy when the price is next to support, not resistance.

If you're front running the pattern you'll want to place your stop loss just below your entry outside of the pattern. The amount of the loss should be no more than a couple percent at the most. Set your stop losses at places where it negates the bullish idea for entering the trade in the first place. If you're buying a breakout or a retest you'll want to place your stop loss just inside the pattern, so if there is a fake out you will be stopped out.

Institutional traders and smart money will do what's called stop hunting where they will attempt to activate your stop loss to bring liquidity back into the market. Exchanges make money when you trade, not when you hold. They are in it to make money. Make sure you put your stop loss far enough down so that a candle wick doesn't come down and stop you out before running up again.

Stop losses can be a blessing and a curse. Sometimes they can prevent you from losing thousands. Other times, however, the price action can come down, stop you out, and then take off to the upside. It can be very frustrating when it happens. When you set your stop loss set an alert for your trigger price. This way you will be sent a notification when you're stopped out, and you can make a decision what you want to do at that time. In a very bullish market you can set alerts instead of stop losses so that when the price reaches a predetermined level you can make the decision at that time.

What's your plan

Before you enter a trade you should have a plan in place. Know ahead of time when you plan on taking profits, and more importantly, know when to sell when the trade is no longer profitable. This will help take the emotion out of your trades because when the time comes to take action you've already made a decision ahead of time instead of in the heat of the moment.

Remember how I showed you how to figure out your take profit levels on the different patterns? You will want to apply that principle to the pattern you're viewing to figure out where to take profits. Resistance levels from previous price history will service as take profit levels. Mark all your take profit levels on your chart, and determine how much of your position you're going to sell when the price action hits the different levels.

If there is no prior price history and the asset is in price exploration you can use the Fibonacci extension tool to find hidden levels of resistance to determine the take profit levels. From there you can either set a stop loss for the trade and set alerts for all your take profit levels, or you can set limit sell orders for your take profit levels and set an alert in case the price action drops to a point where the bullish idea for the trade is negated. This way your investment is protected.

You might decide to sell 25% at your first take profit level, 25% at the next level, 25% at the third, and let the remaining 25% ride. You might decide according to your risk tolerance that you want to sell 50% at the first take profit level and 50% on the second. You could also just keep raising your stop loss as the price goes up and not worry about all the different take profit levels. There is no wrong decision. It's completely up to you when you want to take profits, and it all depends on your risk tolerance. No one can decide that for you.

Don't get too greedy! Take profits when you can and move on to the next set up. Don't waste your time trying to jump back into an asset that's had a good run up. After you make the decision to sell, move on to the next one. Set alerts so you can come back if you need to.

Once your profit level gets to a certain point you could sell only what you have invested and let the rest ride. I know some traders that go this route. Then, at that point you're only trading with the profits you made and you keep your capital for other trades.

When you see 30%+ gains quickly take profits! No matter how strong the coin is it will pull back. Even if you're a long term holder, if one of your assets goes up 30% or more in a day you may want to consider selling and buying back at a lower price. Usually, but not always, traders will take profits after a big run up like that. Are you willing to hold through the dip in price? The price action will most likely fall into some type of pattern, and you don't want to have your money tied up while it's going up and down. Sell at the top, wait for it to fall into some sort of pattern, and set an alert to buy the third touch at the bottom of the pattern.

It is equally important that a trader knows when a trade has failed and when to exit a position. It can be tempting to hang on to a position if you're at a loss, but consider the amount of time it will take to make your gains back while your in an asset that has just lost you money. You could take a loss, put the money into two, three, or more winning trades in the time it takes you to make your gains back with the original asset. Cut your losses quick and ride the winners. It only takes a few bad trades to wipe out a portfolio.

Never have more than a couple trades going at once. It's difficult to watch multiple charts at the same time. If you have a multiple monitor set up this helps, but several trades at once can still be difficult to manage. Only keep a couple open at a time so they are easier to manage.

Some of your trades will fail. That's just how trading goes. You're not going to win 100% of your trades. You just have to do your best to mitigate risk as much as possible. With practice your success ratio will increase. Keep this in mind, you can lose on multiple trades, but one big one can make it all worth it. When I first got started I remember noticing that my portfolio had dwindled down to a fraction of what I had started trading with. I was feeling discouraged. I was feeling like I couldn't get the hang of this trading thing. Then, I was looking at the chart of one of my small caps one day and all of a sudden the price started to rise. Over the course of an hour or so I ended up making what most people would pay for a new car! Never give up. Believe that you can make it happen. Make a decision that you are going to win no matter what happens. You are going to have the mindset that you are going to dedicate whatever time and effort is needed to learn how to trade this market, and nothing that gets in your way is going to stop you.

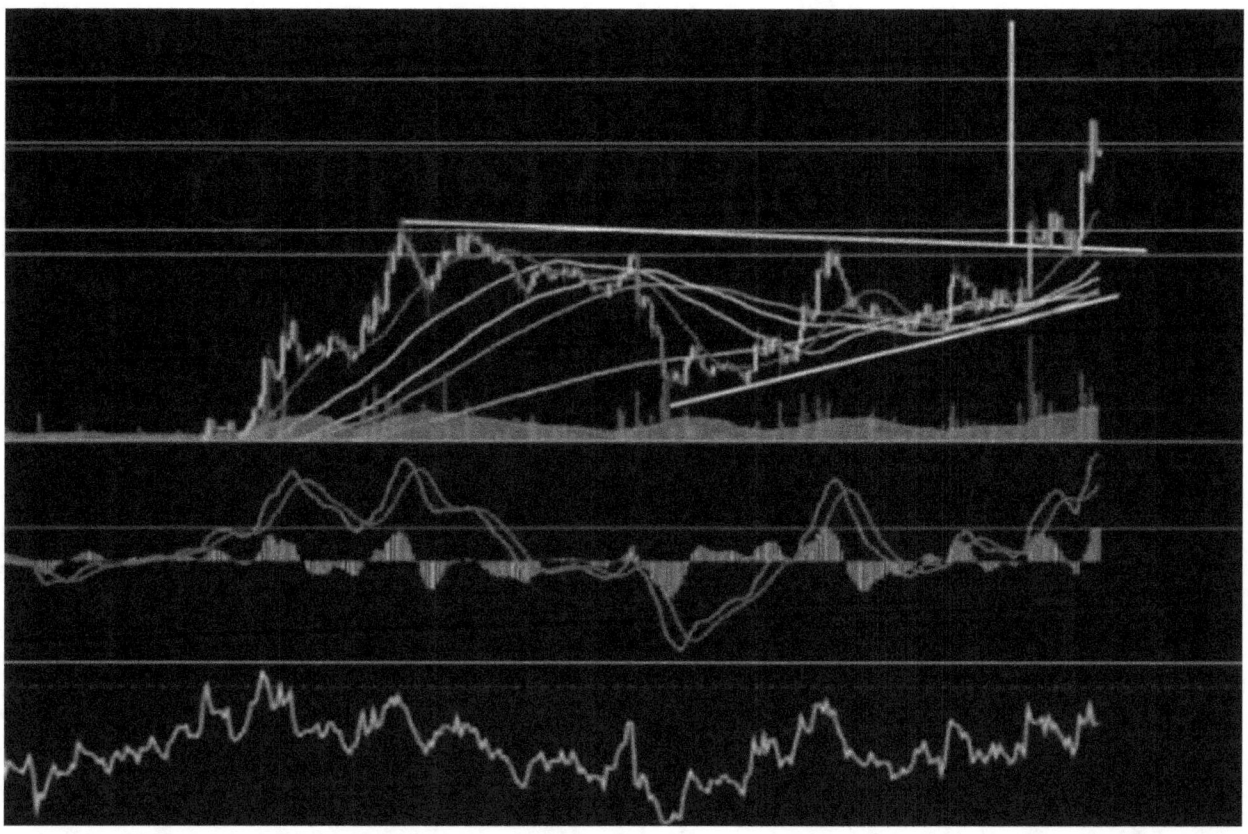

In the example above, we have an ascending triangle pattern that has broken out. As the price action consolidated it ranged back and forth in this pattern from support to resistance. Towards the end of the triangle pattern the price action broke out. Notice the increase in the average volume on the ascending triangle example above when the price broke out of the pattern. The price action broke out of the pattern and at the same time the average volume rose considerably. The price then came back down to retest the previous resistance. Volume dropped momentarily just before the retest and then shot back up again with increased volume. The MACD indicator is showing a cross at the same time of the breakout. The RSI is heading towards oversold levels, but remember it can stay pegged at the top for a while during up trends. A high reading tells us the trend is strengthening. The distance in between the top of the ascending triangle and the bottom at its widest point will give us the possible price potential in the short term. Draw a line between the two and place the line on top of the ascending triangle where the price is breaking out. This will give you the price potential of this move. Resistance levels are take profit levels on the way up. Most of the time the price will only go up three quarters of the length of this line so take profits while you can. This market is trying to take your money and you need to take it before it does.

If there is no breakout you don't open a position. If it does breakout and you open a position you can set a stop loss just below your entry position. Trading this way eliminates most of the risk involved. At first, learn to trade with small amounts. Don't use any more than two percent of your portfolio to trade at a time in the beginning. Then, as you become more successful with your trades you can increase your position sizes. Preserve your capital in the beginning because there is a learning curve involved.

After you gain some experience you can increase your position sizes on set ups that you really believe will take off in price. Make sure to manage your risk to reward ratio. Set a rule for yourself that says if you risk let's say 1%, you want a potential gain of at least 10% to open the trade or it's not worth it. That's a ten to one risk to reward ratio. Most traders only risk one to two percent of their portfolios. Do whatever is comfortable for you. Never give your losses too much room to grow though because they can accumulate quickly. You can always buy back into the trade later if you need to if and when it starts going up again.

Don't chase big green candles either. If there's a hot crypto you really want to buy into but the price has already run up just wait until you see a continuation pattern like a bull flag, and buy the breakout of the bull flag. This way you know things are still trending up. Often there are big run ups and then big pullbacks so you don't want to get stuck buying at the top. Remember Dow's Theory states for every price increase there is around a 50% retrace. Use the Fibonacci retracement tool to find entry.

Don't worry if you take profits and then there's a big run up afterwards. This doesn't happen very often. Stick to the plan and repeat the process with the next one. You can also leave a certain percentage of the position on the table so if the price does take off you won't miss out. Just make sure to keep moving up your stop loss as the price action moves up. You're not going to perfectly time the top and the bottom every time. Just try to get as close as you can.

You'll need to have patience with these set up. Give them time to play out. Sometimes it only takes a few minutes for the price action to take off once I've identified a pattern. Other times it can take a week or so to play out. Once you commit to a trade see it through to the end. Some will play out quicker than others. You just have to be patient. You will know when the set up isn't going anywhere.

In conclusion, breakout trading is a very effective way to trade this market with minimal risk. Locate a good set up by finding a continuation or reversal pattern. Have a list of crypto that you regularly review and look at the charts for all of them. When you find a good set up look at the current trend on a large time frame like the daily to get the big picture of the trend. Is the price trending upwards or downwards? Find your support and resistance levels for your pattern. You want two to three touches minimum on your patterns. Set your alerts so you're not glued to your phone or computer and wait for the breakout. If you would rather wait for the retest when your alert goes off for the breakout set an alert for the retest at that time. Wait for the breakout. Don't buy prematurely unless you are front running the pattern. Then, after the breakout make sure it will hold by waiting for the retest.

Market cycles

Everything in life is cyclical and the crypto market is no exception. bitcoin goes through a continuous cycle of rises, peaks, dips, and then bottoms out before repeating the cycle all over again. When one market cycle finishes another one begins. All the altcoins have their own cycles too. Make sure you always know which phase you are in when you place a trade.

It is essential to know what the market phases are if you're going to be a successful trader. If you can time the market right and buy in at the beginning of the accumulation phase you can earn big profits throughout a bull run. On the other hand if you buy during the distribution phase you could potentially lose a lot of money especially if you don't have stop losses set. Having an understanding of how this market works can help you maximize your gains and minimize your losses.

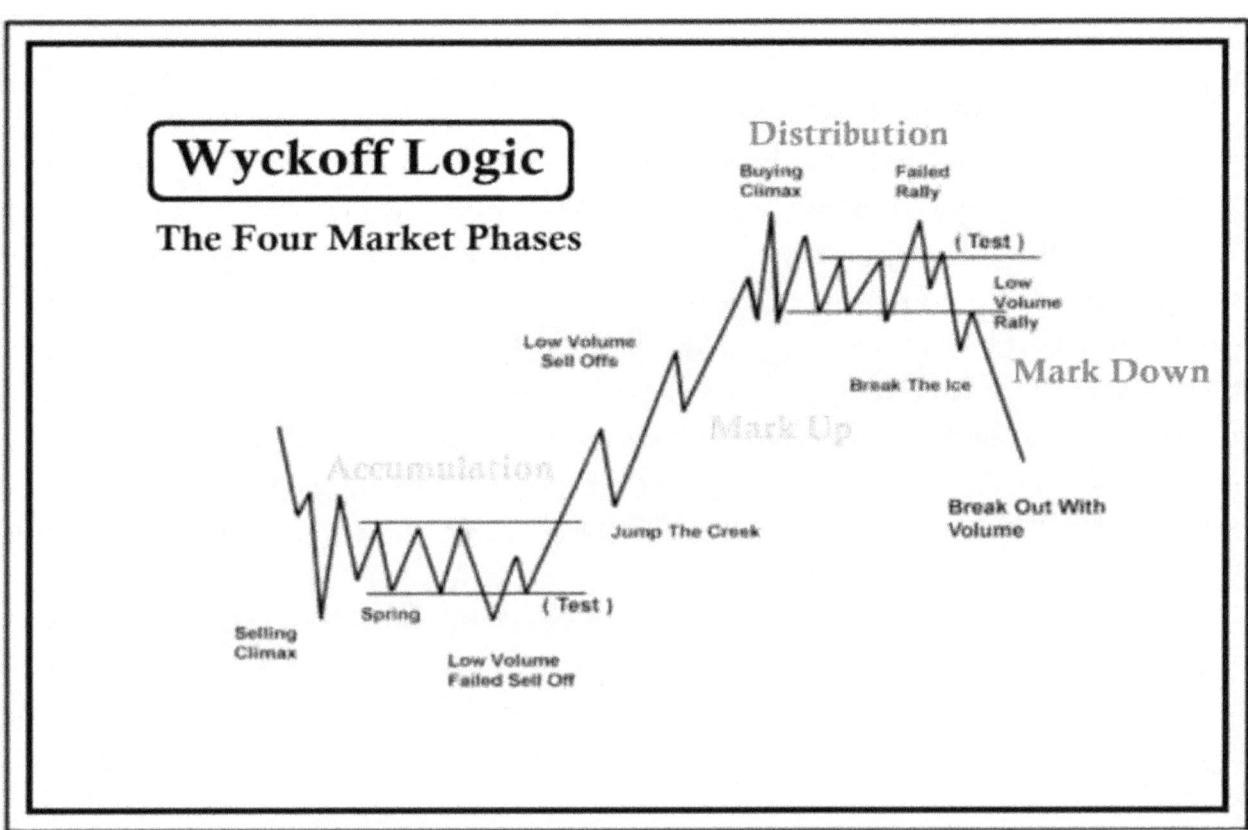

The problem is market cycles can be difficult to identify until after the cycle has actually passed. Luckily, a man named Richard Wyckoff came along and established a set of rules in order to better recognize the transition from one phase to another.

Richard D. Wyckoff (1873–1934) was an early 20th-century stock market authority. His technical approach to studying the stock market led him to be considered one of, "the Titans of Technical Analysis", along side of Charles Henry Dow, William Gann, Ralph Elliott and Arthur Merrill as David Penn wrote in Stock & Commodities.

Wyckoff rubbed shoulders with and studied all the successful traders in his time such as: J.P. Morgan, E.H. Harriman, Jesse Livermore, Otto Kahn, James R. Keene and many others.

Using all the knowledge he gained from his research, conversations, and interviews he developed methods that made him a fortune. Wyckoff used his own capital to implement his strategies in the markets, and eventually amassed his wealth to the point where he owned a mansion with nine and a half acres next door to the Hamptons estate of General Motors president Alfred Sloan in Great Neck, New York.

Wyckoff entered the business at a very early age. In 1888, at the age of fifteen, he began working as a stock runner. He went on to become head of his own financial consulting business in his twenties. In 1907, he founded the first financial magazine in the country, the Magazine of Wall Street. In 1931, he started a business where he offered investing courses to the public which later evolved into the Stock Market Institute. His goal later in life was to teach the public, "the real rules of the game." He was also the author of several books on trading in the stock market. Wyckoff's strategies and techniques are still used today.

Wyckoff formulated the concept of the "Composite Man" which consisted of the idea that an imaginary person was controlling the market from behind the scenes in order to help the average trader better understand the market.

> "…all the fluctuations in the market and in all the various stocks should be studied as if they were the result of one man's operations. Let us call him the Composite Man, who, in theory, sits behind the scenes and manipulates the stocks to your disadvantage if you do not understand the game as he plays it; and to your great profit if you do understand it." (The Richard D. Wyckoff Course in Stock Market Science and Technique, section 9, p. 1-2)

Wyckoff taught traders to play the game as the Composite Man plays it. He painted a picture of the Composite Man methodically planning and executing trades. He said the Composite Man attracts the public to buy a stock which he has already acquired a position in by making many large transactions. The large spike in volume creates a buying frenzy.

Wyckoff and his associates believed that if you could understand the behavior of the Composite Man, you could identify many trading and investment opportunities early enough to profit from them. He outlined ways to identify the four phases in a market cycle: accumulation, markup, distribution, and the mark down phase.

Accumulation phase

The accumulation phase occurs after the market has continuously fallen for several months, even years in some cases. Sentiment slowly changes from bearish to neutral. The price action finally stops falling and begins to trade in a range. Higher lows and higher highs are posted, but the rapid downward momentum due to the amount of fear in the market causes many retail investors to capitulate fearing price will fall even further. The two hundred day moving average while still falling in the beginning starts to flattens out and the price action fluctuates above and below. Many assets are still falling in the beginning of this phase.

Accumulation can last anywhere from a couple weeks up to several years in some cases. While the overall trend is still bearish informed corporate insiders and other smart money begin entering the market around what's called the preliminary support. Retail buyers are quick to sell the uptick in price after the long sell off and we have a selling climax where the price bottoms out immediately followed by an automatic rally. Volume increases are a good indication the down trend is coming to an end. This is the best time to buy. You want to plant your seeds during the accumulation phase and reap your harvest at the end of the bull run season.

The price action will test the previous low a second time before another spring up to the top portion of the trading range. At some point the price will bottom out a second time or make a new low before springing back up, this time out of the top of the range showing a sign of strength.

It can be extremely difficult to spot the accumulation phase because right before the phase ends the price action makes one final new low, shaking out a lot of stop-losses in the process, before the price is propelled into the next phase. This is called a spring because the price action quickly rebounds as the bulls take advantage of the new low pushing the price upwards.

In March 2020, the market bottomed out because of COVID-19. An external event like this can cause the markets to crumble at anytime and start market cycles over from the beginning. A lot of people were fearful saying it was going to go down further. While everyone was still fearful I was buying as much as I could. I purchased where I thought was the bottom after I started seeing a series of higher highs and higher lows with volume. A couple times the price dropped even further than my entry price. When this happened I bought even more. By doing so, I dollar cost averaged into my positions and made even more money on the way up. This was the lowest point before the bull run started. Like Warren Buffet says, "buy while there's blood in the streets."

Wyckoff learned large corporate interests begin purchasing their company holdings during the accumulation phase. When these large financial companies begin to acquire their sizeable positions, they do it slowly so it doesn't alert the competition. They want to acquire a sizeable amount of the supply at the lowest prices possible. If the competition sees the high volume a company is buying they will see the demand and begin purchasing too driving up the price which is counter-intuitive to the objective.

Think of yourself as being one of these corporate insiders when you enter your trades. You don't want to come in and place a huge buy order all at once. You want to slowly buy in to your position to make sure you're able to purchase the amount you want at the lowest price possible. In cryptocurrency an order of even a few thousand dollars can drastically move the price so take it slow. Look at the size of the other orders on the books and place your orders in similar quantity.

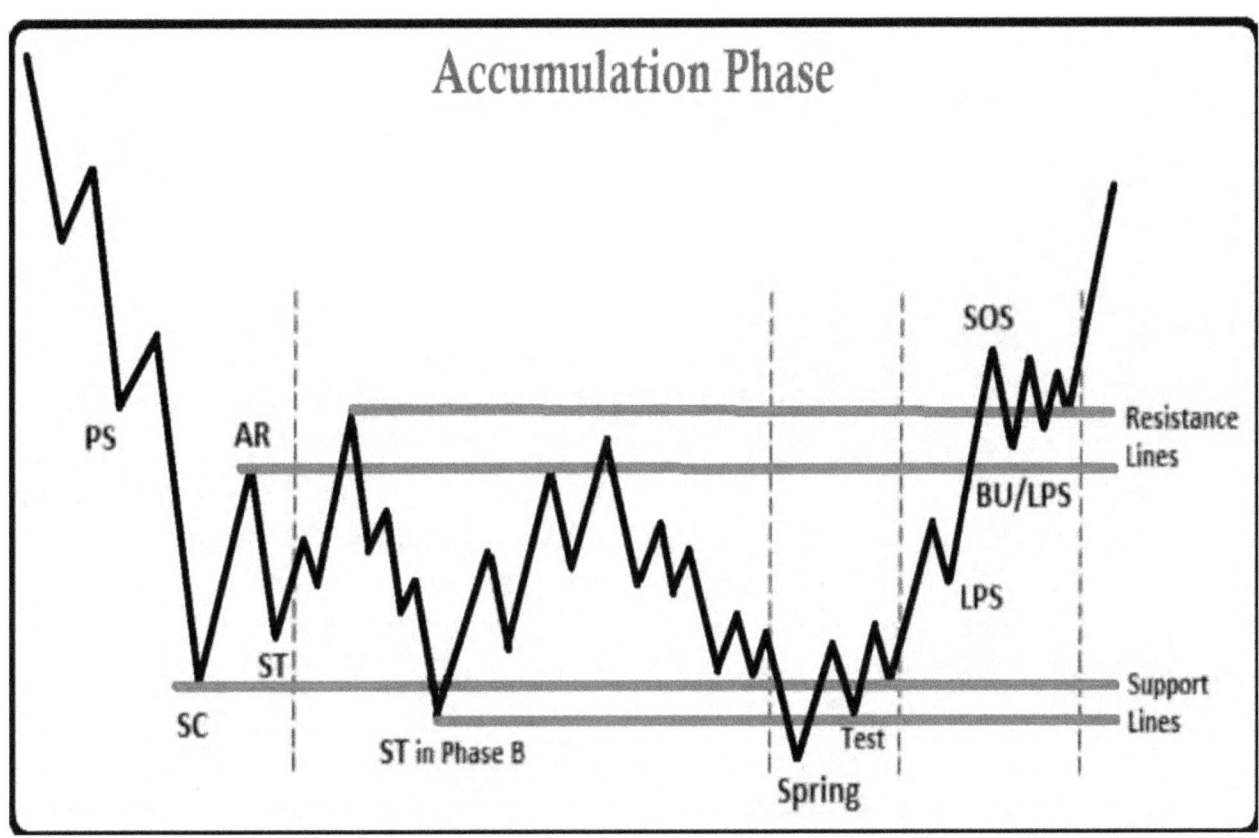

Dollar cost average into the position at or below the preliminary support while accumulation of the asset is being completed. If you're not able to clearly identify the preliminary support, use the middle of the range.

When the phase is nearing the end you will see higher volume as well as higher highs and higher lows as the bulls push the price out of the accumulation range. This is called jumping the creek because the price jumps to the other side from accumulation to mark up.

Markup

When the price action gets enough momentum to break through the resistance in the accumulation phase, the mark up phase begins. Volume increases considerably as more investors become aware the trend has changed. You will notice the price action crossed over the two hundred day moving average to start the uptrend. The bear market has officially ended and the bull market has begun!

The markup phase is the easiest time to trade because upward momentum will propel the price to higher highs with occasional retests along the way where the price action retests the previous resistance as support. Any downtrend during this time is viewed as an opportunity to buy more. When the market goes down below the two hundred day moving average, it's quickly bought back up. Watch out for the retest that occurs after the breakout from the accumulation range. Look for higher highs and higher lows.

After the retest of the accumulation range the price action will shoot up until it eventually falls into what's called the re-accumulation zone. This is where the price action moves sideways in a range for a short period of time forming major support. Investors load up on assets wanting to capitalize on the clear uptrend. As the market climbs it gets more and more media coverage. Astronomical predictions are given out everywhere. Retail investors continuously jump in to try and get their piece of the action. Fearing they will be missing out on the profits, more and more investors pour in repeatedly pushing the price to new highs. On the other hand, some who purchased during the accumulation phase are reluctant to purchase at the new highs not realizing the market is going much higher. They hodl their bags and hang on for the ride.

Demand increases as assets surpass their all time highs and go into price discovery. Retail buyers are buying at all time highs and volume increases substantially. I've seen gains well over 1000% in a day during this phase! Prices then make one last parabolic move, called the buying climax. This is when the largest gains are made in the shortest amount of time. An earnings report or some other good news usually precedes the buying climax, since the large interests require huge demand from the public to sell their shares without decreasing the price.

While retail investors are still pouring into the market in masses, the corporate insiders and smart money begin slowly liquidating their holdings while trying to remain under the radar. This is called the last point of supply. The sell off must happen slowly so it doesn't cause the price to fall too drastically. This sell off is what leads the transition into the distribution phase.

Distribution Phase

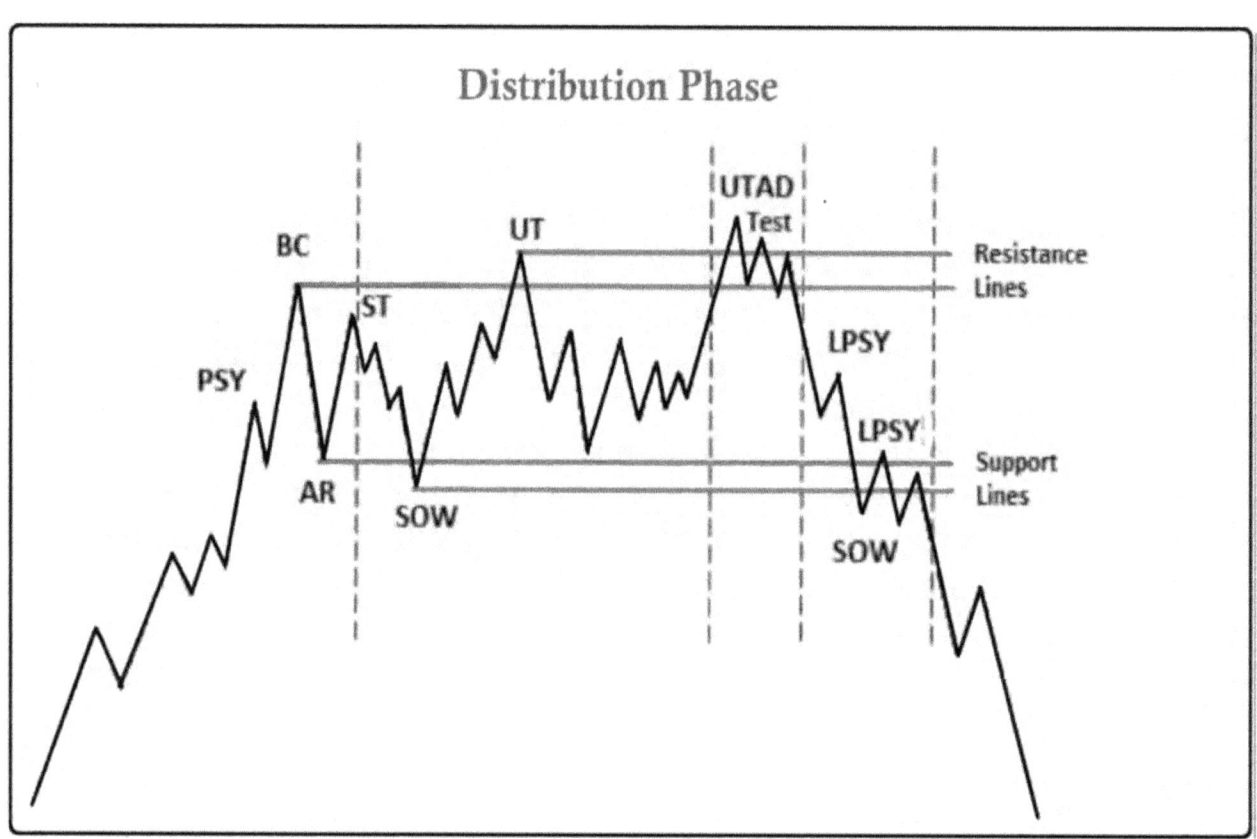

After the buying climax there is a large selloff where the price action falls to the bottom support of the distribution phase, called the automatic reaction. Then the price returns to the area of the buying climax to retest the high. Volume decreases as the price movement approaches the buying climax resistance area. This is called the secondary test.

The secondary test could be a fake out in the form of an upthrust in which the price breaks out above the buying climax resistance area before quickly reversing to close below resistance. After an upthrust the price usually revisits the lower trendline of the trading range.

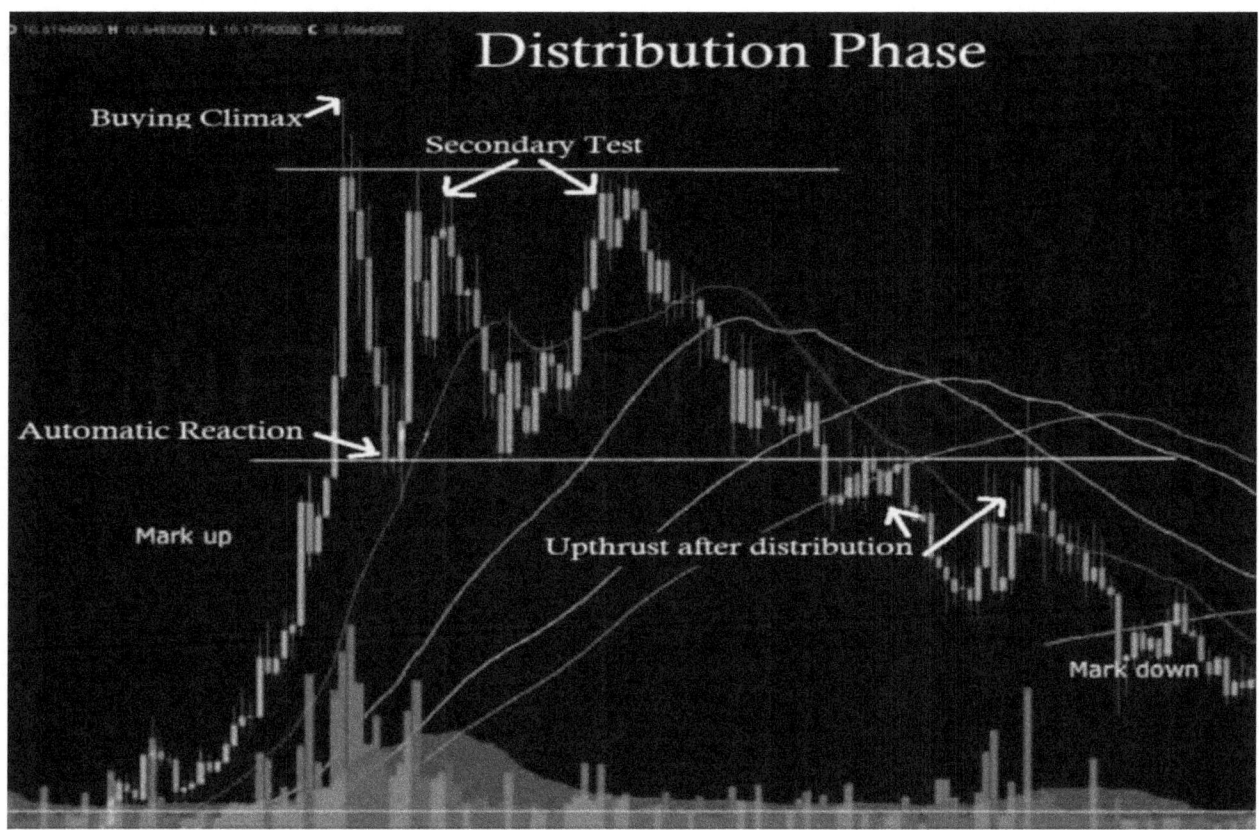

The price action then starts ranging back and forth as the bulls try to push the price above the upward resistance to no avail. Those who purchased during the accumulation phase sell and new retail investors buy into the hype and enter the market. This is a process that can last for weeks in some cases. Smart sellers try to maintain higher prices until they have completely unloaded their positions. As the distribution phase progresses, sentiment transitions between greed, hope, and fear.

Unaware of the market phases some retail investors buy into their positions at or beyond all time highs with the hope the uptrend will continue. Smart money liquidates the last of their positions, and some enter short positions where they bet price will drop further. You want to scale out of any remaining positions you're in too. Just like in the accumulation phase you want to sell your positions slowly to prevent the price from dropping too quickly. Think of what the Composite Man would do.

There are periods of strong selling during the distribution phase, but never a sustained downtrend which makes this phase difficult to identify. When price drops the bulls are slower to respond. Volume is present, but it doesn't move the price very much. Early in the phase the two hundred day moving average is still climbing until the after the buying climax when it begins to level off. When the sell off happens the price will cross below the twenty one day moving average, then the twenty one day moving average will start cross all the until it finally crosses the others. Keep an eye out for common reversal patterns like double tops or head and shoulders patterns on larger time frames. Make sure you watch closely when the price action gets to the lower level. Once the price action breaks the lower support range the distribution phase has ended.

"Don't try to catch falling knives"

In the mark-down phase, the support of the distribution range has broken, and the price action falls below the two hundred day moving average with large momentum as selling pressure increases. This is where traders become long term investors. Sometimes, but not all the time, a major back test will happen right after the downside breakout called the upthrust after distribution. Uninformed traders are buying the dip without knowing where they are in the overall market cycle.

Due to lack of demand the price falls to where it finally finds a little support. The price begins to range sideways. This is called the re-distribution phase, and is an indication of smart money shorting the market. After re-distribution prices fall even further. Corporate insiders and smart money open short positions so they can make money on the way down too. Retail investors that bought the hype and fomo'd in to the market at it's peak during the distribution phase rush to quickly sell their negative positions. However, due to such little demand there's not much volume to buy them! The price is in free fall, and the bear market is in full effect.

Those who were too slow to sell during the distribution phase, or were unable to spot the transition, try to sell and salvage what little capital they have left at a loss. Some traders who purchased during the distribution phase realize their investment has now fallen below what they paid for it, yet in denial they hang on in the hopes that the market will turn back around. In the end, many are shaken out and forced to sell at a massive loss while corporate insiders and smart money look for signs of a bottom like vultures so they can jump back in the market and pick the carcasses of the market clean at rock bottom prices.

There are many investors that either aren't aware that markets are cyclical, or forget to expect the end of the current phase. Even if you are actively watching for market cycles it's impossible to pick the top or bottom. Just do your best to get close as possible. Adjust your stop losses as price climbs, so if there is a big retrace you aren't stuck in a trade with negative profit. Whatever you do don't get stuck holding at the top and don't try to catch the falling knives when prices come tumbling down! Wait for the to hit the ground first and then you can pick them up safely.

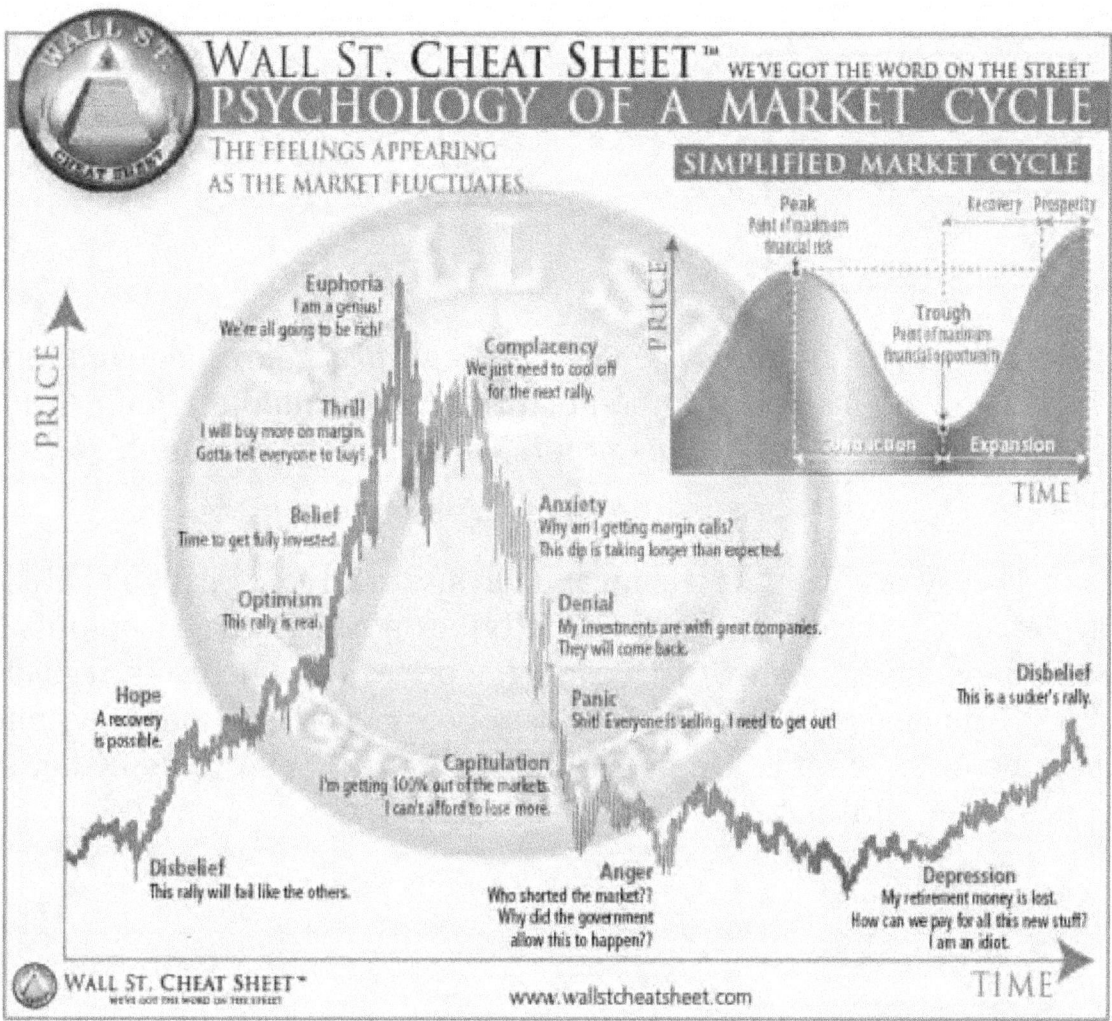

The best way to identify the current market cycle you're in is to study historical market cycles and identify each of the phases. What was the low during accumulation? What was the high during distribution? Record these numbers so you can compare them to the current cycle. Be sure to watch for changes in volume patterns.

Elliot Wave Theory

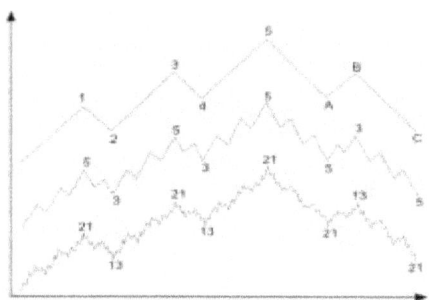

"Because man is subject to rhythmical procedure, calculations having to do with his activities can be projected far into the future with a justification and certainty heretofore unattainable." - Ralph Nelson Elliot

Elliot Wave Theory is a form of technical analysis that traders use to analyze market cycles and forecast trends by identifying moves between optimism and pessimism in investor/crowd psychology, price movement, as well as other factors. Knowledge of the Elliot Wave Theory can help you determine where the price of an asset is heading which will enable you to make better decisions with your portfolio.

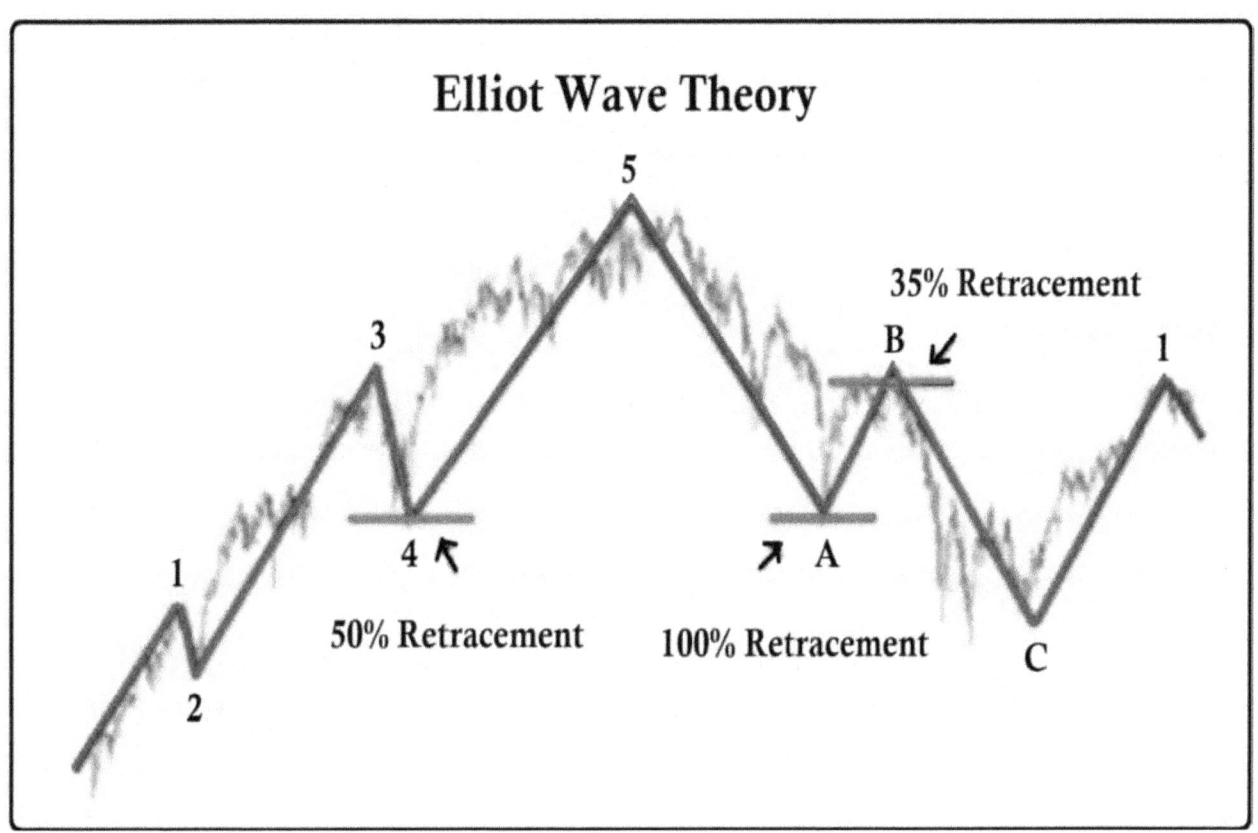

Ralph Nelson Elliot developed the Elliot Wave principle in the 1930s. He theorized that movement in stock prices happen in predictable patterns because large groups of people behave in predictable ways known as herd psychology. Elliot stated that market prices alternate between optimistic impulses and pessimistic corrective phases in a predictable, repeatable way.

Elliot divided the impulses into a set of 5 waves so that waves 1, 3, and 5 are upward impulses and waves 2 and 4 are small corrective retraces that happen throughout the uptrend. At the end of the uptrend is a 3-step corrective wave (A, B, & C) that consists of a retrace, a small impulse, and another retrace. All waves, including the corrective retraces, come together form an Elliot wave. After the wave is over the process starts all over again with wave 1.

After analyzing the mathematical properties of waves and patterns of Elliot Wave Theory it eventually led him to the conclusion that "The Fibonacci Summation Series is the basis of The Wave Principle". Numbers from the Fibonacci sequence are seen repeatedly in Elliott wave patterns, so here we see there importance again. Pay attention to the significance of these numbers! There are other books that go deeper into this subject, but I digress. After Elliot realized there was a correlation to the Fibonacci sequence, he said he had never heard of the Fibonacci sequence before. Elliot had discovered the Fibonacci sequence while working on his theory.

Other financial professionals continued using the Wave Principle and provided forecasts to investors using it after Elliott's death in 1948. Charles Collins, who had published Elliott's "Wave Principle" and helped introduce Elliott's theory to Wall Street, ranked Elliott's contributions to technical analysis on a level with Charles Dow. Elliot wave theory is still used to this day.

Here is a breakdown of the waves in detail:

Wave 1 is very difficult to identify. When the first wave of a new bull market begins, the market sentiment is almost universally negative. The bear market trend is considered to be continuing. Compare wave 1 to the accumulation phase in Wyckoff's market cycles. This is when all the corporate CEO start trying to accumulate their positions without alerting the rest of their competition.

Wave 2 is a correction of the first wave, but can never retrace beyond the starting point of wave one. You will notice the volume is lower in wave 2 than in wave 1. When the price drops it usually doesn't retrace below the 61.8% Fibonacci level. The majority of the market is still bearish at this point.

Wave 3 is usually the biggest and most powerful wave in a trend. Compare this to the mark up phase in Wyckoff's market cycles. At this point large companies let it be known that they have been buying certain assets. News goes from bearish at the start of the wave to positive around halfway through. It is clear now the bull run is underway. Prices rise quickly in wave 3, and corrections are quickly bought up by the bulls. Wave 3 often extends wave 1 by a ratio of 1.618:1.

Wave 4 is another corrective wave. Prices usually retrace less than 38.2% of wave 3. This is a good opportunity to buy before the final wave 5.

Wave 5 is the final stage in the uptrend. The news is positive and everyone is bullish. New investors finally buy in, unfortunately right before the top. Volume is often lower than in wave 3. Momentum indicators slow and start to show bearish divergences warning of a possible reversal.

Corrections are more difficult to identify than impulse moves. The best way is by watching for divergences. The indicators will still show increased volume. After the first 5 waves there are 3 corrective waves that follow:

Wave A - The drop in price is just seen as a correction of the previous bullish uptrend. The wave will either be divided in 3 or 5 waves. If the wave is divided into 3 smaller waves, the price action will go sideways or form a triangle pattern. If the wave is divided into 5 smaller waves it will be more of a zig-zag type.

Wave B - In wave B prices reverse higher. Wave B is a bull trap. Traders jump in to "buy the dip", which many see as a resumption of the new long-gone bull market. You might begin to see the right side of a head and shoulders pattern forming here. The volume during wave B should be lower than in wave A. This should be an indication that the price is going to fall.

Wave C - Prices move lower rapidly in 5 phases. Selling volume increases and usually by the 3rd phase everyone realizes the bear market has started. Wave C is typically at least as large as wave A and often extend to 1.618 times wave A or beyond. Prices continue to move impulsively lower until the Elliot wave starts all over again from the beginning.

A correct Elliot wave count must observe these three rules:

1. Wave 2 can never retrace more than 100% of wave 1.
2. Wave 3 cannot be the shortest of the three impulse waves, namely waves 1,3,and 3. Wave 4 cannot overlap the price action of wave 1, except in the rare case of a diagonal triangle formation.

In addition to these rules there are several guidelines to consider:

A common guideline called alternation states that sometimes waves alternate positions. The guideline of alternation within an impulse states that waves 2 and 4 often alternate. If for example, there's a simple sharp move in wave 2, that suggests wave 4 will have more of a sideways type of move. If wave 2 moves sideways, wave 4 will have a sharp correction. Alternation can occur in impulsive and corrective waves.

The guideline of alternation within a correction states that sometimes the forms for wave A and wave B alternate. If wave A is a zig-zag type of correction, wave B will be more of a sideways correction and vice versa. Alternation gives traders an idea of what not to expect when analyzing wave formations.

Elliott observed that alternate waves of the same degree must be distinctive and unique in price, time, severity, and construction. All formations can guide influences on market action. The time period covered by each formation, however, is the major deciding factor in the full manifestation of the Rule of Alternation.

The standard order of degrees (approximate durations given):

- Grand supercycle: multi-century
- Supercycle: multi-decade (about 40–70 years)
- Cycle: one year to several years (or even several decades under an Elliott Extension)
- Primary: a few months to a couple of years
- Intermediate: weeks to months
- Minor: weeks
- Minute: days
- Minuette: hours
- Subminuette: minutes

The guideline of depth of corrective waves states that when the price action retraces it will often retrace back into the territory of wave 4.

The guideline of channeling is used to identify the end of waves within impulses.

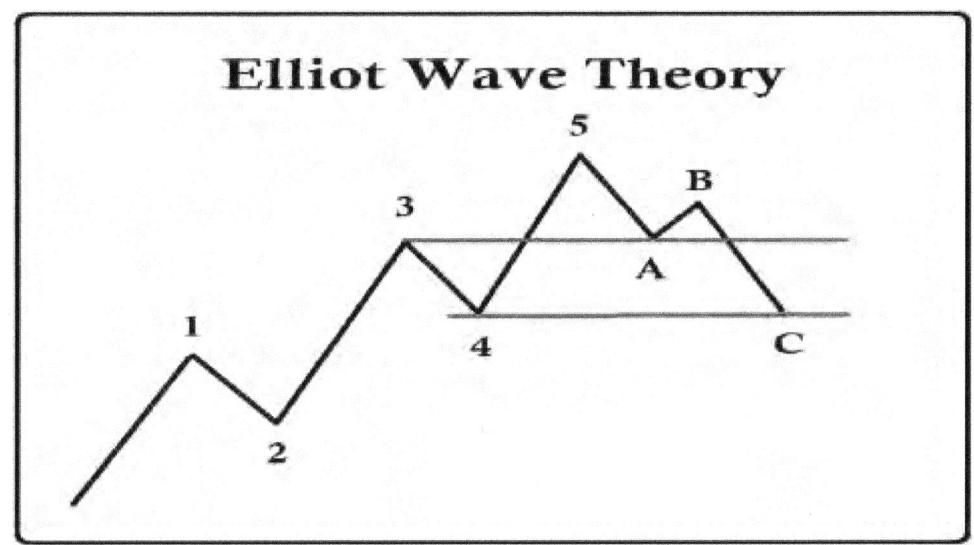

The guideline of channeling is a technique used to predict the end of waves within impulses. Ellioit stated that parallel trend channels usually mark the upper and lower boundaries of impulse waves.

Connect the ends of waves 2 and 4. the upper parallel predicts the end of wave 5 when drawn touching the peak of wave 3.

Within parallel channels and the converging lines of diagonal triangles, if a fifth wave approaches its upper trendline on declining volume, it is an indication that the end of the wave will meet or fall short of it. If volume is heavy as the fifth wave approaches its upper trendline, it indicates a possible penetration of the upper line, which Elliot called "throw-over." Throw-overs also occur, with the same characteristics, in declining markets.

The guideline of scale states that you should use an arithmetic scale chart and a semi-log scale chart when analyzing Elliot waves.

Corrective wave patterns can take on forms known as zigzags, flats, or triangles. In turn these corrective patterns can come together to form more complex corrections. Similarly, a triangular corrective pattern is formed usually in wave 4, but very rarely in wave 2, and is the indication of the end of a correction.

Robin Wilkin, Ex-Global Head of FX and Commodity Technical Strategy at JPMorgan Chase, says "the Elliott Wave Principle ... provides a probability framework as to when to enter a particular market and where to get out, whether for a profit or a loss."

Use the Elliot wave theory in combination with other forms of market analysis. Study this theory and its guidelines so you can use it to understand where you are in the market cycle. Knowing where you are in the market cycle is absolutely essential for any trader. With practice you can learn how to time your trades perfectly using the Elliot wave theory.

"The most contrarian thing of all is not to oppose the crowd but to think for yourself." - Peter Thiel

Resources and support

Apps -
Atomic Wallet
Binance
Binance.US
Bitrue
Kucoin
Bittrex
Kraken
Coinbase
Coinbase Pro
Coinmarketcap
Tradingview
Coin app
Coin stats
Crypto.com
Pi network
Electroneum
StormX
Cryptopanic

News
Coinmarketcal.com/en/ great place to get all the upcoming news
Cryptopanic.com - scrapes twitter and reddit for crypto news

The Daily Hodl

Cointelegraph
Lunarcrush.com
Coindesk.com
coinmarketcap.com
Crypto-news-flash.com
Cryptonews.net
Cryptodiffer.com

Tools
Tradingview
Coinigy
Cryptoalerts.ai - go to oversold RSI under 20, buy divergence
https://www.blockchaincenter.net/bitcoin-rainbow-chart/
Multicoincharts.com
Brave Browser
Coinmarketcap.com
Coingecko
Coinpaprika
Tokenmetrics.com
Studio.Glassnode.com
Cryptobubbles.net
alternative.me/crypto/fear-and-greed-index/
Binance Academy

Security
Different VPN's - Nord, PureVPN
Anti-virus - Nortons, Webroot,
Anti-malware - Malwarebytes

Exchanges
Binance
Binance.US - Enter referral code 35081808 for a bonus
Bitrue - Enter invitation code VAAHEG for a bonus
Coinbase
CoinbasePro
Crypto.com - Enter referral code 3fh4nshqrr
KuCoin - Enter referral code 2RQ8JbM for a bonus

Uniswap

Wallets
Atomic Wallet
Cobo Wallet
Tezor Wallet

Reference Books
Thomas Bulkowski, Encyclopedia of Candlestick Patterns
Thomas Bulkowski, Encyclopedia of Chart Patterns

www.ingramcontent.com/pod-product-compliance
Lightning Source LLC
LaVergne TN
LVHW081532060526
838200LV00048B/2059